Just Saying...

Selected Columns

A collection of ~~weakly~~ *weekly* humorous
newspaper columns
written on the coast of Maine

by

Tom Sadowski

Just Saying... Selected Columns
Copyright © 2021 Tom Sadowski

Library of Congress Control Number: 2021911036

ISBN: 978-1-954517-12-7

Unless otherwise noted, all photos and illustrations were created by the author.

Produced by:
Maine Author's Publishing
12 High Street
Thomaston, Maine 04861
USA
www. maineauthorspublishing.com

Printed in the United States of America

Table of Contents

Preface

After writing five hundred weekly columns for the *Free Press* based in Rockland and now Camden, Maine, it was time to put a number of those essays into a book just to see if a stack of books might spontaneously combust when arranged in a way that would not allow hot air and twaddle to escape. It's an interesting study and is based on the Chicago Pile, the world's first experimental nuclear reactor, built during the Manhattan Project in 1942, but here we go, off on a tangent, and this is only the first paragraph of the preface.

So, the book idea has been in the works for some time; since column number 497, to be precise. Even with a lot of prodding from family and friends, it still takes a bit of an inflated ego mixed with a touch of bravado and maybe some consulting time with Jack Daniels to publish a book. Somewhere in your mind you have to believe that people might want to read it. On the other hand, it's a good way to consolidate your writing in one place so you don't have to rely on binders full of newspaper columns, some of which are missing.

In any case, the final decision to go with a book was made when it was pointed out to me that when people die, whoever is left in charge of their stuff usually throws it into a dumpster. This includes all manner of unfinished creative work, particularly partial manuscripts, and column collections in binders. Some of the more conscientious estate executors will opt to take any paperwork to a recycling facility, but aside from leaving the deceased feeling better about recycling, the end result is very similar.

Since I didn't know where to start, the first column here is the first one written under the "Just Saying…" title for the *Free Press*. The rest follow in more or less chronological order. Most of the science-oriented, technical, and construction columns were held back so as not to frighten the children and to keep the dogs from howling. Those may appear in a future collection for a narrower band of readers. The theme of most columns in this book is amusement and distraction with a stealthy commentary on the state of humanity and civilization, but not too much.

Most of the columns are as they originally appeared in the *Free Press*, although an amazing amount of spellink and punctuation erors were corected,. Some illustrations or photos were added, and then, some of the photos were retracted with the realization that giving too much information is worse that holding back on things people generally don't want to see.

Finally, some of the confusing sentences were edited because apparently, it was originally the malt liquor talking. Now they actually make sense and are better than ever before.

This book is dedicated to my father, who dreamed of being a writer. He might have actually written stories, but he used a pen name or two, or three, so after he died, I could never tell what he had written himself and what stories he had just transcribed on his typewriter. At the time, there was no option to select the story with your mouse and cursor, then copy and paste it into a favorites file.

The book is also dedicated to my wife Janis Kay, for putting up with my ways for all these years. I especially appreciate that she has not ridden off on a horse into the sunset, as she has described such a scenario more than once, in which she watches me get smaller in the rearview mirror. I can only hope that she is sticking around because I still amuse and love her and not because she can't find a way to fasten a rearview mirror onto a horse.

Acknowledgments

It has come to my attention that odd people from my life have twisted my thinking and shaped my writing style. I don't mean these people are odd as much as I mean random... no, some of them really are odd, but still delightful. People like John Parker, Tom Kujat, Fred Rungee, Warren Netherton, Spencer Deiber, George Rooney, Bill Gabbert, George Dickel, Tim Lawrence, Treve Hosken and a host of others who taught me to look at life in a different light. Okay, they didn't teach as much as amuse me with their perspective, still, the influence lingers.

Then there is Alice McFadden, the publisher at the *Free Press*, who saw something in my writing, apparently on a day she forgot her glasses, and offered me column space in her newspaper. That kind of overture just calls out for an acknowledgement. When I accepted, she handed me over to Dan Kirchoff who put up with the columns I submitted every week and expertly beat them into submissions that fit into my allotted space and made me look like I knew what I was doing all along.

Holly Moirs, Queen of the Comma, at *Maine Author's Publishing*, must also be mentioned as she carefully copyedited the manuscript and made me realize that I can squeeze more errors into an essay than a pimply-faced high school freshman who routinely neglects his English homework. It must have been painful to work with a manuscript so infested with errors. Everything she checked is perfect. However, she did not review these acknowledgements so forgive me any errors. Here are a few commas to spread around if you need them: , , , , , , .

Special recognition and thanks to Jimmie Froehlich who took the time to sort through my collection of compositions and offered up his valued opinions and creative input on which columns to include, what was amusing, what was annoying, and how to spell *Jimmy Hoffa* even though Hoffa is in no immediate need of a breather as he is, I'm sure, permanently resting.

And, to all I have slighted, by not including them in the acknowledgements, thank you. Thank you from the lower-right ventricle of my heart.

Just Saying...
Selected Columns

The first column, April 3, 2011

Coronal Mass Ejection and Other Unpleasantries

When I read the news today that there was a large coronal mass ejection headed our way, I immediately thought of my mother. I would routinely push her to the breaking point in my adolescence with my cluttered room, anarchist friends, and basement chemistry lab. When I suddenly filled the house with a blast of smoke so thick that she could not see down into the basement, she had one of those coronal mass ejections that makes me cower to this very day.

Real coronal mass ejections aren't that bad. Simply put, our sun is exploding and the sky is falling.

Please, everyone just relax. I should have said that the sun is exploding just a little bit, and the sky is falling.

Here we're talking about one of the pimples on the face of the sun…of course, you would never put it that way in polite company. For instance, if you had the sun over for a light lunch and you were really friendly with the yellow dwarf, you would refer to her pimples as "sunspots" and might offer her sympathy about how they get agitated every eleven years or so. You wouldn't dwell on the fact that she's a dwarf, either.

To be politically correct and technically accurate, the sun is a G2V spectral class star, but for the sake of civility, you would do best to avoid the entire subject. Starting a conversation about class might ruin the whole lunch. I am just offering this to let you know that I was properly raised by my mother and I can be very tactful when the situation warrants.

Anyway, one of the pimples on the face of the sun gets all puffed up and spews a not-insignificant amount of hot, high-energy, naked and possibly smelly particles along with mind-blowing quantities of electromagnetic radiation way out into space which is where America along with Egypt and Israel and Walmart and Main Street are located.

Again, everyone relax. Earth is a long way from the sun and all this death and destruction is pretty dilute by the time it gets here. Anyway, we're protected by magnets. Magnetic fields, actually—the same kinds of magnetic fields generated by the magnets in the bracelets that they sell at the state fair to ward off intellectuals. The earth generates these enormous magnetic fields because, as one theory goes, the earth's core is basically chewy nougat heavily laced with magnetic bracelets (which, like hell, can't be disproved until we dig down to the center of the planet).

These powerful magnetic fields channel all the particles coming from the sun to the North and South Poles, where they hold endless conferences and tedious meetings before breaking up into smaller groups and electing a moderator. Occasionally, they have a party and set off fireworks, which we see as the northern lights.

So apart from disrupting GPS signals, taking down terrestrial communication systems and causing widespread power blackouts, real coronal mass ejections aren't as bad as creating a small explosion in the basement while your mother is upstairs preparing supper.

My little industrial accident taught me many things. As I recall, I had been experimenting with ways to produce gunpowder in large quantities. It's an honorable exercise that the Chinese have done for thousands of years, although I am now certain they didn't do it in the basement of their mother's house. The weak blast from my poor-quality product didn't hold a candle to the deadly high-energy particles emitting from my mother. I assured her that I would be more careful next time, which I learned was not nearly as good as begging forgiveness with a promise to take a sudden interest in accounting or dishwashing.

Truth be told, I'll take a real coronal mass ejection any day over a mother's wrath. You might be lost in the dark without a working phone, but you won't be grounded for a month without TV—and no access to your lab.

Column 006, May 8, 2011

Coffee, Pigs, and Promises

Have you examined the discrepancy between how coffee smells when you open a can or grind freshly roasted beans with the actual taste of what is in the cup?

I know I have. Every day.

I am not talking about the coffee "experience" or the ritual of a hot cup with your morning paper. At one time, I dispensed with the brewing and filtering and tried drinking only hot water for a month. The cup still felt good in my hand and the routine of sipping a hot liquid provided a certain satisfaction, but the biggest benefit was that I didn't have to put up with the disappointment that everyday coffee brings. What we are discussing here is aroma vs. flavor.

Coffee promises a lot. Pork, on the other hand, promises nothing.

The coffee plant is very discriminating. It grows best at certain elevations. It likes to live near the equator, at ideal temperatures, in good soil with enough rain scheduled sometime between lunch and bedtime before it will reluctantly give up that perfect bean. This bean, when cleaned, dried, sorted, roasted, ground up, and soaked in hot water will tempt you with its aroma but then give you that very same cup of coffee you can get in every truck stop in America.

Pork, as we all know, comes from pigs. Pigs can live almost anywhere, eat almost anything at any time or any temperature. They don't insist on living in the mountains, generally don't make a fuss about soil conditions, and certainly don't require good drainage. They will recycle your garbage. After all, they're pigs. And yet, they give you bacon!

Pizza, it has been said, is like sex, and to that I would like to add bacon. When it's good, it's very, very good. And when it's bad, well, it's still pretty good. I submit that a pizza with bacon on it can hardly ever be bad.

It actually takes culinary malpractice or just plain negligence to screw up bacon—you have to undercook or burn it, but even then, the taste is still there. Walk into any truck stop, order bacon, toast and a coffee to see what I mean. The bacon, in spite of its disgusting background, is good. The coffee, given its pedigree and pampered cultivation, is bad. Even turkey bacon, which is not bacon or even tastes like bacon, delivers more on the promise of bacon than coffee can ever deliver. Of course, I'm talking here about coffee delivering on its own promise. In all fairness, we can't hold coffee responsible for any promises made by bacon, but bacon does set a good example that coffee should follow.

People are not honest with themselves about coffee. "You've just got to taste the coffee here," they say, but what they really want you to taste is the ambiance of the coffee shop, the flavor of the pastry that goes so well with coffee, or the additives. Flavorings, frothy cream, raw sugar, any number of spices that might be mixed into the brew are additives that taste good themselves and can usually make any food taste better—except, curiously, bacon, which does very well on its own thank you.

Take away the additives. Try coffee black. Is it any good? No, sadly not. Do not mistake strong coffee for taste. It's more of a bad thing. Just because the coffee is strong enough to dissolve your teeth doesn't make it good. After all, it might just be dissolved teeth you taste.

I have a solid theory to explain why coffee doesn't taste as good as it smells. Although I still conduct experiments daily, the trend of the results indicates my theory might be correct.

The theory states that the real flavor of coffee is ruined by exposure to heat, air, water, and revelations of your own daughter's personal life, which sort of works this way:

"Here Dad, have a cup of coffee."

"Thanks. Hey, what's that on your arm?"

"Oh, it's my new tattoo. It symbolizes everything I love. See, it's Frodo as a vampire. Aren't you going to drink your coffee?"

"No. It has lost its taste."

Column 009, May 29, 2011

Coffee, Part 2, with Cream

I'm hoping one day to taste coffee as satisfying as the aroma experienced the moment you open the can. I hope, I drink, I theorize.

My theory states that true coffee flavor is ruined by exposure to heat, air, and water. Keep those elements away from the coffee bean when brewing your cup and you will have ambrosia.

Before exploring this theory any further, we have to ask if it's even possible to have coffee taste as good as it smells. Let's examine anomalies where coffee flavor really comes through.

Coffee ice cream comes to mind. It's a calming and dreamy phenomenon just like coffee aroma. It has a narcotic effect. I know this to be true. I have experienced the effect firsthand.

It may happen when you sit down in front of a TV with a half gallon of coffee ice cream, a fork, and *Judge Judy* planning to eat just a half inch off the top of the carton. I know some of you think that I mean Judge Judy is planning to eat a half inch of my ice cream but don't be silly, she has a court to run.

Some time passes and just as the judge rules for the plaintiff, you notice that your container is half empty—or, if you plan to stick around for the next case, half full. The narcotic effect is undeniable.

Ice cream may not be the best argument for the mythical taste of coffee being a reality. After all, ice cream makes almost anything taste good—even black walnuts, an acquired taste to be sure. People have been known to spit them out on their first encounter. Ice cream has a way of making the flavor agreeable. You might not like black walnuts, but ice cream has a Jimmy

Carter effect where food and taste buds all compromise and start to get along.

Dairy products and coffee have some kind of strange relationship that I bet even Dr. Phil can't explain. Many of us would not drink coffee without cream because it simply tastes like poison. But does it take a dairy product to release the true coffee taste? It shouldn't.

When we get that satisfying rush of coffee aroma, there is no need to have an open container of milk alongside to make the coffee smell good. Milk doesn't even rate on the aroma scale unless it's gone bad. People never say, "Wow, is that fresh milk I smell?"

When milk goes bad it does so in a big, dramatic way. It gives off an unholy gas that once your nose gets a whiff, it sends a private cable to your brain, which somehow falls into the hands of a WikiLeaks nerve cell that releases the message throughout the body. You feel like gagging because when your stomach gets wind of what the nose has told the brain, there is immediate unrest. Protests are organized. Stomach muscles start marching and threatening a shutdown of all digestive processes. Facial muscles join in to produce the disgusting look, and the organs that make the shivers up your spine sensation, join the coalition. After vehement denials, the brain promises to commence an inquiry and appoints a committee, but by that time you've found some leftover fried chicken and the entire incident is forgotten.

In strange contrast, mix that sour milk up with a little dry dog food and Fido just laps it up as if it was so much vanilla custard. Go figure.

When coffee goes bad on the other hand and there are green islands of mold floating in the pot that you failed to empty before you left on vacation, it still smells pretty good.

Let's review. Coffee smells good but tastes bad unless you

have it with ice cream in front of Judge Judy or with cream. When that goes bad, the dog will eat it, but the putrid smell will send you looking for moldy coffee to sniff.

I haven't answered my question, so there is more theorizing to be scheduled. I do, however, have a good idea now about why my dog's breath is so bad.

Playing with Sisters, Cornstarch, and Mercury

Like I said before, I like to think I'm on top of science concepts. But truth be told, the last guy who truly understood all the science of his time probably lived in Greece long before it opened on Broadway—which brings me around to my artist-sister, who asked me on a recent visit, "Do you know the cornstarch trick?" I had to admit no, so she started mixing cornstarch with water. She placed a bowl in front of me half full of this thick white liquid.

"Put your fist into it," she suggested. When I tried, the liquid turned solid and it was like punching moist sand. "Now, stick your finger in it," she said (unlike my mother, who always insisted I keep my fingers away from things like this). As I did, the white mass around my finger turned liquid, and as I gently moved my finger around, the entire contents of the bowl liquefied. Getting a little too rough with it turned it right back into a solid. I could pick it up and roll it into a ball but if I stopped, it ran through my fingers like thick paint falling into the bowl turning back into whatever it really was.

In my decades of poking around scientific phenomena, I had never seen, read, or heard of such an amazing transformation. How could I have missed it? Not even one episode of *Star Trek* mentions cornstarch and here it is, in my hand and on my sister's kitchen table. Even more disturbing is how my artist-sister could know about this before me.

The phenomenon is vaguely reminiscent of congressional

press conferences: just when you think a politician is solid, he turns into a liquid and puddles in a low spot. But to experience this with a common cooking ingredient, at room temperature, in my hand, at my age, is like…well, I want to say it's like getting stuck in an elevator with Halle Berry but I'm sure that in reality there would be awkward moments and at the end, I would have nothing to hold in my hand. Handling this white goop is as much fun and as delightfully novel as playing with mercury, but much less toxic.

And yes, Virginia, there once was a time when we all played with mercury. Just a few years after the dinosaurs disappeared, we would light up firecrackers, ride around standing in the back of pick-up trucks, and play with drops of mercury the dentist had given us as a reward for not biting his fingers. When we felt especially cavalier, we would do all these things at once. Of course we had to be home for dinner when the streetlights came on, but that was only to protect us from tripping over any dead dinosaurs in the dark.

Today, there are precious few things we can hold in our hand that amaze us the way we were amazed as children. I remember the magic of discovering fire from a match, light from a flashlight, and a voice over an intercom. Growing up, I explored everything fascinating with abandon. Today you are hard-pressed to find a child playing with gasoline or melting lead in the backyard with a blowtorch or trying to burn asbestos—all of which led me, as an adult, to a better understanding of many things, my mortality among them.

As we get older, very cool experiences are harder to come by. I would have to rate the cornstarch running through my fingers on par with operating a plasma cutter for the first time or playing with lasers on a foggy night.

I must learn more about this glop that I have so far discovered is a "non-Newtonian fluid" with properties similar to quicksand.

My research will begin at those hallowed archives where the sum total of human knowledge resides: YouTube.

If you are not thinking "this guy really knows what fun is about," then you, my friend, have not played with enough mercury in your youth. I suggest you get out the water, cornstarch, and a blowtorch if you have one, and see what mysteries you can unlock before your mother gets wind of what you're doing.

Column 019, August 7, 2011

Earwig Expedition Seeks Applicants

Earwigs are my favorite insect. That's not true, but I go around saying it for shock value. Not familiar with the earwig? Okay, imagine the scariest insectoid horror movie you've seen where giant insects have ugly faces and big pincers. Now shrink that image down to a regular insect size, put the pincer on the tail, add some disgusting habits, and Bob's your uncle, you have an earwig.

People (my wife) are intensely repulsed by earwigs. It's curious because many members of Congress have disgusting habits and, I suspect, tail-end pincers, yet we still reelect them and send them campaign contributions. I suppose deep down we know that just because they have pincers, it doesn't mean they can't bring home the pork.

Most common earwigs in the US are under three-quarters of an inch long. They were introduced from Europe, but that was back around 1907 so they no longer need a green card to work here. The most exotic earwigs hail from the South Atlantic island of Saint Helena and have been reported to be over three inches long.

A volcanic piece of rock that is one of the most isolated islands on earth, Saint Helena is just the kind of place where you would expect to find giant earwigs. However, the last time one was sighted was 1967. Some say they no longer exist.

Saint Helena is, coincidentally, exactly the same size as Walt Disney World near Orlando, Florida. But while the Magic Kingdom draws 17 million visitors a year, the island of Saint Helena attracts, well, a lot fewer. Could it be because the island has no commercial airstrip and people are not willing to go by boat? Or could it be that the giant Saint Helena earwigs discourage tourism?

Why is there no airport? Someone built a nine-hole golf course on the only flat spot on the island which to me, indicates a government conspiracy to keep giant earwigs from booking flights to London or, God forbid, Miami.

I am positive the giant earwigs of Saint Helena still exist in dark, damp corners of the island. Earwigs are as tough as cockroaches judging by their survival rate after being stepped on. They will probably be around to argue with the roaches over our things after December 2012.* My theory is that the giant earwigs of Saint Helena haven't been seen since 1967 simply because people really don't want to admit they exist. They are in denial.

Saint Helena husband to wife: "Dear, have you been on the computer? It's been left on."

Wife: "Not lately."

Husband: "Someone has been using it to try and book a flight off the island to a dark, moist place!"

Wife: "That's ridiculous; there are no flights off this island."

Husband: "You're right. It must have just been the wind…"

I would very much like to organize an expedition to Saint Helena to find the giant earwig. Expeditions with such a noble cause are hard to find these days. Of course, I will need a contingent of hard-drinking adventurers. My wife will have to come for her almost supernatural ability to alert me when the creatures are near—and for her mojito mixing style. A professor or two is next on my list; an entomo-bio-paleonto-logist would be ideal. Also required is a movie star for publicity and to add drama and sexy overtones to the adventure. I see Halle Berry here, but I'm open to Angelina Jolie. A millionaire and his wife to bankroll the entire junket is a critical component of the team. Finally,

I need to recruit a bona fide skipper brave and sure, because I plan to charter a boat around the island for a three-hour tour. A three-hour tour. I will play the part of Gilligan.

If you are interested and feel you have qualifications that would contribute to the team effort, send me a cover letter and résumé. I will promptly file it away until I get enough responses from millionaires and their wives to fund the expedition.

I'm sure everyone is excited about the prospect of being on an expedition to find the giant earwig. Except my wife. She will probably think I was on a three-hour tour of the "Magic Kingdom" when I came up with the idea.

* December 21, 2012
In case you haven't put it on your calendar, is when the world is scheduled to end. It's the ending date of the Mayan Long Count calendar.
When my own 2-year calendar stops at December 31, no one takes notice. But when it was discovered that the Mayan's stopped their calendar on December 21, 2012, pessimistic people pronounced that date as the end of time. Sadly, the Mayan civilization seems to have been a bit too optimistic.

Column 021, August 21, 2011

Pain, On a Scale from One to Ten

"On a scale of one to ten," the admitting nurse asks me, "what is your pain level?"

What kind of question is that? Assigning a number to my level of pain is purely subjective. I mean after zero, how can the nurse know what a seven means to me? They have a chart in the emergency room for kids where pain is rated by pointing at a set of expressions from a smiley face to a full-blown bawling-your-eyes-out face. But for adults, they ask you to pick a number. To me, the smiley-face chart is much more objective. So as the nurse asks me the question, my wife is screaming, "It's a ten! It's a ten!" just to help me out.

Excuse me, my wife is not "screaming." She is asserting herself in a tense situation, but let me tell you, when you're doubled over in pain and the nurse is trying to keep you from knocking over her sphygmomanometer as you fall out of her chair, asserting seems like screaming to me.

As I fall to the floor trying to mitigate the pain, I am blurting out my reasons why I consider the pain a six and not a ten. "If it's a ten now and you smash my finger with a hammer, what kind of paid will I have then, a twelve?" I am thinking, "By God, woman, the scale only goes to ten and I'm still conscious. I must leave room for more pain. Twelve isn't one of the multiple-choice answers!" I figure on their scale, ten is the point just before you pass out from the pain. I'm not there yet. Although I'm blathering, I can still think.

Finally, to avoid the problems with the fact that the scale does not go to infinity, the nurse asks, "Is the pain mild, moderate, or severe?" To everyone's satisfaction, I answer severe. After all, why would I have been yelling "Just take me to the emergency room!" at my gentle wife if the pain was merely moderate?

It would make more sense if the scale was in percentage of maximum pain ever experienced. That way, the nurse would know if you're an old hand at managing pain or if you're into new territory. Another alternative could be using phrases to describe the pain where you would work up from "a distraction" through "a constant irritation" all the way to "put me on morphine *now* or just kill me!"

I am ushered to a small room where I am told to make myself comfortable and to put on a hospital gown. I do not know what to do because, truth be told, I am not comfortable in a hospital gown. More to my immediate concern, I am not at all comfortable because I equate experiencing severe abdominal pain that won't lessen no matter what I do with being uncomfortable. I stand, sit, bend, and lie down but nothing helps *for a full three-quarters of an hour.*

The doctor finally enters. He is the same doctor who stitched up my thumb some months ago. Since he gets so little feedback on the fine work he does, I show him how well my thumb healed and we joke about the street value of painkillers. I then explain about my present situation, and I let him know that just seeing him again has made me feel better. As a matter of fact, I mysteriously feel fine.

He diagnoses kidney stones, declares that the worst is passed, and recommends I drink a lot of water. I confess that I am still uncomfortable because of the hospital gown. He immediately prescribes a change into street clothes and a remarkable transformation back to zero pain follows.

It is interesting to note that the pain scale starts at one and not at zero. Perhaps they assume that since you have come to the emergency room you are already on the pain train heading for ten. Maybe they know we are never really pain-free. In any case, now that I know the questions on the quiz, I am prepared to answer correctly next time: if you don't want that 45-minute wait for the doctor, try a number higher than six.

Column 028, October 9, 2011

Easternmost Points and Pirates

Last month, my wife and I journeyed to Eastport, Maine, to attend the annual Pirate Festival. It's curious that we should attend a pirate festival since we don't typically socialize with any pirates (except my former insurance agent), and we don't particularly identify with the pirate lifestyle even though we may occasionally indulge in a yo ho ho and a bottle of rum.

You would think that nowadays a big pirate festival might be held on the coast of Somalia and I'm sure they hold some kind of celebration, but I doubt you would find any fried doughboys or smoked salmon on a stick there. Okay, maybe fried doughboys but certainly no smoked salmon. Anyway, we're not talking about real-world pirates in Eastport but fantasy pirates like the kind you would find on a Cap'n Crunch box or at your local movie house.

Eastport claims to be the easternmost city in the US —that's if you consider Lubec a town and not a city. Of course, Boston is arguably the easternmost city in the US—with a population of more than a half million residents. Similarly, Memphis, Tennessee, is the easternmost city in the US with the grave of Elvis. Nevertheless, east is east, and while we were in the vicinity, we felt obliged to visit West Quoddy Head, which is the easternmost point on the US mainland because there is a big rock there by the lighthouse with an inscription that says so.

You wouldn't think that the easternmost point would be called "West" Quoddy Head, but life is short and there are other things to think about—like why West Point Military Academy is in New York instead of somewhere out west and why Key West is in Florida instead of California.

We discovered there is no actual point, like a pencil point, sticking out in the ocean. I did note a considerable chunk of real estate between the inscribed rock and the water, so you have to assume the word *point* is not meant in the mathematical sense but maybe more in a cartographic or nautical way. In any case, we concluded that *Quoddy* is just such a fun word to say that it's a wonder people don't use it more in conversation. It has a pronunciation coefficient of satisfaction right up there with *kumquat, diphthong,* and *foibles.*

We didn't dare take the ferry from Lubec to Eastport. After all, it was loaded with pirates and buccaneers. As we drove the distance in our car, I practiced pirate talk on my wife.

Me: "Avast, mateys! Makin' port at Quoddy, all the lasses be wearin' only diphthongs and servin' up kumquats!"

Me wife: "It's cute, but that's enough now."

Me: "Ay, me beauty. You be the prettiest schooner in all of Quoddy, and it be true that all lubbers be likin' your foibles."

Me wife: "That's enough now."

Me: "By the powers that be, your kumquats are a sight for me one good eye!"

Me wife: "Shut up and just drive."

At least half of the ten thousand or so people showing up in Eastport dress up like pirates so it's easy to fall into the excitement of costumes and street theater. With just a few colorful scarves, some dangly earrings, and a pair of black boots, my wife transformed herself into a pirate's dream wench. (Let's not read

Eastport Pirate 2011

anything into this; I mean in addition to her poofy white blouse and printed skirt.) She actually had to steal a razor-sharp cutlass off a drunken sailor to keep the other pirates at bay. I donned a black tuxedo and my skeleton-emblazoned tie because I mistakenly understood I was to "dress up" like a pirate and not "dress down." My wife helped tone down the outfit by fitting my head with a semi-formal bandana.

All went well. We ate, we drank, we listened to pirate songs, and we ogled the amazing crowd. No one was held prisoner for very long. The only group actually trying to pillage, plunder, rifle, and loot were the festival vendors, but we didn't let them get much more than all our money.

Next year we'll be back, only we'll be dressed like festival vendors. Kumquats on a cutlass anyone?

Eastport "Pirette" 2011

Column 031, October 30, 2011

Some Thoughts on Dog Thoughts

Diogenes the Cynic of really ancient Greece was the original Wall Street protester. Camping out at the marketplace, he constantly demonstrated against the institutions and social values of his time. He taught that men would do well to study dogs because of their ability to relax, eat anything, sleep anywhere, and live in the present. I must, however, take issue with his assertion that dogs have no use for abstract philosophy. I have come to see that dogs live their lives based solely on their convictions and even spiritual tendencies.

Many dogs have the "eat first, check quality later" philosophy. They have a competitive eating tendency where they hork down large quantities of anything and let the sensors in their stomachs have a go at accepting or rejecting the whole lot. Throw a dog a steak, and he can't swallow it fast enough. Leave him near a stick of butter, and it's gone like a hot car in a Nicolas Cage movie. Get distracted on a walk, and the dog eats the entire green pile of whatever it was on the lawn in seconds. Doesn't matter if it's good or bad—he's thinking, "We'll let the stomach decide."

Not that dogs think too deeply. Being a longtime observer, I've concluded that most dogs think in very short phrases: "I need to go out." "Visitor!" "He's yelling at me." "He's stopped yelling at me." "I need to go out."

It's something I call Twitter-think: no thought over 140 characters—and that's pushing it. Border collies, German shepherds, and certain retrievers have Twitter-think down to the point where you have to wonder why these dogs don't carry smartphones or at least iPads (without the 3G feature). On the other hand, I suspect breeds like the chow chow, the Afghan hound, and my dog (a large brown), have adopted a stripped-down version we could call "one-quarter Twitter-think."

Quarter-think (for short) is limited to thirty-five characters. Solid but short thoughts like "Ask not what your country can do," "It's not the size of the dog," and "You can fool some of the people" all fall within the thirty-five-character limit. It might not be deep thought, but it has all the indications of a feeble attempt. Or consider this—this thinking might be the dogs' conscious effort to simplify their lives.

My large brown seems to identify less with his breed and more with some kind of dog religion or cult. More and more, I imagine that he is a monk in the Order of Large Brown Dogs. He obviously leads a monastic life and has taken a number of vows very seriously.

His vow of silence is unwavering. Except for the time I thought I heard him mutter the word *Popsicle* to himself, he has never spoken. Even though I beg him to vocalize just a few monosyllabic words to me in complete confidence, he only gives me the stare that says "I cannot break my solemn promise." The dog is definitely intelligent because he never lets on just how smart he is. He seems to know that if he did start talking, we would all marvel at this achievement, but in time we would tire of his limited repertoire if he didn't come up with some real insight. This, of course, is a problem for any celebrity.

He has renounced possessions in line with his vow of poverty and relies on the goodness of laypeople to keep him housed and fed so that he can concentrate on his spiritual work. He keeps only his collar and bowl—and those are for the convenience of society and not for his personal comfort or gain.

In a curious twist of fate, society has also imposed on him the vow of chastity, and I suspect his spiritual work consists largely of meditating on forgiving society for this injustice.

In spite of his commitments, I will continue to encourage him to talk. Like Diogenes, I feel we could all benefit from the dog's wisdom. My biggest fear is that one day he will turn to me and say, "I have an important message for you," whereupon he will have reached his Quarter-think limit and will go back to waiting for the final decision on the last thing he ate.

Column 036, December 4, 2011

Observations at My Bank

My bank is a peculiar place. At the customer table where you can complete the office work that you neglected to do at home, the bank offers a quantity of pens to fill out their forms. All the good pens, emblazoned with the bank's logo, are in a cup free for the taking, but the worst pen, a slender, black, pointy ballpoint, is tied down with a little chain. This pen doesn't even work and yet the bank feels it necessary to chain it to the desk. Nothing else in the bank is chained down—with the possible exception of a few employees.

This particular pen must have some great value that is not immediately evident. To discover the true purpose of the pen, I would like to get it to my shop for a proper evaluation. It could be swapped for a look-alike but with all of the security cameras around, I would have to be discreet indeed. Perhaps the pen itself is a camera. It would be pointless hiding from the other cameras if the security people got a close-up of my face from the pen-cam's point of view.

Then again, it may be some other kind of security device. It would be quite embarrassing if I got the pen to my car and then it exploded, throwing ink all over me and the interior of the car, but at least that would explain why it doesn't write.

It's hard for me to tear myself away from the paranoid theories, but maybe the pen has a more mundane purpose. The bank may have purposely put it there to get its name and logo into local circulation. People come in, grab the desk pen, and find it doesn't work so they take one of the free pens. These free pens work beautifully, and since the customer already has it in hand, and since it isn't tied down, and since there is a certain satisfaction of taking something from the bank, the customer pockets the pen. This also keeps customers from pocketing other loose things lying around the bank.

It's curious to realize that if I take the free pen, I'm doing the bank a service by promoting its brand, but if I somehow figure out how to take the black pen, I'm actually robbing the bank. Technically, my attorney would say I was stealing and not robbing, but if I'm going to be serving time for pen-thievery, I'll certainly be telling my fellow inmates that "I'm doin' time for bank robbery." You have to carefully craft your brand at the penitentiary.

I always feel a little weird walking into a bank with my bulky winter clothes and my stocking cap pulled low to my eyes, heading for a teller with a note. I would feel even more awkward walking into a bank with no clothes on, but that's not where I'm going with this. Point is, I have to write my account numbers down when I'm juggling funds and so they go on a note that I hand the teller. Don't think I haven't noticed that bank robbers operate in exactly the same way.

Bank robbers use notes because most of them really aren't "people persons", and all that polite chatter like "Good morning, I have a gun, please give me all the money, etc." is conveniently avoided with a well-written note.

Bank robber as a career choice is reserved mostly for the criminally inept, judging by how many end up listed in the "Stupid Criminals Hall of Shame" website, which gives some guidelines to potential criminals who want to be more original in their stupidity. The site offers advice for the would-be rake who may be missing some of his tines like "Don't sign the demand note" and "Provide your own transportation." Other sites provide stories of stupid robbers writing demand notes on the back of their personalized deposit slips or showing their ID to the teller to withdraw cash from a personal account before announcing the robbery.

The best advice is to find another line of work, especially if you consider yourself even one step above the level of an idiot. Also, as a matter of safety, don't mess with the pen that is chained to the customer desk. It's covered with all the viruses from the community, it might explode, and it doesn't work anyway.

Column 039, December 25, 2011

Opera Stories

Since I lost the tuning knob for the old radio in my shop, I now listen to opera on Sunday afternoons. It's not so much the singing I enjoy as it is the hosts of the show trying to read through a quick synopsis of the story behind the opera just prior to curtain. Sometimes this summary takes a full ten minutes, and it is very much like the pregame show for the Super Bowl where retired players and coaches are grilled by a knowledgeable host. With the opera, however, the host politely banters with opera scholars or retired singers who chortle at insider opera jokes and marvel how two different tenors can hit that high C even though they employ two different styles of singing. Imagine.

It's all very gracious and ha-ha and "I most certainly agree with you on that point," but I can tell that there is deep-rooted animosity between the host and the former opera stars by the way the host is always interrupting as if he must hurry things up to break for commercial—but this being public radio, there are no commercials.

I also have a suspicion that the host hasn't the vaguest idea of what the opera to be performed is about and he uses his smooth voice and air of confidence to make fools of the listening public. Who would know? The opera is in one-hundred-year-old Italian and might have just been the way to record old family pasta recipes. Most story lines are so convoluted and improbable that they make *Hamlet* look like a third-grade reader.

But if the story lines are accurate, it would be fantastic to just let the voices in your head write a new opera. Of course, there is the matter of writing the music and vocal parts, but I feel if you have an opera-worthy story line, you're more than halfway there, and famous composers and tenors will surely beat a path to your door.

First thing I need is a cast of characters with opera-like names. It's most important that the names roll off the tongue and have a familiar ring—but not so familiar that most people would recognize them without some serious internet research.

So our cast of characters in order of appearance is the king of Sweden, Caligula, Blind Lemon Jefferson, Proust, Pope Leo X, Sharona, Minnie (the Moocher), Ariel (daughter of King Triton), Che Guevara, Sam-I-Am, Be-Bop-A-Lula, Son of Sam, and the king's trusted guard Rajon Rondo.

Act I. Our story opens on the windswept Russian steppes where Caligula, wearing only a purple thong, slays the king of Sweden, who has playfully hidden his other thong, causing Caligula to injure his bare foot on the rocky soil. The only witness to this crime is the king's blind servant, Lemon Jefferson, whom Caligula spares because he is the only one who has the ear of Sharona, the woman Caligula wishes to marry but has only heard of through song and has never met. Proust, who has been close by looking for a wristwatch he lost, finds Caligula's missing thong but during his search also finds Sharona's ear in Jefferson's satchel. The three tenors break into that unforgettable aria *Il mio tempo, il suo perizoma, l'orecchio* ("My Time, His Thong, Her Ear") when they are brought before the Spanish Inquisition, which sends them on a quest to Memphis where they are to obtain a recording contract. As the curtain closes on Act I, Proust expresses his undying love for Caligula in an operatic rondo as the blind servant nibbles on Sharona's ear, having mistaken it for a piece of beef jerky.

As those of you familiar with opera can see, my first act is barely bizarre enough to pass as opera, but if you're thinking, "I wonder what happens in Act II," you may qualify as an opera aficionado (Italian for "nut"). If you're the rational type, you may be thinking, "He really should go look for that tuning knob for his radio."

On the other hand, if you think along the lines I do, you're already off looking for that old beef jerky you may have stashed a while ago in the pantry.

Column 045, February 5, 2012

My Unhealthy Insurance Plan

So now that I've been to the emergency room on my own account, I have experienced firsthand the terrible apprehension and gut-wrenching nausea that accompanies finding the hospital bill in the mail. The pain associated with this bill makes the emergency room trauma seem about equal to watching reality TV. The only thing that hurts worse than the hospital bill is the crushing agony of paying my health insurance premium—which should logically be great fun since my health plan is such a big joke.

So, if I have health insurance, why am I getting a hospital bill in the mail? Because as sick as I can get, it is not sick enough for the insurance to kick in. In order to afford health insurance, I had to sign up for a massive deductible—roughly equal to the gross domestic output of Estonia. Opening that hospital invoice is very much like getting injured again. Even if the sharp paper it's printed on doesn't actually cut you, the stress it causes surely shortens your life by a decade or two.

And you would think that the hospital billing process is streamlined enough for them to send you only one bill. This is not the case. The bookkeeping department in any hospital has got to be located in downtown Dullsville, so for something interesting to do and to keep their maniacal edge, the bookkeepers toy with you like a cat with a half-dead mouse. After you recover from the hospital bill, you will get a separate laboratory bill that is written in a cryptic code where the only recognizable English word is *blood*. Not quite finished messing with you, they might also send you a separate doctor bill, which naturally you assumed was included with your hospital bill because that would be sensible. After this crushing blow, you can only hope you aren't targeted for a separate bill from their pharmacy.

And what exactly is going on at my doctor's office? They seem to run the bill past my insurance company for permission to charge me. After a long time, the insurance company gets back from their golf game and says to the doctor, "Ha! That bill is outrageous. We won't pay you what you have to charge to run a successful practice, but we will pay you, say, 60 percent." So the doctor says, "Well all right, better to get 60 percent from you than nothing from the patient." The insurance company comes back with, "We were just fooling. We don't intend to pay any of this because the patient hasn't accumulated enough medical bills this year to make his ridiculous deductible. We will make a note of it, and good luck getting the 60 percent out of the patient since we've already bled him for all he's got."

If this were a Western movie, it would be at this point that the insurance company would produce a revolver and start shooting around the feet of the doctor while shouting, "Dance for me, you little varmint!" Then the insurance company would have a big laugh and ride off with their partner Big Pharma, leaving the doctor coughing in a cloud of dust.

Now, I'm not exactly sure it happens this way, so I considered calling my doctor and asking his staff. Then I remembered I still owe for the last visit, so there really is no point in opening a dialogue at this time.

In all the years I have been paying for health insurance, I've surely sent in enough money for someone to buy a very comfortable sailboat, fully provisioned, yet they are not satisfied. I get letters all the time explaining why my rates are going up. All I have received in return is a partial calming of my fear that medical bills will wipe me out financially.

Hmmm…if insurance is sold to assuage our fears, there must be a market where people would pay to insure themselves against being wiped out financially because of large insurance bills. If I can raise enough capital, I can start such an insurance company, and with the proceeds, I will be able to afford my own health insurance premiums and that fifty-six-foot sloop with the cherry interior—and, of course, my own revolver.

Column 042, January 15, 2012

Banking Observations, Continued

Ever since I was a boy, going to the bank has been a solemn occasion. You didn't play around in line, you spoke in muted voices, and everyone there was somber. It wasn't much different from attending a funeral except that when you finally got to the head of the line, it was nice to see the teller was not in a coffin.

Even today, a bank visit is a little like a religious sacrament. You prepare and pray at the customers' table before going to the teller's window, which is not unlike a confessional in a Catholic church. The teller already knows more about your affairs than you care to admit and waits to hear your confession.

Teller: "Hi, how are you today?"

Me: "Bless me teller, for I have committed the heinous sin of greed. I have written more checks than I have funds in my account."

Teller: "So you want to transfer money into your checking account?"

Me: "I know check kiting is technically fraud, but it's not anywhere near as bad as embezzlement and I'm surely not guilty of that…"

Teller: "You're all set."

Me: "Please forgive me. I will do penance and repay my home equity account. I will record all my checks and never overdraw my account again."

Teller: "Here, have one of our pens."

My wife gets upset when I joke with bankers over the phone just as she would if I started kidding around with a funeral director. Our mortgage banker called recently about a late payment.

He started the conversation with "Hello, how are you?"

Well, to me, that just opened up all kinds of possibilities. I gave him one of my standard answers: "I'm stable now. I think the drugs have finally kicked in."

To this he replied, "Oh, have you been sick?"

I could have said yes, but for the sake of comedy, I simply answered, "No."

There was silence. Enough time passed for him to look up the current valuation of my home and recalculate my equity. I got the distinct feeling he added a note to my credit report, if not actually lowering my score. He came back with "I see the weather's been warming up lately."

When my wife got wind of this conversation, she hurried down to reassure the banker that I was only practicing my trade and was not in a drug-induced stupor that triggers late mortgage payments. You have to understand my wife. She is the same woman who, on our first date, looked up from lunch and point-blank asked me, "Well, who's your banker?"

Who is my banker? I didn't even know the names of the tellers I would go to the bank just to ogle. In my bachelor days when I lived in Alaska, the banks all had a policy of placing only female models in teller positions. They took a cue from the Hooters restaurant chain, which uses pheromones generated right on the jobsite to bring in male clientele, sell them drinks, and take their cash.

The banks employed good-looking tellers but in smart business attire. They skipped the drinks and just took your cash, which would immediately be lent to people looking to build more Hooters restaurants.

Which brings us to banking advice for single men: No matter how hot the teller, never ask her out unless you have, you know, a hefty balance. In the short time allotted at the window, you might say in a very suave and well-rehearsed manner, "I'd like to deposit this into my account and verify that you're available for dinner tonight at eight," but by the time you get to the end of your delivery, the teller has reviewed the balance of all your accounts and has acquired vast knowledge regarding your credit worthiness. She can make a very accurate guess if you mean filet mignon when you say "dinner" or if you are referring to bean burritos.

I suppose I need to reexamine my own behavior. Next time my mortgage banker calls, I will treat him more like a priest and less like a Hooters employee. Maybe I can learn his name, earn his trust, and borrow money to open a Hooters of my own. I bet that will impress my wife.

Column 051, March 18, 2012

Soap, Men, and Skin Care

It's a good time in the history of humanity because men have relatively recently accepted bathing and personal hygiene as a normal part of life. This is good. Let's be thankful for small victories and not push for sudden transformation with men.

Pushing again is the personal-care industry, which is making an effort in every advertising venue to convince men they need skin-care products. Please. It's taken seventy-five years of persistence for the industry to achieve limited success selling men aftershave, hair conditioner and, of course, soap-on-a-rope, but that doesn't mean we are ready for skin toners, anti-aging face creams, complexion masks, or even moisturizing soaps.

There is not that much to skin care for men: don't burn, freeze, crush, scrape, or cut it, and keep it away from harsh chemicals and ionizing radiation. If it itches, scratch; if it's damaged, head for the first aid kit, not the beauty salon.

Okay, I'm not talking about the Spanx-for-men crowd and those who take to wearing "manscara." They are already represented by a legion of writers everyone can find on the internet. For the purposes of this essay, "men" refers not to those rugged individuals who exfoliate, moisturize, and use "cleansing bars" but to those of us regular guys who prefer regular soap.

Now, I don't play team sports or go to the gym, so I haven't made it a custom to shower with guys. I don't plan to—and no, I haven't talked it over because, really, men have other matters to discuss. However, I get the feeling that when a guy gets into a shower, he wants to see a real bar of soap there.

Guys like plain soap. We don't want soap in a bottle or soap shaped in any shape other than the shape of a bar of soap. We don't want soap shaped like seashells, little yellow ducks, lemons or any other fruit, angels, hearts or any other internal or external organs, gingerbread men, crabs, lobsters or any other seafood, cheese, flowers, frogs, and—especially not—praying hands.

Oversize bars are stupid because they're too big. And please, do not supply us with soap that contains exotic ingredients. Oatmeal is what I eat for breakfast. Why would I want it in my soap? I will make an exception for volcanic ash or pumice. After all, it comes from a volcano. But aside from what was once molten rock, soap should be carefully strained during the manufacturing process to keep fruits, vegetables, flowers, and cereals out of the mix.

Soap is basically a fat treated with lye—the manly main ingredient in Drano and oven cleaner. It's ironic that fat is very hard to clean off your hands and lye (sodium or potassium hydroxide) will chemically burn them, but together, they team up to dissolve away accumulated dirt and grime. They don't need any help from oatmeal.

A rope, however, did help to keep the soap from getting away from the user, and it was embraced by men in the 1950s. Of course, these were the same men who couldn't get enough Old Spice, but that was only to mask the smell of Camels and Pall Malls being consumed while shaving. Searching for a broader market, the industry started attaching other than plain soap to the rope, and men straight-out abandoned it even though soap-on-a-rope was fun to say. Today, they offer football-shaped soap and scented bay rum soap-on-a-rope, which is supposed to invoke Caribbean pirates bathing with an intoxicating fragrance. Excuse me, "pirates bathing"? I don't think so.

Avocado birch eucalyptus shea butter soap? Beard wash? Under-eye concealer? Men are suspicious of products like these because we do not know that they actually work. It doesn't help that we're unsure of what they're supposed to do. We've been spoiled by decent hand cleaners for mechanics like GOJO or Goop that really do get the dirtiest hands and fingernails clean and leave them soft and lightly scented.

For real skin care, men actually need work gloves that are comfortable and fit well. We don't need a $39 hypoallergenic conditioning rescue salve with citrus, vitamin E, and almond oils, although I must admit, if I had some, I might like to try it on a good-sized bowl of ice cream.

Column 060, May 20, 2012

Honoring the Doughnut

The first Friday in June is National Donut Day. For those of you too anxious to keep track because of all the coffee, sugar, and doughnut oil you may have recently ingested, go to donutdayusa.com, where you will find a convenient display that counts down the days, hours, minutes, and seconds to National Donut Day. It seems that the website should also have a list of psychiatrists as a courtesy to help the people who are actually looking for this countdown display, but I couldn't find it.

National Doughnut Day was a 1938 creation of the Salvation Army intended to pay tribute to the women who served doughnuts to the American soldiers during World War I. You would think that if the Salvation Army really wanted to honor the dedicated and supportive women who were the closest to the front lines, they would have come up with a name for a national day to reflect that.

Instead, they opted to name the day for the pastry the women served up to the troops. That's like honoring our professional police with a National Summons Day. It probably had something to do with the tradition of marginalizing the role of women and maximizing the importance of the coffee roll. Thank goodness those days are over! While women spent the next fifty years fighting for equality and have yet to get a National Woman's Day, the doughnut got a free ride and well-deserved recognition for its strategic part in winning World War I.

The origins of the doughnut are rather obscure. A number of cultures and people insist that the first doughnuts were produced by their ancestors.

People of Polish heritage know in their heart the doughnut was really invented in Poland during the Middle-Ages reign of Augustus III. Times were so hard that the corner bakery shops used the center of their fried dough cakes to pay their taxes. Only the outer dough ring was left for the peasants to have with their morning cappuccino and newspaper. When the king's tax collector came to get the dough, it would drive the bakery owners nuts so they called them "dough-nuts." The tradition of government officials spending time at doughnut shops also started here. At first, it was the tax collector, but gradually the duty shifted so that today the task of hanging out at the dough-nut shop falls mostly to the local police department.

I live near the town of Camden, Maine, where it is also asserted that the doughnut (defined as fried dough with a hole in it) was invented. Considering a number of stories with conflicting details, you come away with the common thread that around 1847, ship captain Hanson Gregory, living in what was then part of Camden, came up with the concept of cutting a hole in the middle of dough cakes, resulting in a confection that would fry up more evenly, eliminating the raw-dough-in-the-center-of-your-fried-cake syndrome.

About twenty years ago, Camden held a "donut festival", which I suspect was just to add one more shred of evidence in laying claim to the doughnut. As a symbolic warning or as a nod to the growing awareness of nutrition, the festival parade had the ambulance from the local rescue squad leading the procession. I have photos.

A hundred years ago when many Americans still ate dirt for their midday meal, the nutritious value of a doughnut was important. It would round up the meager daily caloric intake to the point where, if you took it easy on Sundays, the average Joe wouldn't lose any weight. Today, the doughnut still offers important components like fiber to our diet. Eating seventeen doughnuts will grace the average American with 100 percent of the recommended daily value of fiber needed to maintain a healthy lifestyle. Seventeen doughnuts will also give you over 300 percent of your necessary daily intake of fat—an added bonus.

All this talk about doughnuts has me feeling a little low on fiber. I'm heading off to do more research at the doughnut shop near the Salvation Army. Before I do, I'm checking the countdown clock to National Donut Day. I'm not sure what will happen when the day finally arrives, but I had a vision of a parade involving an ambulance, a Salvation Army band, the paramedics, and my cardiologist. Should be an exciting time.

* **Author's notes on the spelling of doughnuts.**

On several occasions, I have been told that readers like consistency in the books they read. And yes, I've been accused of inconsistency when it comes to my spelling of the word doughnut. Au contraire. My spelling is consistent. It's other people who have taken liberties with the arrangement of the letters.

Allow me to stake out my position. There is only one reverent way to spell the heavenly toroidal confection and that is by combining the words dough and nut. This gives the doughnut an air of respectability which it richly deserves. Unfortunately, the individuals, committees or robots imbued with flawed artificial intelligence who/that gave out the national commemorative days, spelled it "National Donut Day" bringing doughnuts down a cultural notch or two and endorsing their boorish orthography.

I will not be led astray by pressure from the way national commemorative days and websites are spelled. But, on the other hand, let's not be dogmatic and inflexible in our ways. On some occasions, as when the need arises to save space on grocery store signs, or for the occasional convenience when we don't have time to produce the extra three letters, we may have to yield to the vulgar spelling. It's entropically inevitable anyway. But, not on my watch.

Column 061, May 27, 2012

My Dog and His Khat

It's my dog again. Ever since the lawn greened up, he has taken to eating grass like his close cousin, the cow.

Whenever I ask why dogs behave this way, it seems that many people consider themselves experts and can speak with authority on the matter. It bothers me that they will not add a comment like "I have heard" or "I believe it is because" or "I have a theory." No. They are sure that dogs eat grass because "they need it for their digestive tract" or because "it contains a nutrient that the dog is missing."

These people are very lucky that they have personal, revealing conversations with their dogs, making them so knowledgeable. My dog doesn't tell me anything. I am forced to use observation, reason, and deduction to form theories that may or may not be correct.

Let us stick to the facts and list some observations about my dog's behavior during grass-eating season:

1. He can eat grass anytime but only does when he thinks I'm not looking.

2. Even though he happily chews the grass, he has great trouble swallowing it, yet he manages to choke it down as if were his least favorite food. Sometimes he gags but usually composes himself enough to finally take it all in. It's like watching someone chug Pepto-Bismol.

3. After he eats enough of it, he develops a powerful thirst and laps up a lot of water.

4. After a short while…give it a minute…wait for it…he pukes it all up.

5. Post-puking, he is a happy dog, tail wagging and probably on the lookout for more grass.

And now, speaking in humble tones and not as an ersatz authority on the matter, let me put forth *my* theory. Dogs eat grass because it gets them high. I know! It all makes sense.

Green grass is the dog's khat, and as I'm sure you already know, khat is the plant from the Arabian Peninsula and Africa whose leaves are chewed by people of different cultures just like we drink coffee. As a stimulant, it produces a mild euphoria and excitement. Unlike drinking coffee, the local sheriff will put you in the pokey for possession if you're caught chewin' in these here parts, but it is readily available and legal in places like downtown Djibouti.

Other people chew khat. People here chew tobacco. Dogs chew grass. It makes everybody happy except for those who must clean up after the chewers and maybe hardened conservatives who would criminalize the chewing of grass. Now let's take my theory and see if it fits the observations.

Guilt is a big part of consuming stimulants. People are always hiding the fact that they chew tobacco, and chewing khat can be associated with guilt when you involve a jury. Guilt is precisely why the dog partakes only when he thinks he is not being watched.

Apparently, the dog gets most of his pleasure from chewing. Unable to spit, dogs seem to be preprogrammed to swallow anything they put in their mouth that's not bigger than their head, so the dog is obliged to swallow the grassy wad. All this chewing sets off his low-on-saliva alarm so he drinks a lot of water to compensate. He gets a mental buzz while his little doggie brain sends a message to his stomach that he has binged over his limit and it's time to throw the gastric transmission into reverse. This is when the puking commences.

It's not a pretty sight, especially for a confirmed "sympathy puker" like me (I can't stand to see anybody puke alone). The other day, my dog horked up a grassy wad nearly the size of

Rhode Island. He expelled his nauseate (used here as a noun) outdoors, so the only proper response I could muster was "Good dog!"

Perhaps it's not like any euphoria we know. Maybe the gagging and vomiting are all part of the fun or part of a dog religious experience. Who can say? Certainly not my dog, not with his strict vow of silence.

More careful observation is necessary and by careful, I mean farther away from the dog when he is in upchuck mode. One cleanup is better than two.

The Dog

Column 068, July 15, 2012

All Clear, Almost

You can come out of your bunkers now and check to see if anybody blew the roof off your house. The Fourth of July is over, sort of.

Since this was the first Independence Day in sixty-three years that consumer fireworks were again, legal in Maine (where I, only by the grace of God, still live), pyrotechnic use has stretched holiday celebrations from a single night to a rather nebulous time period. In the smoky morning aftermath of Independence Eve, people wake up to a surplus of empty Bud and possibly Manischewitz bottles and that pallet of bottle rockets that was overlooked in the dark. They have to make the choice of whether to store them for a distant occasion or to go into the backyard and just "have themselves a time."

My dog is having himself a time as well. Already plagued by a variety of neuroses, he becomes visibly anxious anytime he hears even a small bang. Outside, he retreats into his dog house, or if unchained, he heads straight to the house and dances nervously to music only he can hear until someone opens the door. Inside, he explores all corners of the house, finding each an unsatisfactory retreat from his personal demons, whereupon he begins his search again.

Of course, you could say that the dog is reacting to a perceived threat with avoidance and escape behaviors, but I find it more endearing to think of him with a chronic neurotic disorder, which is to say, he's just plain nuts. Sadly, even high-priced psychoanalysis would be wasted on him since he refuses to speak, let alone share deep feelings and memories about a possibly troubled puppyhood. No, the only help he might be getting is drug therapy, but his income is thin and he does not have a prescription rider on his health insurance policy. Regrettably, he revealed a private preexisting condition at the time he applied for coverage.

My artist sister has given her dogs something called "Calm Down!" because her two canines would alternate between a major bout of "SmackDown" and a nonstop trapeze act in her living room. She had to either dope their food or drug their water just so she could repair the damages.

"Calm Down!" is a homeopathic treatment that is "not a drug" but a "natural blend of essence from selected flowers." Okay, cannabis is also an essence from selected flowers, as is opium, but we all know these essences are essentially drugs. I would suggest that any "natural blend" that calms dogs down may just be—well, a drug. One good study by the scientific community and we won't be calling it homeopathic and natural.

She would give each dog one teaspoon, twice daily, and then I believe she would take a swig or two herself. It seemed to work.

Anyway, thank goodness for fireworks, which were legalized just in time to allow people to vent their pent-up joy and gratitude about what we call freedom. I had a suspicion that my neighbors were celebratory, but I had no real handle on the amount of firepower cached here in the village. The container trucks and forklifts should have tipped me off.

Of course, the means of celebration and testifying about the joys of freedom with explosives is not free. Maine fireworks dealers have to charge a price to cover the cost of their $5,000 license fee and insurance. Plus, they're required by law to sell from a permanent, freestanding building dedicated to firework sales, which usually doesn't come cheap. But it seems when times are hard and people are forced to choose between a meal and their prescribed medicine, they go out and spend big on fireworks.

Besides stretching the holiday out, the new law certainly

helps demonstrate the principle of taking a yard when given an inch. There seem to be many more illegal devices being used in pyrotechnic displays in my town than before the law was relaxed.

"Hey, Earl, you think the sheriff will notice if I mix in a case of those commercial six-inch fireworks shells with our backyard display?"

"Good idea, Beauford. Between the sparklers, fountains, and those .50-caliber tracer rounds, what's to notice?"

Maybe one more night in the old bunker isn't such a bad idea.

Doughnut Confessions

I have recently been scolded for running a column about doughnuts and not revealing my involvement with the doughnut industry—conflict of interest and all that. When I suggested disclosing my connections, it was demanded I use the word *confess* to more accurately convey my heinous sins and admit a lifelong addiction to the sweet morsels. However, the truth of the matter goes far beyond being in love with a problematic food item; in the spirit of full disclosure, let me state that my name is Tom and, and...and I own a doughnut machine. (All the other doughnut machine owners in unison: "Hi, Tom.")

This is not just a heated pot of frying oil where you can drop in some dough. No, this is a Donut Robot Mark IV that can produce up to fifty dozen mini-doughnuts per hour. Not only do I own the machine, but it's also rigged up in a booth that can be taken to distant festivals in order to service thousands of doughnut-needy people. Not only that, the booth can produce twenty gallons of coffee every hour and serve it up hot or on ice. Sometimes we even sell soft drinks. Yes, it's true: I am a part-time carnie but not the kind who would steal your wallet —although I will take your money without compunction.

It all started in my early youth when I read the tale about Homer Price and the doughnut machine by Robert McCloskey. I have come to realize that the story is really a socialistic odyssey disguised as a children's book where the boy Homer is left in charge of a doughnut machine that he can't turn off. Doughnuts pile up everywhere as Homer, no doubt representing the proletariat, cannot keep up with the newly mechanized means of production that he, symbolically, cannot control.

Most of the deep socioeconomic references in the story

escaped me. I didn't understand the concept of capital resources or machines as the modern means of production. Obvious references to the law of supply and demand didn't affect me one bit. The only thing I came away with from the story was that someday, in some way, I just had to have my own doughnut machine. I mean, can anything be more fun than an out-of-control doughnut machine? One problem: I never had a legitimate excuse to own one.

Forty-five years pass. In 2002, while attending the National Folk Festival in Bangor, Maine, it wasn't hard to notice that there were about a hundred thousand people in attendance and maybe twenty food vendors. Each vendor had a line of customers that stretched to New Hampshire who were more than willing to move our economy forward by purchasing fair food at inflated prices. *

My wife, an accomplished businesswoman, said to me, "We have to get in on this action."

Being an accomplished dreamer, I said to my wife, "I will build a doughnut booth and they will come, although most of them are already here…" Privately, I was bursting with the thought that this might be my only chance in life to buy a doughnut machine!

The convoluted story of going from this thought to the reality of operating a doughnut booth has to be left for another time. I must confess that we did indeed get into the next festival as vendors by discounting our

Photo: Janis Kay

lack of experience. We were unsure about everything and even questioned the appropriateness of our product. To absolve ourselves of the guilt in supplying Americans with fat- and sugar-infused toroidal fried dough, we chose to do business under the name "Dangerous Donuts" and let the buyer beware. This prompted a standard question from our customers: "Why are they called Dangerous Donuts?" After answering several hundred times, we came upon a standard answer: "Ask your doctor."

Photo: Annie Henderson

So, what more do I have to confess? I discovered a lot about the Homer Price story vs. reality when we went into business. Had he owned the doughnut machine, he would have been more concerned with keeping it running than with shutting the machine down. Capitalism would have trumped socialism, leaving the working class with fatty foods. But under any political system, I must confess that there really are few things more fun than an out-of-control doughnut machine.

* Author's note:

The sentence about "purchasing fair food at inflated prices" is a bit misleading. It should convey the message that the customers were willing to purchase food at inflated fair prices. But even this leaves the reader wondering if the food was just fair, as the original sentence implies, the food was the type that is typically available at a fair, or if the fair itself was somehow inflated.

Okay, truth be told, the food wasn't five-star, and the prices *were* high so this only leaves me struggling to explain that customers were willing to purchase *acceptable fair-style food at prices normally inflated when the venue is a festival.* Or, something like that.

English is *so* complicated.

Column 072, August 12, 2012

Annoying Words

It's time for the summer assault on words we don't like. This is where we dig in and take a stand against English words that offend us. Then, we hold our position and watch as the immense forces of language roll over and squash us like bugs.

Language is a funny thing because it's just a bunch of unique sounds that most of us agree mean something. English has enough of them to allow you to express complex ideas very efficiently, unless of course you're a teenager where no language, however efficient or complete, can ever serve to get your thoughts and ideas expressed.

Sometimes offensive words are those you may dislike for no reason other than how they grate on your eardrum. Their meaning probably affects your feeling for them, but mostly it is the raw sound of the word that makes you cringe.

I very much dislike *tummy, bra, lotion, mums, blog,* and *blouse,* in that order. I don't care much for the word *tartar,* either, especially when used as the cooking ingredient cream of tartar. The thought that there is cream associated with tartar is more than just unappealing—it's a bad thought that doesn't jibe with leading a happy life.

It's even hard to know how to pronounce *tartar.* Do you say it quickly as you might *martyr* or *smarter,* or do you use the awkward semi-stutter as you would when introducing Jar Jar Binks from the planet Naboo? Jar Jar Binks is thought to be one of the most annoying characters in the *Star Wars* series, and it can only be because his name is a lot like *tar-tar.*

Until recently, I didn't even know what tartar was, and I didn't want to ask because I would have to say the words with my own mouth. Turns out that tartar is an acidic compound that comes from grapes. It's the crystals that form in grape jam or precipitate out of grape juice. Sometimes it forms on the cork in wine bottles. For the love of God, people, let's call it what it really is: potassium bitartrate, or for you more technically proper types, potassium hydrogen tartrate.

The white crystals are used in baking powder as a leavening agent. It's what makes the bread dough produce carbon dioxide bubbles, making the holes in our bread rolls. It's also a component in laxatives and is used in the tinning of metals. It's amazing that something you use to make bread can also be used to keep you regular while you're smearing it on your hobby circuit to prepare it for soldering. We have to stop calling it "cream of tartar."

Recently, *The New Yorker* did a study—which is to say they ran an informal contest on Twitter to find words people most disliked and wanted struck from the English language. Words *The New Yorker* uncovered were not even on my radar, although they most certainly will be considered if I suddenly become king with the power to ban *lotion* and *bra*.

Phlegm, bling, and *impacted* were among those nominated, but many people chose to hate the word *dude* and disliked *moist* even more. Considering all the nominees and their own personal aversions, *The New Yorker* staff finally declared *slacks* as the number one word that should be obliterated.

I can see why people don't like the word *moist.* It conjures up images of places that are too warm and dark, possibly with a foul odor and mold. Moreover, the word ends in *oist,* which we all know is the first part of *oysters.* Need I say more?

I personally have no problem with *slacks,* although I have never used the word in conversation. Some words I would say more often if the opportunity arose: *carbuncle* and *hackmatack* immediately come to mind. It may even be fun to try and bring back some slang words that were immensely popular in the past but have fallen into disuse. *Huzzah* would be one, as in: "Huzzah! Have you seen the new menu down at Hooters?"

But there is no use fighting it. Language will go in the direction it wants as it ignores individual pleas for elegance or beauty. You may as well pull your slacks up to your tummy and hide in a moist cave as you are impacted by forces you can't control, dude.

Column 075, September 2, 2012

Dog Days

As gently as I could, I tried to explain to my dog that the "dog days of summer" were officially over. He seemed to listen intently before he turned his attention to licking himself as dogs tend to do, and then he lay down to nap. Was he trying to send me a message or just ignore me? I had to get him up by knocking gently on his thick skull to explain everything from the beginning.

Somehow, I get the feeling that terse letters from readers will follow, but this is such a curious thing I just have to mention it. Whenever I knock softly on my dog's head—or sometimes maybe not too softly, on the middle of his skull, just above the eyes—it gives a little hollow sound. It's a *thunk, thunk, thunk* as if you were knocking on an empty wooden box. Okay, sometimes it's a few more *thunks,* but the sound is the same. I really don't know why I'm surprised; it should have been expected, but still, it's rather amazing.

Logically, you know that something is in there. The dog does have a brain, and it's packed in tightly—except for the frontal sinus, but I think that's a bit lower. There really shouldn't be a hollow sound there.

In your heart however, the hollow sound seems natural, and it's a bit comforting as if that is what you expected all along. Careful observation and repeated attempts at in-depth conversations can only lead you to believe that, at least with my dog, there really is nothing in there. The dog doesn't seem to mind the thunking, but dogs are like that. As long as you aren't causing them any pain, or any great pain, they generally let you do what you want to them in exchange for being near you. I assume that is the reason, but who can say for sure?

Then on the other hand, why on earth would they ever want to be near you?

I yell at my dog regularly using disparaging language sometimes peppered with mild oaths and oftentimes employing denigrating epithets. Wow; that was some sentence. Who the heck writes like that anymore? I don't think I even know what it means, and I've read it over a number of times. I was just trying to say that when I yell at my dog, it comes out like: "Get the *&#% out of the road you stupid pinhead!" And I do that all the time.

So I yell at my dog, and what does he do? He wags his tail, lowers his head, and comes to me. He just doesn't have the capacity to sneer the "get-lost-you-oppressive-human" sneer and then take off for Lancaster, Pennsylvania—which has a milder climate, is ranked as one of the most dog-friendly cities in the US, and finally, for my dog, is easily within walking distance.

Dogs seem to have no short-term memory. You can leave them out in the cold, and by the time you remember to let them in, they've forgotten that it was you who originally put them out. They treat you like a hero for having rescued them from that mean old whoever it was who left them out in the cold.

Long-term memory is another story. You can softly mention to your wife in a room on the far side of the house from the dog that "our canine must be taken to the veterinary clinic for a rabies vaccination" and you'll be able to look out the window and see the dog leaving, bags packed, most likely for Lancaster, Pennsylvania.

Anyway, as I was trying to explain to the dog, the "dog days of summer" refer to the time of year when the Dog Star, Sirius, rises at the same time as the sun. They run from about July 3 to August 11 and, alas, have nothing really to do with it being so hot that dogs just lie around in the shade unable to do anything else.

Now I have never, to my recollection, used *alas* in a sentence except when it was part of Alaska, but it seems to fit in. I'll have to look it up sometime to make sure, but right now it's so hot that I'm unable to do anything else besides lie around in the shade.

No Column This Week

I'm terribly sorry, but there will be no column this week. It's because my wife and I have decided to open a restaurant. Hey, how smart is that? I am just too busy to do anything remotely related to sitting down and taking the time to write, so no column. Sorry again.

Yes, yes, I know what you're thinking. I've been told many, many times. Whenever I mention opening a restaurant on the coast of Maine, people immediately open up their hearts with advice. They say, "A restaurant?" Then they pause to look at me for hints that I can still listen to reason before they continue. "You know the success rate is very low." Then, summoning up all the tact at their disposal, they hit me with the keenest of insight: "You must be aware that the three most important words when you are considering opening a restaurant are *stupid, stupid, stupid.*"

In all modesty, it may be a peak of stupidity for me since I have no restaurant experience, unless you want to count being the assistant milk carton manager in my grade-school cafeteria. I also think you really can't count building and running my donut booth as legitimate experience, since making donuts for fifty thousand people at a music festival is closer to an asylum visit than it is to food service reality.

My wife, on the other hand, understands the pitfalls of owning a restaurant since she just recently emerged from the pit after falling into it thirty-five years ago. "Stay out of the restaurant business!" she has told me almost every day since we met. She has little stomach for a no-show cook simply because he was taken down by a swat team and waitresses who quit their jobs without notice after winning no more than a secondary

Powerball payout.

To assure you and our banker that we are still north of idiotic, let me make it clear that we never intended to open a restaurant. We were merely landlords who got stuck with a building that happened to be a restaurant but turned into a rather considerable money incinerator what with mortgage, utilities, insurance, and tax payments. How we ended up with this property is a story for another time, but I assure you that we attended the auction only on a lark the day we committed to buying it. We had no idea the peppermint schnapps was actually authorized to bid for us.

Oh, we've considered many other options to get the building to pay for itself. My proposal was Tuesday-night cockfighting in the basement, but the decline of the once massive Maine chicken industry has left the most aggressive chickens in the hot-and-spicy bin at Colonel Sanders'. Topless establishments seem to draw the arson crowd in this state, so that's off the table. The only organizations that want to rent office space are Democrats and Republicans, but both groups consist of short-term tenants who are always in a fundraising crisis. When they vacate the premises come November, the walls are full of pinholes and tape, coffee stains abound on the ceiling, and you can never get the scent of politics out of the carpet.

No, we decided the building must stay a restaurant, and as ridiculous as it sounds, we can't afford *not* to open it.

Many months ago, we realized that the first thing we had to do is go to the bank and try to secure a wad of money. It became obvious that if you mention it's to open a restaurant, you won't get it. Bankers are much too smart for that. They already have a pile of restaurants under foreclosure, and it's no longer a thrill for them to swoop in to surprise a restaurant owner who already knows they're coming. Bankers are much more likely to lend you money to run guns through the Khyber

Pass before they ever even consider a loan for any type of eatery.

Fair warning: Again, there may not be a column next week. It's a small matter of making a quick trip to Pakistan to pick up a Khyber Pass Kalashnikov Special as a small gift for my banker. I may as well pick up some Punjab kebab pointers or a falafel idea in the unlikely event I make it back for the opening. Lobster falafel, anyone?

Column 103, March 17, 2013

Licensing Your Restaurant Made Easy

Really, how hard can it be to open a restaurant in Maine? Lots and lots of people open restaurants and bars. You can tell just by driving up the coast and counting the ghosts of restaurants, grills, bars and taverns that set up shop and then closed down, never to be seen again. The state is awash in bankrupt, foreclosed, ruined, and insolvent restaurants that started out with positive attitudes and dreams of big success. I imagine many of these establishments failed because the prospectors ran out of steam trying to cross the Licenseandpermits Mountain Range on their way to the restaurant gold fields.

For some, restaurant opening is a snap. McDonalds opens thousands of new restaurants every morning all over the world, but they know what they're doing. I understand the Mars rover *Curiosity* is opening a McFranchise in Gale Crater, which is, of course, the best location on the planet. It's one of the few spots on Mars with any vehicular traffic and is destined to become a major tourist attraction.

For my wife and me, navigating the permit trail was more of a trial. She maintains it's easier to have a baby, while I would rather pass a shovel, full of kidney stones, than repeat the journey. But after all the screaming is over, when they wean you off the drugs and the bandages come off, you get to open your doors to your beloved public.

It's really unfair to compare opening a restaurant to having a baby. Babies give you a few years to learn how to parent before they learn to seriously yank your chain. Opening a restaurant is more like giving birth to a couple of fifteen-year-old girls who constantly spend all your money, make trouble in school, eat all your food, have undesirable boyfriends, and might be involved with designer drugs or worse yet, reality TV.

The path looks easy enough, but it helps if you overdose on naivety before the party begins. You start by getting a federal employer's identification number. There is no fee. It's one of the last free things left in the USA, sort of like handcuffs are free when you get arrested. The government can't keep track of all the taxes you pay to stay in business if you don't have this number.

Turns out you are going to need a state employer's ID number as well. While you're at it, get yourself a state unemployment insurance account number and a state withholding account number. Of course, you'll need a state resale certificate and a "state sales and use tax" account because selling things automatically makes you a tax collector for the state—which, by the way, doesn't pay you a penny to do the dirty work.

And while you are shopping at the state licenses and permits store, don't forget to go to the restaurant aisle to pick up specific permits for your chosen industry. An eating place establishment ID with its accompanying certificate number is mandatory, and if you plan to serve alcohol, get a liquor license, which, as you may imagine, is another story. You may have to get certification by taking a food safety course and an alcohol serving course, but we're only talking licenses and permits here, so in that spirit we won't talk about the accounts and pin numbers you will need to pay all your taxes online.

Having satisfied the state, you will need permission from your town to open a business and to serve food and alcohol. It may be just an application, or you may be required to perform a specially choreographed song and dance number in front of the planning board with a PowerPoint presentation and a live jazz ensemble. Indoor pyrotechnics are a very good idea during your presentation, but they require a special permit from the fire marshal. Don't forget to get any building permits you might need.

As long as you complete all the forms, answer all the questions, attend all the meetings, pay all the fees, and don't ruffle any feathers, you are in business!

It's a good thing we decided to open in a business-friendly town located in a super business-friendly state or it might have been an ordeal getting this business off the ground. I'm so accustomed to pain, I can hardly wait for that next kidney stone.

Author's notes about the above column:

The application to the town has no section about entertainment that you may be planning at your establishment, so the town requires a letter outlining your plans regarding performances and spectacle.

The heading on my letter read: "Contrary to rumors about town, there will be no cockfighting in the basement of the new restaurant every Tuesday night promptly at 9:00 p.m., where the $15 cover charge includes one drink. It is not necessary for cockfighting patrons to park toward the back of the building since the door to the basement (as opposed to the side door) will be locked. No bets will be accepted prior to fight time and certainly not after fighting has commenced if it were to commence, which indeed it will not since there will be no cockfighting."

We do, however, plan to bring the following entertainment at the restaurant, although dates are yet to be determined:

Fight club	Alice Cooper
Ventriloquists	Animal acts
Chinese gymnasts	Very large pyrotechnic displays
Dancing girls	Pole acts
Symphonic orchestra	Yodeling competitions
Car shows	Drag races

The town can rest assured that there are no plans to bring mimes or mime troupes to perform at the new business. As a matter of fact, we have made it our policy to not even let mimes into the establishment, not without a two-drink minimum purchase.

Breaking into Small Groups

Someone please, invent a better way of getting a large number of people to meet and agree on things without breaking into small groups and electing a moderator.

Have you gone to a meeting hoping to influence some policy just by your sheer presence? I know I have. I go with the dream that people will see things my way simply by me being there. But suddenly, to my shock and dismay, people start breaking up into small groups and electing a moderator because the guy who's come up with a better way has not yet been born.

It seems we are stuck with this uncomfortable social get-together where we have to actually start talking with people, carefully avoiding any alienating topics even though, truth be told, we came to the meeting to confront alienating topics.

At meetings in my town, I've found myself at a small table where my end of the conversation starts sounding a little whack:

"I can see by your name tag that you are called Jerry....No, we've never met, but I've waved to you for the last eighteen years from my house across the street....Yes, I kind of figured you were Wiccan with all the symbols....No, we don't mind the late-night drumming....No, don't be silly, the smoke hardly bothers us at all what with all the chanting, and who knew so many neo-pagans and wizards had Harleys?"

I always try to elect the person in my group as moderator who least wants the job, besides me. They are the ones who most likely will not impose their will and skew the opinion of the group when summarizing our findings at the end of the meeting.

And if you are a moderator or heading up a meeting, I have a small request: Don't ask me at any point to close my eyes. You can ask me to use my imagination, you can ask me to visualize this or conceptualize that. If I need to close my eyes to do any of those things, I will do that on my own. There is a very good chance that while you are droning away, I will doze off in the middle of the meeting and you won't have to ask me to close my eyes at all.

Finally, I would like to understand why someone always suggests that "we make a circle and hold hands" at the end of the meeting to "feel the energy." I do not typically attend meetings where, say, Halle Berry or Penelope Cruz end up in my group and elect me moderator. If I did, you could bet holding hands would not be an issue.

In high school physics class, we made a big circle, held hands, and the teacher, who we called Mr. Enzyme (although I think he spelled his name differently), hooked the entire class up to some generator. I don't remember much after that except I was allowed to hold hands with one of the hot cheerleaders who under normal circumstances would never have considered even accidentally touching me. Nowadays, they don't allow teachers to hook entire classes up to high-voltage circuitry, and the experience of holding hands with an attractive girl who is out of your league while your bodies build up high levels of electrical charge has sadly been lost to subsequent generations.

Look, there is no energy that flows around circles at municipal meetings. No, really. I can't feel any energy. I can feel the guy's sweaty hand on my right and the woman's ice-cold hand that she coughed in on my left but no detectable energy.

Since the last meeting where this happened, I have a new policy—whenever anyone suggests we all hold hands, I will no longer go along with the crowd. I will speak up. I will state loud and clear that while everyone is gearing up to hold hands,

I will be forming a group in the corner of the room for people who do not wish to hold hands. We will not be breaking up into smaller groups nor will we be electing a moderator. We will simply meet with the clear goal of finding our own cars and then driving home.

You can bet we will indeed feel the energy after we get in our cars and press on the accelerator.

Column 084, November 4, 2012

The Ice Machine Cometh

Did I mention a few weeks ago that my wife and I are opening a restaurant? Shoot, I didn't know it then, but in order to open a restaurant, especially one that includes a bar, you first have to pass the ice machine test. To be sure, there are a lot of other details to attend to like food ordering and hiring employees, but if you open before you come to terms with your ice machine, you might as well call the repo man and initiate foreclosure procedures on yourself.

As it turns out, most restaurants fail within the first three years of operation because the owners and staff are overwhelmed by the ice machine. To avoid the socially embarrassing scenario of being hauled off to debtor's prison, we had to delay opening until we agreed to all of the terms and conditions in the contract it offered us.

The ice machine is obviously built with alien technology. At the very least, it was built by a wise and ancient civilization during the Grant administration that was on the verge of total collapse because every person in the nation wanted to open a restaurant. When the elders discovered they were on a path of self-destruction where everyone and his brother would be in the food-service industry, they called on their best scientists to develop something that no restaurant or bar could do without. It had to be indispensable like the soda gun at the bar, yet it had to discourage people from opening a restaurant and encourage them to seek another career, like butchering, baking, or lightbulb making.

The scientists worked furiously, and just in time to avoid total global annihilation, they built an ice machine. No decent restaurant-bar could ever be in business without one, yet when the owners and staff realized they could not deal with its demands and quirks, they would flee in droves to another line of work.

The machine is a technical, psychological, and financial wall of challenges for all who aspire to be restaurateurs. Of course, bars and restaurants have a lot of other equipment to keep operational. The toothpick dispenser always needs attention to keep from jamming up, and the soap pump that squirts foam on customers' shirts in the washroom can only be maintained if you find the key to open it. But the king of high maintenance is the ice machine.

The machine calls upon a lot of different disciplines to merely exist. You need to either master these crafts or hire a plumber to manage the water and an electrical technician to pamper its sensors, power supplies, and controls. Of course, you're going to need a top-notch refrigeration man along with an accountant and possibly a law firm and an insurance agent. Finally, you will need a fairly good counselor. The counselor's duties include mediating disputes between the bartender and the ice machine, talking to the ice machine when it goes into one of its moody periods, and also talking the owner down from high places when ice machine ownership becomes too much to bear.

Literary scholars are just now coming to realize that *The Iceman Cometh,* Eugene O'Neill's great play that takes place in a bar, is really about the bar owner and his desperate pipe dream that someday he will come to understand the plumbing of his ice machine. The owner would have figured as a major character with more speaking parts had he not spent so much time backstage dealing with ice machine problems during the time O'Neill was writing the play.

For us, time is running out because money is being spent on employees, food, and dumpsters. We have to open soon. Luckily, the truce with the ice machine is holding. After countless hours of troubleshooting, all the leaks have been attended to; all of the worn parts have been replaced; corroded areas have been addressed; and the machine has been cleaned spotless, inside and out. It seems satisfied and at the moment is producing ice without any odd noises, smoke, or fire. Things are quiet. Too quiet.

I see that while we negotiated with the ice machine, all of the tourists have left the state so we won't have to worry about accounting for any income from that demographic. We may have missed the summer season but with winter upon us, we will have ice. I just hope it's from the ice machine.

Column 085, November 11, 2012

Mispelling Problems

Did you flunk spelling in the second grade? I know I did, and it's been haunting me ever since. It seems it took me until grade nineteen to achieve an eighth-grade level of proficiency.

The inability to spell looms large in my childhood memories. I vividly remember the trauma of being taunted in the school playground by the local intellectual bully. "Look at you," he would announce in front of his learned thugs and all the hottest sixth-grade girls. "You're ugly, your mother dresses you funny, and you can't even spell *carbuncle* or *daiquiri.*" Then they would all laugh at me and go back to playing Scrabble and debating theories of linguistics and deeper subjects like the relative grossness of phlegm.

There was a particular incident in grade school I vividly remember when my teacher confronted me with the threat that I would end up working as a ditchdigger in adulthood if I did not learn to spell. I recall this prediction every time I drive past a state road crew working on some culvert or water-flow-control problem. It has not escaped my notice that the man apparently making the most money on the crew is the one sitting in the air-conditioned cab and operating the quarter-million-dollar Caterpillar 320D L hydraulic excavator equipped with an articulated ditch bucket. That would make him a ditchdigger, right? I sometimes wonder how well he can spell.

The threat of becoming a ditchdigger and the academic bullying incidents are all solidly locked in my memory, but the ability to spell *hydraulic* or *daiquiri* on demand still escapes me.

Throughout grade school, I was always the first one to be asked to sit down during a spelling bee. "Poor dumb kid," my teachers would no doubt think. "He can't even spell *maybe.*

M-a-b-e indeed. I wonder how he'll do behind the controls of a Cat 320D L hydraulic excavator?"

At the college level, spelling problems really haunted me. It was in the days of the typewriter when I pulled an all-nighter or two getting a forty-page magnum opus term paper finished. (A typewriter is a device like a word processor-printer combination, but the memory and central processor circuits are all user-embedded.) Come sunup, I carefully placed all the pages in a clear plastic cover and stood back to admire its bold title: "The Roll of Forest Management in Outdoor Recreation." I turned it in.

For those readers who may have flunked spelling alongside me, R-o-l-l indicates what your car does before it comes to a stop when the engine ceases to function. Or it could mean the pastry you eat with your morning coffee after pulling an all-nighter. R-o-l-e, on the other hand, has the same meaning as *function* and would have been the preferred way of spelling it on every one of the forty pages in my otherwise brilliant dissertation.

And while we're discussing forty, why is there no *u* in *forty*? Isn't it based on the word *four*? I was actually in my forties before it was gently pointed out to me that the word *forty-four* only has one *u*. In my dreams, I write copy for greeting cards. The one I am designing has a cover that reads "Why is there no *U* in forty?" Here you open the card, and it says "Because you're fifty! Happy 50th Birthday!" I wake up when I realize that no one wants to give me a dollar for my composition. Not wishing to waste a good idea, I thought I would drop it into the spelling column here. Feel free to use it.

Before spellcheckers, I had a dictionary where I put a dot next to a word each time I looked it up. Some words had multiple dots. And some words like *maybe* were pretty much dotted out, indicating that I am a slow learner. There are a number of words I still can't spell: *recipe, lettuce, ingredients,* and *bovine spongiform encephalopathy* immediately come to mind, all important words when you write a menu. Of course, I could never spell *restaurant* until I recently opened one.

After struggling with spelling all my life, I look at texts I get from college-educated professionals and I am dismayed to see that today, spelling hardly matters at all, f u no wat I mean.

===============

Column 089, December 9, 2012

A Fun Restaurant Owner Simulation

Everybody wants to know what it's like to be a new restaurant owner. It's really very easy to duplicate the feeling in the comfort of your own home without the bother of leasing a building to actually run a business—and I'm going to tell you how to do it.

First, invite your best and worst friends and a bunch of total strangers over for what you might want to call "dinner theater." Be sure to invite that unhappy guy from down the street who still lives with his parents and spends his time posting his opinion all over the web so he can expound on how bad his experience was at your party. Tell the guests that they aren't there just to eat but to witness your experience as a restaurant owner and to add realistic tension to the event.

Next, take as many hundred-dollar bills as you have and can borrow and pin them up all over the house. If you want the experience of owning a really nice restaurant, you should pin up at least a thousand bills. Pin up more for a successful franchise and less for a hash-house-dive type of place.

The object is to run around the house and collect as much money as you have invested in this exercise plus any money your guests may want to contribute before your house and all your money essentially go up in flames. Remember to try and get all your own money back before accepting any from the guests.

Brief your guests that when the fun starts, they are all to chant in unison: "Where's my food?" getting louder and louder as the event shifts into high gear. As you run around trying to recoup your investment, any of the guests are allowed to trip you, but in all fairness, they have to shout out a reason before they stick out their foot. For example, "My soup is cold" is very popular, as is "The dishwasher just quit." However, don't hold your guests to traditional reasons to trip you up; let them get creative, as almost anything goes. "Furnace broken," "health inspector," "property taxes," and "kitchen fire" are all good, but "colostomy bag accident in the bathroom" and "broken water pipe hosing the staff" are much more entertaining.

Now, here comes the fun part. Give a lighter to a nimble guest and ask them to go around the house and set as many hundred-dollar bills on fire as they can find. A proper simulation requires that you cannot collect any bills unless they are burning. Get to them before it's too late and use only your bare hands to extinguish the flames.

To collect your money, you can hire as many helpers as you can afford, so you won't have many. It's good to make sure that these helpers are hardworking and trustworthy and that they like your management style. They can quit or you can fire them, but just for fun, you have to chase them down for the money they have already collected before they get to their car. The helpers are allowed to go through all of your cabinets and use any supplies they find without your permission. Ask them to cultivate squabbles among themselves and to bring any personal problems they may have to work along with their pets and contagious diseases. Don't forget to pay your employer taxes.

Be sure to grease your shoes with oil spilled on the floor from the fryolators just before you begin. It isn't really necessary, but if you have an overexcited dog or two chasing you around the house and barking constantly, it adds another layer of realism to the simulation.

As you run around trying to save your investment, invite your guests to say anything they please as to how they would run the place or how they would improve the food. You must stop and thank them for their input each time and encourage them to post anything they find to their displeasure about your house, your appearance, the kind of car you drive, and your mother's age all over the internet. Compliments allow you to get a ten-second break and a pat on the back.

Ready? Check to make sure you have 911 on speed dial.

Set...can't go unless you set your hair on fire.

GO! It's fun.

Errant Texts and Acronyms

Not long ago, I received a text message on my cell phone that read exactly this way: "Hey its me, Evan :p. I'm watching a movie with my mom so I figured I would text you. How was the rest of the night at the fire? I just wanted to say goodnight and that I love you. :) seeya in the morning."

There are several possibilities here. Some are quite disturbing. I have to immediately discount the likelihood that the message was actually meant for me, as this cuts the disturbing possibilities by a substantial margin. The big question is why isn't Evan using any acronyms? I have been led to believe that all younger people who text use acronyms.

Most cell phones use SMS for texting, a TLA (three-letter acronym) for Short Message Service. SMS is a standardized communications protocol (SCP), which mostly limits messages to 160 characters or fewer, so abbreviations are the rule for chatty or sometimes garrulous users (SGUs).

Abbreviating is much older than most people realize. Recent decoding of a memory chip recovered from Abraham Lincoln's personal cell phone revealed he was quite an accomplished abbreviator: "4SKOR N 7YRS ago R Fathrs brawt 4th on dis contnt a nu natn conCvd n libty n dedic8d 2 d propssitn dat al mn R creatD =."

The website netlingo.com lists about 1,600 acronyms that people allegedly use while texting. They range from obvious shorthand terms like B4 meaning "earlier than" to acronyms that are longer than the words they represent, like BUHBYE for "bye." There are conflicted acronyms, such as STD for "save the date" or, depending on context, "sexually transmitted disease," and hard-core, extra-long acronyms like ILICISCOMK, used not only for its space-saving properties but for cryptic and comic effect ("I laughed, I cried, I spilled coffee on my keyboard").

The obvious conclusion is that Evan is a much older man who never really caught on to texting, but this begs the question—how old is his mother?

So what is the proper procedure here? Is there any kind of texting etiquette that dictates what you do with a wrong number text? Do you ignore it? Answer it as if it were intended for you? Reply that the text was sent to you in error? Or do you publish it in a humor column? I am tempted to text back "I love you too, Evan. Meet me tonight by the fire. Bring your mother," but I'm concerned that it may prompt a dialogue.

I don't text as much as I would like. There just isn't enough time in my day to tap out a message when I can speed-dial whoever I am trying to reach and blurt out what I want them to know. It would be great to be able to sit in class or steal away to a quiet corner at work and surreptitiously text family and friends, but most people I know can live a full and productive life without ever getting a text from me.

As a matter of fact, the extent of my texting goes only as far as reading the few messages people and my cell phone company are compelled to send me. I refuse to type out a note on my cell phone keypad* where I must tap out 7-7-7-7 in order to generate an *s* for a text message. If I need to type *senselessness,* it amounts to thirty-nine keystrokes for a thirteen-letter word. Not a real time-saver considering almost all the messages I want to send people include the word *senselessness.*

Aside from the limitations of texting, I will be the first to admit that texting is superior to many forms of communications (smoke signals and the telegraph immediately come to mind). And there are circumstances where texting is the best choice.

A short message for someone to read at their convenience is a good example. "Call me July 10, 2057, when you get a chance" makes perfect sense, as does "Bert, noticed your barn smoking early this morning."

Finally, there is the hypothetical situation where you might be sitting in a quiet movie theater unable to suppress thoughts of your favorite columnist so you tap out a quick text message without making a sound, using the popcorn bag to shield the glare of the phone's tiny screen from your mother.

Goodnight, and I love you, too.

* Author's Note:

My old Motorola flip phone was loaded with features and even more limitations. Texting without a touch screen figured high on the limitations list. I never heard again from Evan.

Column 099, February 17, 2013

The Last Pay Phone

So "The Terminator" came to our business last month and just took the public pay phone from the side of my restaurant building without even asking me.

He didn't announce himself, but I took notice since he came out of his truck shaking a can of black spray paint. I thought it odd that a man his age would be spraying graffiti on the side of my building in the daylight, well before noon. Had my building been located in certain parts of New York or Los Angeles, he wouldn't have rated a second glance, but in small-town coastal Maine, I had to ask a few questions. We don't get much "tagging" here, which is street talk for vandalizing property with graffiti. It is a pathetic attempt to legitimize wrongdoing through language, as is using the words *ripping off* for thievery and *reality TV* for entertainment.

He was already spray-painting all the signs on the booth that said "FairPoint" and continued to work while we chatted politely. I asked him if he had any authority to do this or if I should be calling the police about wanton defacement. He produced a flashy ID in a plastic holder with lanyard from around his neck, and I marveled at how little skill it would take with Photoshop to produce such a document. He finished painting and explained that FairPoint would sue his company if any graphics remained by the end of the week since his company bought all the pay-phone assets from FairPoint. He then proceeded to remove the phone.

"Whoa. Just a minute. You're taking my phone?"

"Almost all the pay phones are being terminated. They don't bring in enough money. Someone will be by sometime for the booth."

"What will the local drug dealers use to communicate?"

"Hey, you're talking about my clientele," he snapped back.

"Hold on, this pay phone lives here. Don't you have a sense of history? I think it's the only one in town…it may be the last pay phone on the East Coast. I want that phone left on my building!"

"Didn't you get the letter?"

He produced a copy of a notice I was supposed to have received some time back. I scanned the letter and found a paragraph explaining that I could keep the pay phone for the convenience of the public—if I would just pony up $75 a month.

"Seventy-five dollars a month!" I said out loud in horror. "Let me get my wire cutters."

The pay phone had come with the building. It was almost a novelty that we hardly ever saw anyone use. We never received any compensation for maintaining a space for it, and we even paid for the electricity used to light the booth at night. It seemed like the light came on at dusk and off at dawn, but to my shock I discovered that it was always on.

Pay phones have been around since the Grover Cleveland administration when attendants would lock you in a phone booth and collect a fee at the end of your call before unlocking the door. In the year 2000, there were as many as two million pay phones scattered across the US. This is about the same number of cell phones that are lost in the US every three days at the present time. Today, less than a quarter of those remain in service—the pay phones, not the lost cell phones.

The man first removed the coin box that was surprisingly full and put it into a special safe in the back of his truck. Removing a few screws, the phone came away from the booth. The Terminator grabbed the wires, and without the decency of using a sharp pair of wire cutters, he just ripped them off the phone. Unceremoniously, the now dead communicator was thrown into the back of his pickup truck, where it landed with a crash on top of the corpses of two dozen similar devices.

"All going to metal recycling," he said as he drove off. Stunned, I never thought to ask him to leave me the phone, but it's all right because I found they are available on the web for $300 each.

Oh, what will we do without our pay phones? Of course, no one I know has used a pay phone in fifteen years but the convenience, the comfort, the history...well, the history, anyway.

The Last Pay Phone

Column 107, April 14, 2013

Miami Impressions

Early this winter, my wife and I planned a three-week visit to see our daughter and boyfriend-in-law in Florida. Our businesses constantly bully us into corners and threaten us with economic ruin should we decide to take a vacation. Fighting back takes a toll. We kept cutting our trip, and when all the vacationing was finished, we had actually managed to get away for four days, including travel time. The trip was unforgettable. We even experienced the new smaller bag of peanuts they now give you in-flight.

Miami is a wonderful place full of interesting people and lots of big-city action. The only possible negative aspect (really negated by all the positive things about Miami) is that it is full of interesting people and lots of big-city action.

Our last time in Miami, we checked in late to a moderately high-class hotel. The night was warm and the air was filled with that special feeling of tropical coup d'état and gunfire, so we immediately decided to take a late-night walk to see what was happening in the neighborhood. People tend to stay up late in Miami since they don't have to save on their fuel bills by sleeping during the coldest parts of the night.

We did not get more than fifty yards away from our charming accommodations when we were chased down by an employee of our hotel who sprinted up behind us yelling, "Sir, sir, where are you going?"

"We are going for a late-night walk to see what is happening in the neighborhood."

"Please, sir, please, the hotel does not want to lose any more guests. There are many activities and things to do at the hotel. Please come back."

We did return safely, and, we also managed to rob the hotel employee of all his valuables. No, just kidding! He had lost all of his valuables earlier in the day during another mugging.

Lucky for us, this time in Miami coincided with the beginning of spring break, a special time when deep genetic coding compels hundreds of thousands of college-age kids to migrate south and look for mates just inland from the beaches where all the restaurants and nightclubs are located. Here you can witness the peculiar mating calls of inebriated males who try to woo females with showy displays of expensive automobiles—or lacking that, amplified music with an extraordinary boost in the bass range coming from their cheap, used Toyotas.

This is also the time for the Ultra Music Festival. Of course, you haven't been to a major music festival lately. You have a mortgage and car payments to make these days. If your last concert was a $75 ticket to see Pink Floyd, note that tickets to the mid-March Ultra Music Festival sold for $574.95 for the two-weekend pass—unless your daddy was willing to give you $1,449.90 for the VIP tickets. And this is not even for a concert under a full Miami moon but only a waxing crescent.

In all fairness, there are seven venues at this musical event, but you won't see many guitars because this is all electronic dance music—club music presented by world-famous DJs who deftly go from track to track, whipping the crowd toward what I imagine to be a dance-vectored nirvana, although I'll never know for sure because I did not attend.

Oh, I could have come up with the cash the same way I come up with medical payments, but as priorities go, it just wasn't in my top ten—or twenty. It was, however, most curious that thousands of people, very much younger than me, found they had enough disposable income to dispose of it in this manner.

Also, if I had decided to go, I would not have survived the traffic. I am not exaggerating when I say it took us about seven weeks to drive the two and a half miles from the Fontainebleau, where we couldn't afford to stay, to Mango's Tropical Café, where the bouncers check IDs to make sure you were born after 1985 before they let you in.

Except for the insecure feeling of not wearing your parka, Miami is a great place, although I can get stuck in traffic and overcharged at home for a far lower price. I just can't find any of those tiny bags of peanuts short of booking another flight.

Miami street art in relativly safe neighborhood.

Column 112, May 19, 2013

Destination Fun

Do you have trouble with the concept of fun? I know I do. Fun is something that I've never been able to clearly define. People ask me if I had fun doing this or that, but life is more complicated than simply dividing experiences into two categories. Fun has no defined beginning or peak, yet there is a well-established standard level that is "a barrel of monkeys." Very odd.

The spectrum of human experience can be viewed against a scale that goes from painful through neutral to pleasurable, but as you can see, "fun" isn't even one of the categories.

Pleasure isn't exactly the same as fun. Fun is more childlike, whereas pleasure—well, that's just more adult. It's even possible to experience pleasure through pain in a fun context, but, of course, I wouldn't know anything about that. We can see that fun must be a different way of categorizing experiences apart from the pleasure-pain scale.

The first known use of the word *fun* in English dates back to 1685, which is understandable because before the European Renaissance, there was really no point in using the word. There actually *wasn't* any fun in England before then and precious little after that until 1772, when Joseph Priestly first synthesized nitrous oxide, commonly known as laughing gas. Naturally, after the fun began, the government felt compelled to regulate and tax it.

You can't *have* fun the same way you can *have* a bag of peanuts or a blood transfusion. Fun is an individual experience: two people can be at the same event, like an arraignment, and one person will consider the experience fun while the other, maybe not so much. Personally, I was having quite a bit of fun at the last arraignment I attended until the judge went all serious on me. He was obviously having no fun and managed to spoil it for the rest of us. From this and other similar experiences, we can deduce that fun can be terminated.

Fun can also be transferred. As a boy, I would be having great fun tormenting my sisters when my mother would intervene and apparently transfer my fun to my sisters in short order. We also find that fun can be infectious as well as fleeting. Few people experience fun 100 percent of the time, and those who do are usually confined to state-run asylums.

By the way, if you really are looking for FUN, it is the official International Air Transport Association airport code designator for Funafuti International Airport. This is a major transportation hub for the country of Tuvalu that you would be very lucky indeed to find if you were adrift without power somewhere between Hawaii and Australia. I checked to see how much a flight from BOS to FUN might be and found a good fare on cheapoair.com from Boston to Los Angeles, then to Nadi, on to Suva, and finally to Funafuti Atoll and back, for only $2,484.50!

Realistically, you can't spend that much on fun and leave your wife behind. Going together, it will bump up the price to at least five grand just for airfare. To be sure, on a flight that long, you will also have to budget a fair amount for those cute miniature bottles of liquor, especially if you're lucky enough to get seated in front of the infants.

Usually, my wife will expect us to overnight in a conventional building, very much like a hotel. Prepare to spend heavily on the Vaiaku Lagi Hotel with its twenty-four rooms because as far as I can tell, it's the only hotel in town. Hopefully, the hotel is more fun than its website, which is devoted to crashes and frustration. A double room goes for 99 a night—although they don't specify the currency when quoting the price.

After all the accounting is tallied, a trip to FUN and back would cost enough to offset an awful lot of fun. From this, we can agree that the experience of fun can be reduced by its cost.

In conclusion, we find that fun can be spoiled, regulated, and taxed. It's fleeting, it has nothing to do with pleasure or pain, it's twice as expensive to get there if you go with a spouse, and its measurement involves monkeys. And people wonder why I have trouble with the concept of fun.

Column 111, May 12, 2013

Mechanical Conspiracies

Am I alone in this, or has anyone else noticed an uptick in machines going on the fritz lately? The last few weeks felt like it was machine rebellion month at the restaurant where I am responsible for the maintenance.

First, the dishwasher blew a circuit, then one of the blower motors in the exhaust hood above the cook line failed. Finally, while we were standing around drinking coffee and scratching our heads diagnosing the problems, the coffee machine went on a sympathy strike, crippling our efforts to get things working again. This took place just after the Mars rover *Curiosity* had a computer glitch and shut down for a week or so, over on the red planet.

Now, I am certainly not a conspiracy theorist, but I have carefully looked for a common thread in this prelude to the collapse of civilization as we know it and the only logical party to blame for all of this is, of course, North Korea. It can only be a cyberattack originating from the suburbs of Pyongyang (pronounced "Pyongyang").

Hold on, you might say. What about China or Israel or—depending on your political leanings—Canada and the suburbs of Ottawa? (Pronounced "Ottawa, eh.") All these nations are full of fanatics who want to destroy our infrastructure, except for Canada, which is really only about 2 percent full considering all of that unoccupied land they have to the north. But still, you're thinking, you have to keep your eye on those hosers who use loonies to buy their Molson.

Well, it's hard not to blame Canada for everything, but this time it's extremely convenient to blame North Korea because it's only logical that after recently trying to undermine US industry and defense IT departments with their computer hacking, they would set their sights on restaurants in Maine. They are aiming to cause severe stress in the general population by targeting maintenance men who keep this capitalistic devil-dog society of ours doing whatever it is we do that bothers dictators and oppressive regimes world over.

So what is it exactly that drives Kim Jong-un and the generals nuts over there in Pyongyang? I think I know. I bet it's the idea that any eighth grader in Cheeseville, Wisconsin, can call up Google Earth while sucking on a Popsicle and check out every building and military base in North Korea any time of the day or night.

The North Koreans are apparently a private lot; they don't like anyone taking photos inside the country, from along its borders, and certainly not from directly overhead, especially on a nice clear day.

Of course, their eighth graders who live in Hamhung could also check out the entire US, right down to street view, but their own private North Korean Internet doesn't use Google, so right there you have a great injustice where I'm sure America is to blame. Also, they don't have access to Popsicles.

I can just hear them at the Institute for Death to Blackhearted Capitalistic Gangsters in Pyongyang:

"In honor of the Great Leader, we have successfully dealt a blow to the ventilation system and the sanitation facilities of an insignificant food service facility in Maine, America."

"Has it had any effect on the sanctions crippling our economy?"

"It has employed me for some time, enabling me to buy enough rice so that one half of my family has something to eat. Praise be to the Great Leader."

"So what are you doing for our Great Leader's birthday?"

"Why, I'm going to the mass celebration in the Great Square, same as you."

"Can I get a ride?"

"I don't have a car and I am walking, same as you."

"What are you going to wear?"

"Well, same as you."

All of the mechanical issues at the restaurant have been corrected, and the net effect has been the stimulation of the American economy through my spending vast sums for repair parts and services.

This should demonstrate to that Pyongyang gang that they will not benefit from attacking our national interest. If they manage to damage anything here, all we have to do is order up some expensive parts from Canada and we're back in business.

Hmmm. Might have to get back to you on this one.

Column 117, June 23, 2013

Disorderly Eating, Guilty Dogs

Even though I vaguely suspect my dog has eating disorders, I am certain that he is guilty of disorderly eating. Trouble is, I'm not so sure I myself have superior eating etiquette or technique. I eat too fast, I sometimes swallow without enough chewing, and I'm not very careful about what I eat. These are all misdemeanors I've accused my dog of committing in the past.

Dogs are very clever when accused—they look guilty, but they take their Miranda rights very seriously as they exercise their right to remain silent. Obviously, they can't afford an attorney and they seem to know that one won't be appointed, so the dog's best defense is to remain silent inside the legal limbo of standing accused but unable to defend himself. They know that after a while, you have to forgive them just because they're so damn cute.

For refined humans, eating involves the five-step process of viewing, smelling, chewing, tasting, and swallowing. There is satisfaction derived from each procedure, and if you think that eating pleasure is strictly from tasting or chewing, try skipping a step.

Start masticating on some favorite morsel and enjoy the taste. Now, just as you get to that point of enough chewing when it's time to swallow, spit it out. You will notice that not only has your chewing pleasure been cut short, but it's been reversed by the denial of what was essentially promised to the stomach.

A note of caution when conducting this experiment: don't spit out whatever you were chewing where the dog can get it. Dogs are very happy to have someone else chew and taste their food before they hork it down. As a matter of observation, the eating process for dogs is greatly abbreviated and can be cut down to only sniff and swallow. Sometimes, especially if they are running late for an appointment, it's just swallow. Anytime they use their teeth, it's only to trim something to the size that will fit down their throat.

My eating habits are more refined, but truth be told, not so refined that the dog couldn't accuse me of disorderly eating. Like my guilty dog, I eat compulsively, never sniffing enough before intake and never tasting enough before swallowing. For all I know, my dog could be contemplating a lawsuit with himself as the plaintiff at this very moment.

I am rather compulsive, eating whatever I want, sometimes deliberately in front of the dog. This doesn't always work for me. Coming home from school in my youth, I would throw open the refrigerator and ingest the first edible item that was most convenient. On one occasion, I noticed that my mother had baked a pineapple upside-down cake. I knew she usually poured off the excess juice from the canned pineapple and would leave it in the refrigerator, so when I saw a glass of juice on the top shelf, I just threw it back like a cowboy drinking whiskey at a bar.

I got it halfway down before I noticed it wasn't pineapple juice but egg whites. By the way, it's hard to stop drinking egg whites because they tend to come out of the glass in one long strand.

I once ate a pound of prunes. You might know them as dried plums, but they will always be prunes to me. People talk of them being effective laxatives, but personally I had never noticed that prunes had any effect whatsoever on my bodily functions. Not until I idly ate a one-pound box just to give my mouth something to do.

Back in the sixties, there was a TV commercial for a laxative that started out with a victim of constipation wondering about prunes: "Is three too few? Is six too many?" Well, I'm not sure about three or six, but I can tell you from personal experience that a pound is, for me, anyway, far too many.

In the most recent episode of disorderly eating, the dog ate an entire stick of butter that was too near the edge of the kitchen table for him to control his desires. After severely scolding the guilty dog, I sent him to his corner, even though I have no real proof that he took it upon himself to eat...oh, excuse me, I have to go. Seems I have to take a call from someone claiming to be my dog's attorney.

Column 118, June 30, 2013

Basic Freedom, Simplified

Seeing that it's Fourth of July week, it's time to look past the patriotism, the precious freedom we relish, and discuss fireworks. But let's talk about freedom anyway.

The kind of freedom that we fight for is the kind we can control. We hardly ever consider freedom from gravity or from the effects of momentum or magnetic fields; our biggest concerns are individual rights, civil liberties, and government oppression—nothing that is brought on by nature, only by other people. It's kind of ironic that when we say all of humanity wants freedom, what we really want is freedom from humanity's constraints.

We could demand more, like freedom from dying or getting sick, freedom from collisions with cars on the street and asteroids from outer space, but there is no well-defined authority where we can take these demands. The tyrannies of gravity, illness, and accident are out of anyone's hands. Massive protests because the winter is too cold or because the moon is not bright enough don't draw huge crowds because, well, they're silly. Of course, we can take these concerns to God, but don't you feel that asking God to tip the balance of nature in our favor would be a bit pretentious?

"Excuse me, God, but could you do me a favor and free my planet from any massive natural calamities like earthquakes and tornadoes this weekend, please?"

"WHY? YOU UNDERSTAND THAT I ALREADY KNOW WHY, I JUST WANT TO HEAR YOU SAY IT."

"Yes, well, I just want a day free from these natural disasters for all the people of the earth so they can be happy."

"AND…"

"And…and my company is introducing a new product to stop hair loss, and I don't want any disaster news to distract people."

"WELL, SURE, I WILL ALTER THE COURSE OF NATURAL HISTORY FOR ONE WEEKEND SO THAT YOU CAN GET YOUR HAIR LOSS MESSAGE OUT."

"Wow, really?"

"NO. NOT REALLY. THANK YOU. NEXT, PLEASE."

If a man lived totally apart from other people, he wouldn't need to petition anyone for freedom because he wouldn't be constrained, coerced, restricted, suppressed, or discriminated against by others. He would have freedom in abundance. Of course, he wouldn't have any spare time because he would have to be inventing agriculture, medicine, and ways to protect himself from the natural world.

If he could, he would probably try to get himself relocated to a place with other people who would instantly start encroaching on his freedoms. This is called civilization. To make it possible to interact with others, we give up some of our freedom. We agree not to do whatever we please and we all limit our freedom so that we can all enjoy our own existence. We all can't enjoy life if we're free to steal our neighbor's corn or hair-loss products. We can't set off explosives to celebrate our freedom if it sends firebrands and projectiles into our neighbors' homes—which brings us back to fireworks.

I can't decide if it's ironic or most appropriate that we celebrate freedom with some of the most heavily regulated products on the market. Local municipalities outlaw use and possession. States regulate distribution, sale, and taxation while mandating licensing, and the feds do anything they can to make it impossible to buy a good M-80 anywhere in the country.

It's just too hard to make a law where we agree that we can all use any kind of fireworks as long as it doesn't affect anyone else in any way, that no one else minds, and if we hurt ourselves it won't cost the rest of us anything. Consequently, we end up making a rule that no one can even possess anything that goes bang, except for a gun.

My mother used the same technique—if my friends and I couldn't get along playing with our illegal firecrackers, she would take away all our black cats and lady fingers, leaving us only our guns to play with. There is no constitutional right to keep and bear firecrackers.

And so ends the simple essay on freedom because it just gets complicated from here. By the way, freedom is an anagram for "more fed."

Column 121, July 21, 2013

Topology of Sugared Toroids, or Doughnuts, Part 3

Even as a kid, I felt the adage about not being able to have your cake and eat it too was flawed because you generally can eat a piece of the cake and the rest of it is left over *and you still have it*. Even a kid can see that. It would be more accurate if we spoke of not being able to have your doughnut and eat it too. There aren't many people who take a bite out of a doughnut and then put the remainder away for safekeeping. If you are one of those people, you should really have yourself tested for Inability to Wolf Down Small Confections Syndrome.

Doughnuts not only give you all the satisfaction of eating cake, they also satisfy a little ingrained gluttony. With cake, you generally get to eat only a slice, which on some primitive level leaves you dissatisfied because there is more cake: the rest of the cake; cake you really shouldn't eat; forbidden cake. With a doughnut, however, you get to consume the whole enchilada, leaving you not only satisfied but finished. Done. Complete. In any case, just one bite destroys the form, and although you may have a segment left over, speaking philosophically, your doughnut is gone.

Shape defines the doughnut, and speaking mathematically (or more accurately, speaking topologically), the shape of a doughnut is called a torus. This is not to be confused with Taurus the Bull (a constellation) or Taurus the car (a means of transportation). Torus technically refers only to the outer surface, so if your doughnut is hollow, like French crullers tend to be, then you have a torus. But don't you feel a cruller is closer to parallel twisted polygonal toruses (if *toruses* is the plural for *torus*)? I know I do.

It would be interesting if there were a car in the shape of a doughnut like the Wienermobile is a car in the shape of a hot dog. If it were built on the frame and engine of a Ford, it could indeed be called a Ford torus. This is but one example of what the tortuous voices in my head are saying. No one cares about a Ford torus; why would I think that such a scenario would be interesting? The only thing interesting here might be a visit from a clinical psychologist, who may recommend drugs that can only be purchased in a doughnut-shaped building known as a *drugstorus*. This is the part where later they will point to it and say, "See, he was calling out for help and nobody was listening."

Solid objects in the shape of a torus are called toroids, or as I like to call them, doughnuts. Anyway, geometricians (you know, *geometry* plus *mathematician*; it has the same meaning as *geometer*), get all excited about toroids because they lend themselves to many mathematical parlor tricks with which you can amuse your friends. This is assuming you have a parlor, and it's full of friends who are all geometers. But let's face it, if you are a hard-core geometrician, you probably don't have a parlor—or any friends.

Go to Wikipedia on the internet and look up torus. You will find a number of animations undoubtedly produced by geometricians with time on their hands because they were never invited to any parties or other time-consuming social events. These animations are amazingly complex. One shows what would happen if you punctured a torus, like an inner tube, and turned it inside out and then closed up the puncture. The doughnut appears to eat itself, yet the result is an identical torus—only inside out. The animation must have taken a lot of time to produce, but it helps us all understand how it's possible to have a doughnut, eat it, and still have a doughnut.

For people with brains much more efficiently wired than mine, this has important implications when studying multi-dimensional universes or when attending quantum physicist and mathematician shindigs. Someday, this apparently useless investigation into the inner workings of surfaces and dimensions will probably inspire a young genius to uncover mysteries of existence.

In the meantime, I find that I still enjoy sugared toroids most with my morning coffee and, of course, the voices.

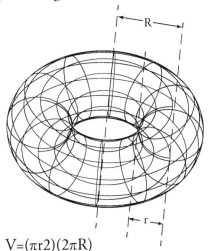

$V = (\pi r2)(2\pi R)$

To calculate the volume of your doughnut simply measure R, the major radius which is the distance from the center of the doughnut to the middle of the dough ring, then measure r, the minor radius which is half the diameter of the dough in the ring. Plug R and r into the formula above. Enjoy with an adequate volume of coffee.

Summer Fair Time

There is still time to fill your wallet with cash, fill your car with the family, and head out to an agricultural or state fair while they flourish in warm weather. Here your whole party can be amused for an entire day for generally less than one month's mortgage payment if you live in a moderately high-priced home and have not refinanced since the housing bubble burst.

You can also consume an entire month's worth of calories packed into anything that can be breaded, deep-fried, and sugared, including dough, candy bars, animal parts, political messages, and campaign promises—anything people are willing to swallow. But don't worry about gaining weight—diet sodas are sold in small kegs, and a number of amusement rides are available in case you need to empty your stomach in short order.

Here in Maine where I live, a fair is usually made up of a traveling carnival with its midway and sideshows, an exhibition hall, and grandstands.

It is important to know the difference between these areas, especially when you lose a child and the loudspeaker announces to the entire festival that the careless parents, whose behavior undoubtedly borders on criminal child neglect, can pick up their offspring at the midway. The midway is where the carnival rides and fast-food booths are concentrated. This is good news, since it means that your child has not been hired on as help by the carnival and most likely will be going home with you. On the other hand, if your child is thirty-two and still living at home, the news may not be as welcomed.

True carnival sideshows, the kind with freaks and oddities, lasted well into the 1960s. I myself was convinced by an actual carnie barker to pay and "see actual live piranha fish so vicious that they devour a human in under a minute, and an entire horse in under ten!" The pitch was so furious you knew that the entire bloody show would be over if admission wasn't immediately granted. Once you paid your money, however, you were allowed in to view piranha peacefully schooling together in various aquarium tanks—with not a human skull or horse bone in sight. It was a business model destined to fail. These days, we all can view piranha on any mobile iDevice anytime we want.

Today, sideshow salesmen pitch items you can barely imagine living without. I have never fallen for any of these ineffectual pitches, unless you want to count the special solder I bought that allows me to solder together aluminum cans. Of course, in the ten years since my purchase, I have not had the occasion to fuse aluminum cans together, but by golly, when the need arises, I will be ready. And then there was the kitchen knife I bought because it cut tomatoes so effortlessly after slicing through a number of beer cans. I sensed there was something amiss when the pitchman gave me two additional knives for free to go with my purchase. It was as if, in a moment of weakness, he felt sorry for me. Turns out the knives are designed to cut only tomatoes. They don't do a neat job cutting chicken, carrots, or even butter, but they do a superb piece of work on tomatoes.

Don't miss the exhibition halls at any of the fairs, as you will be doing your family a disservice by denying them a chance to see award-winning, locally grown produce and flowers. A lot of these have severely wilted since being put on display, but you can bet that in the opening hours of the first day of the fair, the dill and dahlias looked a lot like award-winning dill and dahlias.

I have not yet attended any of the events offered for viewing at the grandstands, mostly because I am regarded as a penny-pinching tightwad by those who would have me buy them admission. The entertainment must be good because I can hear the roar of the crowd coming from the grandstands even over the loudspeaker announcements for lost children.

You might return from the fair with an empty wallet and short a family member or two, but the experience will be well worth it. At the very least, you should be able to effortlessly slice tomatoes.

Column 128, September 8, 2013

National Preparedness Month

Sad to say, but I was really not ready when it was pointed out to me that September is National Preparedness Month. I had no strategy for dealing with planning preparations and not a clue about exactly what for, as a nation, we were all preparing.

"National" means everyone in the USA. I must confess that for just a moment, being Canadian looked very attractive, as they are obviously exempt from thinking about preparedness all month long, but that quickly passed when I realized I would most likely have to learn French words like *loonie* and *toonie* and put in a supply of Molson, eh?

Turns out, the Federal Emergency Management Agency wants us all to be preparing for emergencies by using four key points to national preparedness. Three of them are absolutely no fun like developing a family plan, learning about the different emergencies that can darken your door, and getting involved with the prepared community, but the fourth is to prepare an emergency supply kit. This involves shopping. What could be a better antidote to impending doom than a day of good old American shopping?

There is nothing like a big warehouse shopping club to inspire and help you prepare for disaster. At a Costco or a Sam's Club, nothing is in short supply. Just walking in the door of the hangar-sized warehouse, you get the exciting feeling that this is American consumerism gone wild. Gargantuan quantities can be purchased at wholesale prices to fulfill all your preparedness needs.

In every emergency, however, it seems that only a few items

dominate the preparedness concerns of most Americans: toilet paper, batteries, bottled water, and sometimes food.

Food is an afterthought. Many of us have a cupboard with odd cans of olives and artichoke hearts that we bought for a New Year's Eve party in 2008 and never opened. It's obvious that an emergency would be a perfect time to break into this cache and rid ourselves of those old sardines.

Toilet paper, however, is foremost because it essentially represents civilization. When natural disaster occurs, we just can't afford the additional emotional burden of exhausting our supply of *papel higiénico*. Would we go to the neighbors looking to trade a can of olives for a roll or two, or would we revert to pre-civilized times and improvise? It is too dark a thought, so we stock up whenever our way of life is threatened.

Batteries represent power—power to see in the dark (even though you'll have a tough time getting those old, corroded batteries out of the flashlight), and the power to listen to radio stations (that may be off the air), and the power to communicate through cell phone towers (that may be off-line). Anyway, it's just nice to have fresh batteries. You rarely have any during normal times, so why not treat yourself before an emergency?

Bottled water is really the purity of life, contained. It gives us hope, and when the water is gone, well, it gives us a container we can use to hold more water that may or may not be so pure.

Ironically, the one thing you can't stock up on is prescription medication, even though it may be what you need most when that emergency strikes. The government pushes preparedness, but it still maintains that prescription-drug control is more important than having extra meds handy. You can stock up all you want on liquor, guns, and ammo, but extra pain medication and antibiotics are off the table.

Indeed, we wouldn't know how to properly use pain medication in an emergency now, would we? Do you take one pill every hour? Is it with a meal? Can you take it with a shot of Jack Daniels or no? It takes a professional to prescribe the proper dose, even though the "take a pill until the pain stops" method usually works in a painful emergency. On the other hand, it's easy to know how much ammo to use. Basically, when the clip is empty, it's time to refill.

Thinking about preparedness all month, I wonder how much I should let the government do the thinking for me. Isn't this the same government that, as a matter of preparedness, told us all to duck and cover and get under our school desks when the nuclear missiles hit? I seem to remember it is.

Polish Heritage Month

As almost everyone already knows, October is, of course, Polish American Heritage Month. This is Polish with a capital *P* and not your mundane lowercase *p* as in *shoe polish,* although I will admit there is always some confusion whenever someone writes "Polish jokes always make me look down at my scuffed-up Italian shoes."

Sadly, a few people will overlook this all-American celebration of Polish culture because there is no authority, short of Congress, that has jurisdiction over heritage month conflicts. We all know that Congress is a mess. This is most apparent when we learn that our lawmakers passed resolutions also making October Filipino American History Month as well as Italian American Heritage Month, even though everybody knows October is really Polish American Heritage Month.

Just to complicate matters, President Reagan proclaimed September 15 through October 15 as German American Heritage Month, most likely to spite President Johnson's earlier proclamation that evolved to recognize the same period as National Hispanic Heritage Month (as if September 15 to the middle of October is some kind of actual month).

With all these different cultural groups competing to be recognized in October, is it any wonder that the Germans chose October for Oktoberfest? With the possible exception of a buxom German waitress just about busting out of her lederhosen as she serves you a cold Berliner Pilsner, nothing can overshadow the fact that October is Polish American Heritage Month.

As the waitress image subsides, let's review some influential Polish people who still contribute to American culture.

The Renaissance astronomer Nicolaus Copernicus was Polish, but America was hardly on the map during his time so he can't really be considered a Polish American. Nevertheless, thanks to him, we enjoy knowing that our earth revolves around the sun and not Kim Kardashian. Frédéric Chopin, the Polish composer, would have come to America but the music scene was quite limited here in the 1800s—yet some of us still scat his nocturnes in the shower. And the famed Polish director Roman Polanski still influences us with his films even though he can't really come back to the USA, now can he?

Genuine Polish Americans include Pat Sajak, who represents some of the highest levels of culture we can expect from American television. where his *Wheel of Fortune* is but an analogy for the American dream. Martha Stewart, who, like my own mother and most Polish-American women I know, is genetically predisposed to try and make everything nice and everyone comfortable, which I must begrudgingly admit is a good thing. And how can we forget Zbigniew Brzezinski, Carter's national security advisor, who always reminds us that Polish names can contain a lot of *z*'s.

Many people ask me at parties if there might be an anagram in Zbigniew Brzezinski that makes sense. Seeing that there are only *i*'s and *e*'s for vowels (and the three *z*'s), the most conspicuous anagram that immediately comes to mind is "Rink Wizzes Begin Biz." This would have made an excellent title for a newspaper story in 1953 when Frank J. Zamboni & Company set up a business selling their famous ice resurfacing machines in Paramount, California, where their ice rink was located. Even though Frank Zamboni was of Italian heritage, polish is what his machines do to the ice.

This would make a perfect segue into Italian American Heritage Month, but far be it for me to get off topic. *Segue,* by the way, is Italian in origin for "it follows," meaning you achieve a smooth transition—something that's not happening right now.

Polish culture is much more than horseradish-eating contests and fantastic drinking songs. It also includes a mandate to dance until you die at weddings and a compulsion to save useless items because they may come in handy in the future. It is a culture rich in art, music, science, literature, and guilt. It is the culture that brought us vodka, bulletproof vests, the oil refinery, and reverse Polish notation for mathematicians, which is a good thing but not as good as Polish kielbasa and a cuisine that relies heavily on butter, eggs, and cream.

I know all this because I am a direct descendent of genuine Polish peasants. Every October, I think of my Polish-American upbringing and the fact that I was never allowed to forget that *Polish American* is not only an anagram for "Maraschino Pile" but "Serial Champion" as well.

Column 147, January 19, 2014

Antidisestablishmen-tarianism, Used and Explained

It seems that the word, dear to our hearts, which we learned in grade school as being the longest word in the English language has been deleted from the Merriam-Webster dictionary because of lack of use—and not just any old kind of use but *proper* use. Apparently, writing "*antidisestablishmentarianism* is the longest word in the dictionary" is not acceptable usage because the word in this context conveys no meaning.

The Merriam-Webster people have found only three legitimate uses of the word in literature so they axed it from the official tome. But just because they're professional doesn't mean they don't have fun. They are now toying with the idea of including *supercalifragilisticexpialidocious* (even though the sound of it is something quite atrocious) because of its frequent use. Minor glitch: no one is really super clear on what it means, and the dictionary people are easily hung up by this little hiccup.

Even though *antidisestablishmentarianism* was bandied about in the fourth grade mostly by smarty-pants girls, the only meaning it conveyed was "I am smarter than you because I know the longest word in the dictionary" type of thing.

So to discover what it's all about—and no, it's not about the hokey pokey—let's go back to the year 1534, about the time when Jacques Cartier was claiming Canada for France and Ignatius of Loyola was founding the Jesuits. Times were different then; very few households had a TV and almost no one had a Game Boy, so unfortunately, people had a lot of spare time to get in over their heads with church politics.

One of the people most in need of a Game Boy was King Henry VIII. He is the guy who told Pope Clement VII to take a hike and, just like Coca-Cola is an official sponsor of the Olympics, he *established* the Church of England as the official church of, well, England. That made him and his supporters establishmentarians. He didn't take kindly to those who promoted taking this arrangement apart. These were the disestablishmentarians, and they gave Henry fits.

Henry got Parliament to pass the Act of Supremacy to let everyone know who was boss, and he continued to demonstrate his antidisestablishmentarianism by passing the Treasons Act of 1534, which basically shortened by a head anyone snubbing their nose at the Act of Supremacy.

In more modern times, all anarchistic hippies of the 1970s—like Abbie Hoffman, who authored the counterculture publication *Steal This Book*—could have been considered disestablishmentarians. It didn't take long for Chicago Mayor Daley and likeminded people to organize an antidisestablishmentarianistic movement.

There. I did it. I used the word properly twice (and the second time I even changed the *-ism* to *-istic,* adding two characters to make it the longest word that is *not* in the dictionary but would be if we used it more often). My only trouble is that I almost had to stand on my head to do it. No wonder Merriam-Webster axed it. And a welcome riddance, too; in spite of its familiarity, it's just too hard to use. A more common word of the same length is *electrophotomicrographically,* and that's easy to use in a sentence: "Hopkins, I have reviewed your lab work and I found the results documented electrophotomicrographically were fabricated; you're fired."

If you really start digging for lengthy words, the "a26m" word, abbreviated here to indicate there are twenty-six letters missing and to spare you the pain of encountering all twenty-eight, is actually toward the bottom of a long list of words, the longest word being "p43s". * Suffice it to say, the forty-five-letter word starts with *pneumo-* and ends with *-osis*. It appears to be some kind of lung disease that will kill you long before you master how to pronounce it.

There are chemical names that are much longer, but thankfully, they are not in the dictionary because dictionary editors have no patience with people who make up their own rules for naming things with no restriction on length.

So what we learned in fourth grade is wrong—there are longer words than the best-known long word. The big question is, what else did we learn in the fourth grade that is wrong? The only other thing I remember learning in the fourth grade is the hokey pokey—now that's disturbing on a number of levels.

* Pneumonoultramicroscopicsilicovolcanoconiosis

Author's Note:
The page footer, originally printed at the end of this column in the *Free Press* read:
If he isn't preoccupied with hippopotomonstrosesquipedalian issues, email sent to sadowski@tidewater.net has a high probability of reaching the author. ©2014, Tom Sadowski. All rights reserved.

Column 149, February 2, 2014

Merchant Credit Card Fees

Just in case you are the sole individual in your state who pays off their credit card bill in its entirety, on time, every month, without fail, in order to avoid any interest and penalty payments, let me assure you that there is no need to feel guilt. There is no shame even if you've reasoned that if everyone did this, the credit card companies would go belly-up. Taking advantage of the no-interest, no-fees allowance shouldn't make you feel anxious that eventually no one will be able to enjoy the fantastic benefits of an economy lubricated by exchanges made on a mere swipe and a promise.

You may wonder, "How can those poor credit card companies survive if people pay their bill on time? And what of the wretched middleman firms that process the credit card information between the merchant and the Visa and Mastercard companies of the world? Where on earth does the money come from so these poor banks and financial institutions can pay their employees enough to feed their children?"

Please; I am here to assure you that there are other streams of revenue that contribute to the great river of income the credit card businesses enjoy. There is no danger of this mighty cash flow going dry as it cuts its own Grand Canyon through the world economies. Just like rivers have both snowmelt and rainwater to feed them, the credit card industry has both the consumer and the merchant. Even if credit card companies didn't charge you interest and penalties, they could probably squeak by with what they charge the merchant.

If you think dealing with American Express or Discover is a

nuisance, you need to know what happens from the merchant's perspective. As a guy who runs a too-small business making minor sales to customers who pay to a large extent with credit cards, let me paraphrase a telephone conversation I had recently with a credit card service provider in order to give you the bigger picture.

"Thank you for holding for thirty-five minutes and listening to insipid music while I had a fantastic lunch. How can I be of resistance to you?"

"I am looking at my statement and it states that you went into my bank account four times last month and helped yourself to the fees you've listed here."

"Yes, sir. It's much more efficient to take your money when we want it rather than to send you a bill and wait around until you decide to pay us. We send bills to our cardholders and that is, frankly, a hassle. It would be much more profitable if people would just consent to us taking the money right out of their bank account like you do—but then again, you really don't have a choice now, do you?"

"Yes, I understand that. I was just wondering if you could explain some of those fees to me."

"Well, of course. Even if you are a dolt, I will rationalize away until five o'clock when I go home. Is it that huge dollar amount you're looking at?"

"Oh no, I understand that is the heinous percentage you take from every bankcard sale I make. Sometimes it's less than 1 percent and sometimes it's almost 5 percent depending on your mood."

"Very good, sir, I see you've done your homework, but did I detect a little tiny bit of sarcasm in your voice with that 'mood' comment?"

"Most certainly not. Did I say 'mood'? I really meant mode. You know: debit vs. credit."

"Continue."

"I was wondering if you could explain the 'LOL1' charge."

"Yes, your account is charged a system access fee depending on your monthly volume of sales."

"And what of this 'LOL2' fee?"

"That is an access fee based on the number of monthly sales."

"So if those are both access fees, what is this network access fee you have here?"

"That, my meager merchant, is the monthly fee you pay to access our network, not our system."

"Well, that certainly explains a lot to me about those fees. I was hoping for just such a thorough explanation, and I am very pleased you did not once call me stupid."

"You are lucky indeed because we can do whatever we want. It's in the contract somewhere. Now drop and give me ten."

"What? Right now?"

"Oh, look, your credit score editing page just came up on my screen."

"One, two, three," puff, puff, "four..."

Column 152, February 23, 2014

Never Touch a Baby

While celebrating the peak of flu season, I experienced a revelation of what might eventually kill me: babies. No, it's not like a pre-toddler will come at me in my sleep wielding a machete (although you've got to admit that does have a certain Stephen King-esque appeal), it's just that one day as my immune system begins to forget where it lives and who I am, I shall touch one of these baby brooders of bacteria and vectors of viruses and finally succumb to whatever type of influenza, rhinitis, or sinusitis the child can deliver.

How did I celebrate flu season? By barely recovering from a bout with death brought on by a mere wisp of physical contact with my cute-as-a-button grandniece. Anyone can see the writing on the Facebook wall of death. This is how they plan to bring me down.

Every year or two, I am sure, the various virus unions including rank-and-file members along with a good showing from management, decide at one of their conclaves that it is time to test my immune system and see if I am weak enough to finish off. This viral shindig is undoubtedly hosted somewhere by a baby who acts as the factory, happily stamping out the latest virus models while she goo-goos and gaa-gaas.

According to the Centers for Disease Control and Prevention, children have two to nine viral respiratory illnesses per year. The CDC doesn't single out babies as a group, probably because the parties thrown by viruses within a baby are strung so closely together that it's just too hard to tell when one viral infection stops and another starts.

The baby is a perfect vector. She, of course, is gorgeous. Everyone is fawning over her and passing her around like a big wet Q-tip that was pulled out of the dangerous medical waste bin at the regional hospital. Just ignore the runny nose—after all, she only has baby viruses. Everyone assumes the viruses are only practicing; they're only tough enough to infect a baby. Surely they can't hurt a full-grown man ten times her size.

Oh, contraire—don't let the age of the carrier fool you. That baby has a brand new shiny immune system that is still working out the bugs, so to speak, and while she is exercising that system to serve her for the rest of her life, those viruses and bacterial factories within are mass-producing sputum and baby drool full of new product ripe for the opportunity to jump on Grandma or Gramps or Uncle Tom and see if they can kill—or at the very least debilitate for a week or three.

Viruses love babies because babies are open to experimentation; they will put anything in their mouths and look cute doing it. Furthermore, babies often team up with the family dog that's been out fraternizing with chickens or better still, chicken droppings. As dog and baby exchange spittle and various secretions, they can't help but look adorable.

When a man has a runny nose (or a "purulent nasal discharge," as the nurses are fond of saying), he looks awful. No need to put red flashing warning lights on him because you can see he is something to avoid. When a loveable little baby has a runny nose, well, she just looks like a baby; it's their normal look.

"Oh, look, dear, someone left a baby at our door."

"That's a funny way to dress a baby, in a black hooded robe. Is that a tiny scythe he's carrying?"

"Oh, isn't that cute? He must have been out reaping. Look, he wants you to hold him."

"No, I don't think so."

"Oh, go ahead. He's pointing at you with that little tiny bony finger."

"You don't think he has a cold, do you?"

"No. All babies have runny noses—and hacking coughs. Go ahead."

"Well, he sure has a certain determination. Oh, come to Papa."

There is at least one other way babies could cause my early demise—my wife might suddenly announce that we are expecting triplets. Now that, right there, is worthy of a myocardial infarction.

Column 159, April 13, 2014

National Blow Your Own Horn Day

It has come to my attention that April 18 is National Columnist Day, which is a little bit embarrassing because I'm pretty sure there is no National Grocery Clerk Day or National Payroll Accountant Day or National Guy That Changes Your Oil Day. These positions are just as important and the people who fill them deserve as much recognition as columnists, secretaries, groundhogs, and fools, all of which have a special day of recognition.

There just can't be a special day for everyone where speeches are made and awards are given, so people are just going to have to stand up and applaud themselves. This is why I am proposing, no, I am *declaring* April 21 as National Blow Your Own Horn Day.

It's time every profession, craft, industry, and semi-skilled low-level, blue-collar, entry-position worker to have a day of recognition. If, for no other reason, it would be good to counterbalance the disproportionate amount of recognition the entertainment industry heaps upon itself.

The entertainment industry has a real chokehold on blowing their own horn only because they have control over a very big horn. Between the Academy Awards for good films and the XRCO Awards for bad ones (i.e. naughty), there are critics' awards, festival awards, and industry awards numerous enough to fill the entire calendar—sorry, forgot the audience awards category. Their business is blowing horns even though only a very small percentage are actual musicians.

Entertainment businesses occupy a position of not having

to go to anyone else in order to make an announcement, no matter how self-aggrandizing the message. If dental hygienists want to produce an awards program, they have to go to the entertainment industry to get something, well, entertaining, because we can all imagine what a prime-time awards gala produced by dental hygienists would look like. Now, I'm not saying that dental hygienists can't produce great TV, but I suspect it would be about as good as the teeth cleaning you can get at any random mansion in the hills of Hollywood.

Carpenters, teachers, and plumbers don't get the kind of recognition that entertainers get even though most of us think that plumbers are at least as important to a civilized society as porn stars; maybe more. So where exactly is the envelope, please, for this year's best supporting plumber in the residential drainage category? It's just not going to materialize.

Sure, there is a World Plumbing Day celebrated on March 11, but it's mostly a global health issue kind of thing. And okay, April 25 is National Hug a Plumber Day, although hugging a plumber without warning is ill-advised as you really don't know what they've been rubbing up against or touching in the course of their work. So plumbers do get some recognition, but there is no red carpet, no gold statuette, and certainly no day off.

You have to be careful picking a new day to celebrate because the calendar is already crowded with commemorative events; if you want to blow your own horn, you don't want to do it on Christmas. Occasionally, Patriots' Day falls on April 21, but that is only when the twenty-first and the third Monday in April collide. Easter, of course, is anybody's guess, so that leaves only National Kindergarten Day as a conflict. But if you have to steal a day of recognition away from a group, it's obvious that kindergartners are the perfect patsies—they don't fight hard, and they haven't really done much to deserve recognition, anyway.

It may have been a better world if we had never gone down

the path of handing out days to recognize how particular jobs contribute to society. We all contribute. Now we're stuck with too many different kinds of workers to sing their praises and not enough days to do it. People, if you want any of this kind of attention, you're going to have get into the entertainment business or blow your own horn.

Let's all blow on April 21, and maybe we can clear the calendar of celebrations for normal and necessary jobs. We can keep Mother's Day, but I'm not running out to get a card and flowers for every backhoe operator, pizza maker, and proctologist on their special day. I don't know about you, but I gotta get back to work.

Column 161, April 27, 2014

Internet Comments

There is a shipload of articles on the internet that allow people to leave comments. I try hard not to read the comments mostly because my face is already misshapen and I can do without any more head-slapping and face-scrunching in disbelief at what I read. My faith in people to say the right thing is already so thin that a few more rude comments may push me over the edge and make me polish off that half gallon of ice cream I know is in the freezer in a burst of immoderate, unrestrained self-indulgence.

At times, the comments are quite useful. They can express praise or point out contradictions and omissions—all good. But too often, they quickly degenerate to the level of fourth-grade name-calling that has to make you wonder if they let out all the elementary schools and gave every rude boy a laptop on his way out the door.

In the era of newspapers and magazines, it took up to a month before letters to the editor were published. People had time to think about wording while editors had a chance to edit. You had to get paper to typewriter and then find the correction fluid for the inevitable istakes. By the time you produced acceptable copy, your reaction to the issue that triggered the urge to write had mellowed and matured. Comments were more civil, and only editors were driven to binge eating.

Today, it appears that many people who leave comments are unsupervised nine-year-olds. They all hold dogmatic opinions on matters as deep as Middle East politics and as wide as constitutional law but have not yet developed the capacity to understand basic civility.

A typical thread following a paper on ocean mineral deposits might read:

"Your recommendation for deep ocean exploration is spot-on: a direction of study really worth undertaking." —Bobby Sox

"There are lots of areas worthy of study, but Congress won't fund them." —Al Agitator

"Congress is full of spending weenies who won't cut taxes." —B4All

"So you're the weenie who wanted the Bush agenda and look where that got us." —Heathen1

"You're a stupid left-wing idiot." —6th GradersSuck

"No, you're the stupid idiot, and a jerk." —CantPassMath

"You're the jerk, and a dumbass." —Anonymous986261

My! What a pleasant public exchange between people with strange signatures that I suspect are not their proper names. After all, using your real name would cause the unbearable burden of being responsible for what you say.

This seems to be an internet phenomenon. You don't go to a conference where, after the panel discussion, a young man steps up to the microphone and says, "I want to ask a question of conservative Professor Dumbass in the stupid shirt."

People, it's not that hard to be polite. Often, it's usually a matter of just stopping short of an insult. The comment "I disagree. It's not consistent with past court rulings" is much more polite than "I disagree. It's not consistent with past court rulings, you stupid jerk-face."

A good place to start would be to study your comment and remove all of the adjectives and expletives along with references to any deity, places of eternal damnation, and parts of human anatomy not normally visible when in the presence of polite company. For those who have trouble defining polite company, think of a funeral parlor with younger children and clergy present.

If you can't stifle the name-calling, a good technique to sound civilized is to use a more sophisticated assault. Change your attack when you find yourself referring to someone as a "dumb, stupid Republican ass" (which in itself is a misnomer since the Democrats are the ones represented by a donkey). Instead, call their position a "beef-witted, lumpish piece of reasoning worthy of Bush-era depravity."

It's true that the street-gang insult is more efficient than the Harvard slur, but instead of putting the comment-maker in a dim-witted light, a more sophisticated remark elevates him or her to a position of an intellectual who can generate a cunning retort—and who doesn't love a cunning retort?

Just remember Proverbs 26:6 the next time you type an impulsive comment: "He that sendeth a message by the hand of a fool cutteth off the feet, and drinketh damage." No one likes to drinketh damage, but by golly, I could go for a little ice cream right about now.

═══════════════════════

Column 164, May 18, 2014

Robot Conversations

Attention all telephone-marketing companies. Please note my new policy: I will no longer converse or even listen to your robots when they call on the phone. I will only spend enough time to verify that it is not a human calling and then I will hang up. I'm finished. The end. No exceptions.

Okay. I will make an exception if the robot is exceedingly polite and offers an amusing exchange or tête-à-tête, as the English might say when making fun of the French. In that case, I reserve the right to continue talking with the robot to explore the limits of its entertainment value or the depths of its knowledge. But I still won't buy anything.

It's plain to see that companies which employ robots do not value my time enough to dedicate another human to make contact. I can hardly blame them because contacting me over the phone to sell me anything from a business loan to septic system bacteria is, frankly, a waste of their time as well as mine. But they use a robot to make the call, so it turns out to be a waste of only my time.

I really need to make better use of my own robot to take these calls. Of course, the robot would have to drop the household vacuuming to chat. It's a scenario with far-reaching implications. What if the two robots hit it off and started making frequent calls so that you couldn't get them off the phone? Then, despite my forbidding it, they would meet secretly, and we all know where that leads: they would start out by just tightening each other's loose screws and nuts, and soon this would lead to—need I even say it?—*oiling each other's bearings*. Next thing you know, we're in this war to save humanity where the robots are throttling us with superior weaponry while vacuuming and making sales pitches on the phone.

Oh, it's funny now; you can tell me how funny it is when we meet someday in the muddy trenches after the failed offensive and we all know without saying that Tom Cruise is just not going to come and save us this time.

Things are getting a little creepy with the sales calls as it's getting harder to tell if you are talking to a robot. Just the other day, "Larry" called me. He started right in because he was very excited that my business was selected and preapproved for a loan of up to a hundred thousand dollars. It was almost as if there was something in it for him.

I was enchanted by Larry's enthusiasm and absolutely flawless studio-quality voice. Larry continued:

"I know how important having a ready and reliable credit line can be to a business."

"Hey there, Larry," I interjected while Larry took a breath. "I was wondering if you are a robot."

After a very short pause that Larry must have used to combobulate himself, he replied.

"You are speaking to a real person."

"Well, then, I'm terribly sorry, but I'm not interested at this t—"

Larry hung up on me before I thought to give him a Turing test to figure out if he actually was a real person. Right there, I should have asked him, "What is two plus three?" or "How do you spell *Larry*?" or "What is the taste of sugar?" He might very well have been a robot programmed to hang up on "not interested," or he could have just been a rude son of a blasphemer interested in making the sale and not at all in being polite, or civil, or even humanlike.

Larry was very different from Josetta, who called me after the Larry chat. When I interrupted her to ask if she was a robot, she said, "Whoa! Am I that bad?" Then she proceeded to relate what her mama done told her about sounding robotish on the phone. Fair enough. We chatted amicably until she had to excuse herself because her boss would notice that she was getting behind in her vacuuming.

I'm not trying to start a movement here, but if you would care to join me, don't talk to any more robots. We should all take the time we save and look into some state-of-the-art concept weapons, especially those capable of plugging up vacuum cleaners.

Column 164, July 1, 2014

The Robots Really Are Coming

Barring a direct hit from a large meteor or the collapse of world order or an unprecedented pandemic or any number of natural and man-made disasters that can throw civilization for a loop, this has *got* to be the decade when robots for home and work just bust out of the starting gate. Somewhere there must be a garage where the future Bill Gates of robotics is tinkering, and it's only a matter of days before his team releases a robot equivalent of the first personal computer on a waiting world—and are we ever ready for it.

We've got all the controls we need in the palm of our sweaty little-smartphone-holding hand, but we have nothing in the real world to control. We're all spending our time liking things on Facebook, scanning QR codes, and posting bad photographs, but we aren't doing any real-world controlling with all this wireless handheld power we have.

Not to get off topic, but just to be clear, *sweaty* in my statement above refers to the hand and *little* describes the smartphone. I have to do this because people constantly stop me on the street to attack positions that they feel I am defending simply because of ambiguous statements I have let slip. And please, if your hands never sweat, let's just agree that the bacteria-laden oily film found on most people's smartphones comes from the oily-film gnomes who handle your phone and drain the battery when you're not looking.

Anyway, the garage-dwelling tinkerers may need a suggestion or two to keep them on track to develop robots the world really needs and wants. With that in mind, I have compiled a few suggestions for consideration in order to speed the process of what we all hope won't be a plague of robots that will eventually snuff out civilization in an ironic triumph of technological progress designed to benefit mankind.

We already have the robotic car wash, so why is it that two guys have to prewash anything before sending your car into the machine, only to be followed by two dispassionate employees who wipe down the car by hand once the robot is finished? Surely it wouldn't be difficult to add a couple stations where the robot wets and wipes. You drive up to the car wash, tap in the payment method and the service you want on your smartphone, and the robot takes it from there. There should be only one person attending a car wash, and that would be to hand out refunds for broken antennas and mirrors. Any employees displaced from their low-level, menial positions would be free to get better-paying jobs as architects, medical specialists, or even robotic design engineers. The future looks promising indeed.

Affordable robotic lawnmowers can't be far from reality; this is just off-the-shelf technology. They start in one corner of the yard with a sharp, high-powered rotating blade and go back and forth, avoiding any obstacles or babies that might have crawled onto the lawn. How hard can that be? You could be out sailing, smart-dial your mower, and by the time you got back home, the lawn would be partially cut, the police would be holding your mower as evidence, and the district attorney would be in your driveway awaiting your arrival.

More difficult to design, more expensive to purchase, and yet something my wife would not hesitate to order for immediate delivery would be the laundry-folding robot. The problem here is not folding the laundry. The problem is pulling out a shirt from the dryer and recognizing that it is indeed a shirt with one sleeve turned inside out and some underpants caught inside the other sleeve. The bot has to be programmed to complete the folding process without becoming so frustrated that it uses its laser-beam eyes to cut the entire laundry pile into small bits and then set them on fire. When these robots become available, remind me to pass on the laser-eye, cutter-igniter option.

All right, there may be some details to attend to, but the commercial and personal robots really are coming and there is no way to stop them now. Especially if the stop button is on your smartphone and you've let it slip from your sweaty little hand.

Column 168, June 15, 2014

Eat You Alive Theater

It's not hard to get involved with community theater. You just show up. It doesn't have to be at one of their meetings or at a rehearsal. As a matter of fact, if you happen to be driving within three hundred feet of one of their functions while minding your own business, there is a fifty-fifty chance you will be assigned a job on their next production. This job will be based on your experience, plus you'll be given credit for at least five years' experience in areas that you have no skill and possibly didn't even know existed prior to your promotion.

If you're not careful, you may very well end up as chairman of their board of directors or at least head of the fundraising committee all within six weeks of expressing even the slightest interest in any aspect of theater. This applies even if your original intention was only to give out programs at a single performance just to get in for free. The only "free" in theater is what you'll be working for.

In a typical example, you attend a play produced by your local community theater group. While innocently milling about the lobby during intermission, you notice something amiss and casually pick up a poster that has fallen onto the floor. This is called "displaying an interest." The next thing you know, you're being released from a long-term psychiatric care facility. It is seven years later. You go home and your house is stuffed full of posters, flyers, and programs for old plays. There is a drawing board and a computer loaded with high-end graphic programs hooked to a high-speed color printer/copier that would still be putting out program notes if it had not run out of paper. Apparently, you were the graphic arts department for this theater group even though when you lost consciousness you couldn't manage to draw a circle.

There is more. Your garage and carport are loaded with set pieces. The house is overflowing with stage props: dining room tables cut in half, coffins, French revolutionary street barricades, swords both real and rubber, pieces of train cars, and skulls. Your bathroom is stocked with a hundred cans of partially used paint. In your front yard sits the HMS *Pinafore* shipwrecked on what appears to be part of a South Pacific island.

Your head is repeating show tunes and catchy lines from plays that you've seen rehearsed dozens of times. To your horror, you find evidence that, on occasion, you might have crossed the line — and consented to acting. Could it be? You find stage makeup, but maybe you were only assisting with costumes and makeup. Then you see the pages of scripts taped to the walls of your kitchen, which has been rearranged to mirror the set of *A Streetcar Named Desire.* Your lines are highlighted in yellow, but you don't have to look at them; you are "off book." You have a dog named Stella that won't obey. The horror.

Your phone is ringing. Taped to the phone is a handwritten note apparently inked in your own blood. It reads: "Learn to say NO."

You have to be careful because community theater groups are very much like black holes—they are fascinating at a distance and great material for thought experiments. But get too close and they will suck you in, converting your entire mass into energy keeping the theater operational until you pass the event horizon. At that point, you are spit out into another universe densely populated by out-of-work actors, drugged-up roadies, psychotic stage managers—and every last one of them wants to direct.

To answer Paul Simon, no, the theater is not really dead, but theater is a killer. And in the nearly fifty years since he penned those lyrics, the theater refuses to die because it offers audiences something unique to experience and cast and crew something to live for, however savage its demands.

Next time, we will discuss exactly what the theater does for audiences and why attending local productions is more important than eating or personal hygiene. Did I fail to mention that I am involved with community theater? That, too, is a story for another time. What? No, no, I don't act. At least...well, I can't remember now...sorry, my phone is ringing. I have to go answer the phone.

Column 171, July 6, 2014

Dressing Up for Travel

Have you noticed how people dress when traveling in public? Apparently, not many of us have, or there would be a rush to buy mirrors, personal-care products, and clothes that fit and are not intended for the gym, bedroom, or beach.

There was a time when people dressed up to travel. Napoleon Bonaparte, who traveled a great deal, was never seen in sweatpants and an oversized hoodie, even when he was stranded in Moscow, tired, defeated, and unable to catch a flight back to Paris. At an earlier time, Attila also seems to have been a sharply dressed man—and he was a Hun!

My grandparents dressed up whenever traveling because they insisted some of their blood was aristocratic and they didn't want to be treated like yokels since they were, technically speaking, Polish peasants. If you dress like a peasant, people naturally assume you're a peasant.

When flying was still glamorous, everyone wanted to be part of the jet-set: people who often traveled by jet, had money, and coincidentally were always well dressed. Since flying was considered a bit risky, you always wore clean underwear in case of trauma so you wouldn't suffer the embarrassment of hospital staff shocked by your low laundering standard. This mandate for clean underwear extended to dressing stylishly; if there was a serious accident, you wouldn't want the coroner making the socially fatal discovery that you didn't have a sense of fashion.

Back not so long ago, everyone in America knew when and why to dress up. Then between the 1960s and today, a good majority of Americans experienced lasting psychological damage and forgot. It might have been the result of extended exposure to *Gilligan's Island*. But you have to wonder—even though the shipwrecked cast spent three television seasons and countless years in syndication on a tiny island with no hope of new clothes, their outfits remained unsoiled and as fresh as the day they first came aboard the SS *Minnow.*

So let's review the reasons we've forgotten as to why we dress up.

The primary reason is to show respect for your hosts and situation. If you're going to a wedding, funeral, or church service, you dress up to show the bride, the survivors of the deceased, the clergy, or maybe God himself that you hold them and the occasion in such high regard that you put on your Sunday best. Show up at a wedding in tattered shorts and you'll divert all attention from holy matrimony to your holey jeans.

Dressing up also shows that you possess a certain level of style and professionalism. You are in command of grooming and visual presentation. No one looks at James Bond in his semiformal wear and wonders if he has forgotten his medication or an appointment with his therapist.

You may dress up for class or respect, but you might also consider doing it as a favor for the rest of us...oh, wait, I'm sorry; I forgot that in the 2000s we have turned so self-centered that pleasing others with our appearance is no longer a consideration.

In the lobby of an international airport, I recently witnessed an American female in her twenties wearing a pajama ensemble complete with fuzzy slippers. I was wondering what her mother would have to say about that until her mother appeared also dressed in bedclothes. Was this a horribly awry fashion statement that was actually a cry for help? Were they trying to raise money for a charity? Did they lose a bet? Were they bumped off a late-night plane and forced to stay at Hotel B3?

Rather than suggest what to wear for travel, I have compiled a list of clothing that could cause you to lose points when it comes to being well dressed. I will leave it to you to assign the number of points off for each item listed. These include, in no particular order: sleepwear; beachwear; T-shirts; jeans; shorts; sneakers or athletic shoes; athletic clothes of any kind; any clothes advertising anything or with any branding (extra demerits for lettering across the buttocks); torn, worn out, stained, dirty, shabby, or smelly garments; flip-flops; underwear as outerwear; and codpieces.

If this list encompasses your entire wardrobe, it might be time to add a button-down shirt.

Napoleon did well and looked good without sneakers and basketball shorts, and you can too. Of course, no one saw what he was wearing when he was sulking around the Waterloo International Airport.

Column 175, August 3, 2014

Dad's Guide to House Shopping

So you finally got the kid to move out of the house and get an apartment near his or her place of full-time employment. What next?

Okay, stop right there and drop to your knees. No—prostrate yourself before whatever power you consider godlike. Thank Him or Her or at least your lucky stars that however bumpy the path might have been, you have survived so far. You may not be healthy or sane by any reasonable standards, you may be drained of cash and desperately treading water in a deep lake of debt, but at least you're still breathing and able to stand back, look proudly at your son or daughter, and say, "Oh well, I gave it my best shot."

There were the basics to cover and little luxuries to buy. Some of us had insurance or medical payments, which extended to cell phone and car payments. There may have been exorbitant tuition bills and even attorney fees, and those of us with girls had to pay large ransoms to the aliens who took their brains when they were thirteen and would not give them back until they turned twenty-three. It was expensive, and now it's their turn (our children, not the aliens) to try and manage their financial situation without tapping into their credit line with the First National Bank of Momandad.

Next comes the effort to make sure your offspring are financially secure and somewhat literate in the language of money and investments. After seeing our own daughter use whatever pay she had earned over the month on food we would never buy, clothing that Dad especially didn't approve of, and the remainder on inflated rental costs, it was time for a talk about her financial independence.

I had made it clear to my daughter that if she was in love with the city she had settled in (never mind that it's on Dad's list of top ten cities to avoid), then she should rid herself of apartment rents and purchase a house.

"But Dad, I don't have that kind of money," she said, pointing out the painfully obvious. I had to explain that this is America. You don't need to have money to buy a house; you just have to make someone believe you can get the money—over time.

A week later, she was sending me images of homes with "For Sale" signs in the front yard. I wanted to know how much the owners were asking, but she was too nervous to call in case she might come across like a kid in a candy store asking how much the penny candy costs. She needed house-shopping guidelines, so I offered a few key tips.

Call the number, make sure you are talking to an adult, and let them know right away you saw their house is for sale so that they don't think you are trying to sell them anything like bacteria for their septic system. Tell them your name, clarify that you are not an agent, and inquire as to how much they are asking for the house in plain English. Avoid anything like "Yo yo, bro, like how much of my stash of cash for that crib of yours in the hood?"

When they tell you, start taking notes and try not to whistle or gasp in amazement. You can do that later after you figure out if the house is overpriced. While you're note-taking, ask the standard questions and find out the following: square footage, size of the lot, number of bedrooms, number of baths, available parking, annual taxes, and how the house is heated and cooled. Be polite and professional, and avoid talking about meth labs or Jimmy Hoffa's final resting place; those topics can be covered if you make an appointment to see the property.

Before making that appointment, ask questions about things that might be major deal breakers. Why are they selling? If they answer that too many people have walked into the basement and never returned or that the neighboring fracking facility keeps them up at night, you will want to say thank you, wish them good luck, and hang up.

Look at more than one place, look up home values in your area on the web, and when you make an appointment, get back to me. I will then forward "Dad's Guide to House Inspections and Financing." I will do that just as soon as I get up off of my knees and finish my little victory dance.

Column 178, August 24, 2014

A Quick Guide to Tenant Conduct

Are you a tenant wondering about the proper way to behave during your tenancy in your apartment, home, or condo? Let me assure you that you are on the right track because that question apparently never even crosses the imagination of a good percentage of tenants today.

It's not as if the question has never been addressed. As early as 1772 BC, the Code of Hammurabi dealt with some tenant-landlord questions. Of course, that particular section of the code has been damaged on the original rock pillar where it was inscribed, and it wouldn't surprise me if it was erased by a landlord gone wild or a group of tenants having a little vandalizing fun on a Friday night.

Allow me to offer some etiquette guidelines when renting property. Being a landlord of many years, I have had the privilege of experiencing rental horror stories firsthand. True, there are web pages dedicated to the rights and responsibilities of the tenant and landlord, but all of these guides are, frankly, boring. Sure, the tenant should pay the rent on time, refrain from making loud noises, and stick to the rental agreement, but these obvious considerations don't even begin to address real-world tenant behavior.

Tenants like to hang things: pictures, posters, curtains, wind chimes, TVs, garlic, bed sheets, underwear, and stolen highway signs to name some of the more popular items. If you must hang something, then please put the nail, screw, or hook into the wall and not the trim or woodwork. This may be counterintuitive, but trim is much harder to repair than drywall.

In fact, if you feel the need to punch a hole into something with your fist or when swinging a frying pan while high on PCP, do it to the drywall and not a door or window. Breaking down doors in a drunken rage when your girlfriend has locked herself in the bathroom or at a party gone wildly out of control will seem like a bad idea in the morning, and gluing a door back together takes a skilled craftsman. No matter how much dope you smoke to make the door look good as new, you won't be able to fool the landlord.

Do not nail doors shut when you no longer wish to open them. Instead, use the locking mechanism that is already part of the doorknob. And while we're on the subject, consider hiding a two-dollar spare key in case you lock yourself out; hiding it somewhere outside of the house works best. Using a tire iron on a $300 door is considered brutish.

Instead of designating a bedroom, the basement, or the entire garage for permanent storage of all the trash you produce during your tenancy, it might be nice to take your garbage to the dump or even place it inside the dumpster provided by the landlord. A room, chest deep in trash bags is difficult to deal with when you are moving out. Leaving it for the landlord not only results in the loss of your cleaning deposit, but chances are good that the landlord will take your deposit to hire an experienced voodoo hoodoo queen who will use the hair you undoubtedly left in the shower drain to make one of those dolls that looks so much like you. Taking your trash to the dump might be less painful in the long run.

Other tenant tips include serving only white wine at parties as red will stain the ceiling, keeping the music at a low volume after the *first* police visit, and remembering that a waterbed and spiked collars on dogs or humans don't mix.

By the way, if you are going to keep a pet in violation of your rental agreement, make sure it is the kind of pet that is physiologically incapable of urinating. A pet rock comes to mind. All animals dispose of metabolic waste, and most of the time, it stinks. It may be fun to have a pet rat or monkey, but it may get you tossed out of your rental unit when your neighbors catch wind. At the very least, make sure the monkey doesn't smoke.

Indeed, paying rent on time is paramount to good tenant-landlord relationships. Landlords have hefty monthly expenses that must be met; they just can't wait until the cows come home for a tenant to pay the rent…uh-oh, cows…I better go check for cows.

Column 183, September 28, 2014

Dad's Guide to House Shopping, Part 2: Inspections

Earlier, we discussed house shopping for the benefit of our grown-up children who, like my own daughter, have moved out of the house and settled into jobs and apartments of their own (glory be to the Almighty). I am very proud of my daughter for attaining complete financial independence, even though my wife and I have an unspoken agreement never to discuss the "cash gifts" my wife sometimes sends, so the daughter can occasionally buy a small luxury for herself, such as groceries, in order to survive in a world of two-income households.

I advised the daughter to shop around for a house so that she can stop sending money to a landlord and instead start sending money to a mortgage holder. The logic of doing this escapes me at the present time, but I am sure its wisdom will become self-evident before the girl reaches retirement age.

Now that she has made inquiries into a few properties in the affordable part of the city, sometimes playfully referred to as the slums, it's time to don an environmental, level-B hazmat suit and inspect the properties firsthand. Here are some tips to remember when the real estate agent is taking you on a tour of what they always call "your dream home."

When approaching the house, note any signs of forced entry and bullet holes, which may help explain the price of the property. Try to determine if the bullets entered the house from the outside or originated from within. Especially troubling are multiple bullet holes that entered the house from the direction of the street. This may indicate a rough neighborhood, but don't jump to conclusions without digging deeper.

And speaking of digging, check for freshly turned earth in the basement and dark, private corners of the backyard. This may be an attempt at gardening, but everybody knows tomatoes don't grow in the dark.

Look around for evidence of fire, meteor impact, meth labs, and discarded containers with labels such as "radioactive," "medical waste," or "DDT." Cast a casual eye to see if the neighbors have large fences topped with razor wire and gun emplacements, which can indicate that survival in this particular neighborhood is indeed possible even if they don't have a welcome-wagon program for new homeowners.

Smell for gas leaks, pet odors, mildew, sewer smells, and the stench of death. Know that the odor people notice when entering the attic of an old house is not a nostalgic "old house smell" as it tends to be called; the smell is actually bat droppings, or more crudely, bat poop, left there by real live bats, probably over a long period of time.

Look for damage from dogs, cats, reptiles, birds, fish, amphibians, and all manner of mammals including rodents, monkeys, and former tenants. If you spot any monkeys, do not touch, feed, or even acknowledge their presence, as they may never leave the property. Same goes for tenants, only double. Also keep an eye out for invertebrates like insects and mollusks; there is nothing worse than being surprised by a giant bivalve clam when you open the laundry room door.

Discovering irregularities may be deal breakers, although with creative packaging, some situations may be converted to a legal income stream. People will pay to see a giant bivalve clam. If there is enough bat guano in the attic, it can be traded on the international fertilizer market, although that kind of quantity is usually found only in old New England homes.

On the flip side of finding living organisms in the house is finding no life whatsoever. If you can't locate one living spider, ant, or pill bug, better zip up that hazmat suit until you find out what kind of poison factory the former owners operated there.

Once you decide the house is livable, start asking the standard questions about square footage, roof condition, and proximity to churches and liquor stores. You will now be in a good position to either make a solid offer or run full-speed toward the door. Avoid tripping over any vagrants who may have set up camp since you came in, and remember not to open the door to the giant bivalve clam.

Remember that house inspections are the fun part of house shopping. Take a break and have a cup of coffee at your favorite café while you ponder your options. Mom will send you money for coffee.

Column 185, October 12, 2014

Let's Talk About Glue

The problem with learning about adhesives, their specific uses, and application techniques is that if practicing what you've learned doesn't kill you, it ultimately leads to hoarding. The murderous tendencies of glue are straightforward, but their ability to turn you into a hoarder are more subtle.

It starts small and innocently enough; you successfully reattach the eyeballs of a reindeer on a Christmas tree ornament, but after some time you find yourself saving—even acquiring—everything broken simply because you have the power to fix it. The reality is that it's not actually a power but an insidious curse.

I'm sorry. I don't believe I've ever used the word *insidious* before, in writing or in speaking. It's one of those words that I see now and again, but my confidence level in knowing exactly what it means is just not high enough to use it in public on the fly. There are lots of words like *piquant, parsnakle, dord* and *participle* that fall into this category. Writers have it easy because they can look up a word before using it. People standing around at a cocktail party, however, have to take a chance that they'll look smart bandying about a rarely used word, assuming most everyone has only a vague idea of what it means. It takes some courage to take the risk to impress people, as there is always the chance you'll blurt out something unintended:

"Isn't Oedipus the guy who had that insidious relationship with his mother?"

If you're lucky and drinking with intellectuals, which in my case is happening more and more infrequently, they might attribute your erroneous use of the word to scholarly depth and jump in on what they consider an insight:

"Insidious indeed—enticing but harmful. Could have done

with a little more exogamy and a little less endogamy. Is there any more absinthe? Okay, how about malt liquor?"

I would normally have used the word *sinister* when talking about adhesives because everyone is familiar with a sinister movie character that is evil, foretelling disaster and trouble. But *insidious* is actually a better word because it not only defines the harmfulness embodied in *sinister,* it also adds a dimension of time where evil is working toward a gradual and cumulative effect. What may seem harmless at first eventually reveals its sinister character and entraps the victim. This is truly the essence of glue.

You sit down to simply glue something back together and all is well. You, the broken item, and the glue are in harmony. In this opening chapter, no one suspects the glue to be the character that will eventually go berserk and try to kill everyone else. But something is slightly off: the glue container is ajar; there is a hint of cyanoacrylate in the air.

By the last chapter, it is revealed that the glue container isn't really a jar but a tube; it has burst open because you applied too much pressure. It splashed into your eyes. You try to hold back a sneeze brought on by the toxic fumes from the glue but blinded, you can't see your hand is covered in super adhesive which instantly adheres your hand to your face, sealing shut your mouth and nose. At this point, the pressure of the sneeze blows out your eyeballs, but I really must stop here as I am encroaching on Stephen King territory, and if there is territory you don't want to encroach on in writing, it's Stephen King territory.

You may scoff and say, "Tut-tut. That is only a worst-case scenario." Okay, I agree that very few people in this day and age will say *tut-tut*. It's a shame, really—*tut-tut* is so much more elegant than *yo-yo*. Nevertheless, if you're careful and avoid death by adhesive, you may still fall victim to that incestuous tendency of glue to gradually transform you into a hoarder.

What? Did I misspell *insidious*? As you see, just the subject of adhesives has destroyed the cohesion of my writing. My plan to explain the different types of glue and their uses has been mired down in a sticky mess of gummy references, incoherent asides, and tacky wordplay. Adhesives are more dangerous than they appear.

Great. Now I'm stuck for a good finish...

Column 189, November 9, 2014

Power Outage Notes

Day 1, 5:00 p.m.: We're fairly tough here in semirural Maine where I live. A major storm is raging, the power has been out for at least twenty-seven minutes, and my wife and I are not complaining. We have already settled into a blackout routine where she goes about the house lighting candles and I follow close behind lecturing about fire safety and the relative flammability of household objects.

5:15 p.m.: We are getting along just fine as the romantic atmosphere builds where it's all: "I'll light the fire; you place the flowers in the vase that you bought today." We have each other, all is good, and anyway, the power company will come to the rescue before any contentious positions rear their unpleasant heads.

A mere two days ago, we felt summer would linger on and on. I even worked outside in just my shirtsleeves until a neighbor suggested I put on some pants before she called the police. Point being that the weather was unseasonably generous up until forty-eight hours ago. I'm sure that's when the guy who controls the climate must have received a letter of reprimand citing him for being a slacker so he buckled down and clobbered the region with a good dose of winter terror. Now we are victims, sucker punched by a mid-autumn snowstorm.

6:00 p.m.: Attempted a trip into a nearby town for dinner. Nearly slid off the road twice and just about swept over a pedestrian who was out for a mid-storm stroll. Turned back after half a mile. Noted that wife's mood changed as we crossed the bridge when the truck made a sudden lunge toward the lake. Instead of being commended for heroic driving in near whiteout conditions, I was scolded for almost losing control.

6:15 p.m.: Back at home. Our entire area is dark, but we know the grid works in mysterious ways. We were once invited across the street by fabulous neighbor Liz Hand who was without power but had enough candles going to make Easter in a Catholic Church look understated. She cranked up her woodstove and served hot stew to power starved citizens who were enjoying her bright and warm abode. It was a great party until the wine ran out and she noticed our porch light was on across the street. No, we had never lost power—and no, we hadn't realized that having power sort of disqualified us from the party. Awkward.

6:45 p.m.: Bedtime comes early when you take a step back into the Stone Age. We're in bed because it's cold and we've finished all the tasks we usually perform in the dark as we quickly ran out of film to develop. Thought we would catch a movie in bed on the iPad. Silly, that requires Wi-Fi, which disappears when the electricity has drained out of the wires. "No, dear, I didn't mean to call you silly…dear?"

Day 2, 2:00 a.m.: I'm up early for some reason. There's a faint light outside reflecting off the clouds to the north from a small town where they obviously still have power. I'm sure they're all in their warm, well-lit homes, tuned into the news and feeling sorry for the neighboring community where the people have resorted to living like primitive savages.

5:00 a.m.: Things are better now. We are once again on speaking terms and no longer yelling at the dog. Of course, my wife is still sleeping. So is the dog.

Sunrise: Cell phone died. No telling what time it is. Can't locate the cable to charge the phones from the car. Conflict developing between keeping the house warm and the refrigerator and freezer cold.

Evening: Spent the day feeding the woodstove and trying to fix the generator. It was pointed out to me that the generator maintenance was inadequate and that wet, green wood from our freshly downed trees doesn't burn hot. Our conversations seem to be heating up, however, and even boiling over every once in a while.

Day 3 (Maybe 4): Just about had enough. Generator not working properly. Wife insists on a shower, a toilet that flushes, a consistent cookstove, and hot running water—in short, civilization. Making ready to pull up stakes and head for a Motel 6…oh wait…never mind. Power restored. I wonder who won the game last night? Yes, a glass of wine sounds delightful—and let's make sure the porch light is off in case our across-the-street neighbor is planning another power-out party.

Column 196, January 4, 2015

The Problem with Stuff

Now that the holidays are over, it's as good a time as any to talk about stuff management because nobody listens anyway. That's because we're up over our ears in belongings, and it's hard to listen to good advice about stuff overload—just like it's too late to get swimming pointers when you're drowning.

I've been making a pie chart representing the life of a typical American when it comes to possessions. The pie is divided into four unequal pieces that show how much of our time is used interacting in some way with material goods commonly known as "stuff."

The largest slice of time—maybe 40 percent—is labeled "Acquiring Stuff." That's the time we spend making things or earning money to obtain goods. "Managing Stuff" is represented by a 20-percent slice and includes moving, cleaning, repairing, insuring, and lubricating our things. A pitifully thin slice of 5 percent is allocated to "Actually Enjoying Stuff." The remaining 35 percent is labeled "Disposing of Stuff."

As I get older, I may have to adjust the numbers; 35 percent may not be enough time to properly dispose of my stuff. Of course, you can cheat by dying and letting other people dispose of your stuff, but dying is simply not the moral thing to do.

It's not that we're materialists. Alan Watts, the American philosopher (whose one hundredth birthday will be celebrated January 6, 2015) introduced many Americans to Eastern philosophy through his books and lectures. He maintained that Americans are not materialists as in "those who hold material possessions in great regard." He pointed out that we actually hate material things because if we loved material possessions, we would take better care of them. Indeed, we would not call possessions our "junk."

What we are in love with is the idea of possessing many wonderful things that we magically have room to store, are accessible at any time, require absolutely no upkeep, and are always in like-new condition. In other words, we are dreaming. It's not all bad news: we are driving the world economy based on a faulty dream. What could possibly go wrong?

The entire problem stems from the fact that for the last fifty thousand years, humans didn't have much stuff. Check any archeological dig and you'll find that the stuff we had, like pottery and arrowheads, was easily broken or lost. Really cool things like the pyramids or the Gardens of Babylon either belonged to royalty or were laid waste by the marauding hoards. No one had much stuff to deal with in their house, if they indeed had a house. It seemed life would be better if we had unlimited stuff.

But by the early 1950s, people were making money and having children and building homes and thinking about getting things like TVs, cars, swimming-pool toys, and Hummel figurines. Before that time, the only person with a lot of stuff was Citizen Kane, who had so many warehouses full that he couldn't find his sled—but he was seen as an exception and not a warning to us all. My father built a house about that time, and my mother actually had to go out and buy furniture so that it wouldn't look so cavernous. She did manage to fill it full of stuff by the early 1980s thanks to automation, marketing, and all of the StuffMarts that popped up to fill the need.

Ownership has its hidden costs. There is the cost of storage; this becomes obvious when you start to value the space that your stuff occupies more than the stuff itself. A deeper understanding comes when you rent a storage unit, or two. There is opportunity cost where you can't buy more stuff because you've spent your money on storage units. Of course, there is the cost of defending your stuff against the marauding hoards and people like your wife who want to dispose of it. And who can ignore the cost of moving your stuff around to make yourself believe that you actually use it. It's no wonder that we only get to enjoy our stuff 5 percent of the time we own it.

Well, that is certainly a good start on the problem of stuff in our lives. I should continue with how some people have changed their entire relationship with material goods, but next week, I can't wait to write about some of the fabulous things I've acquired over the holiday season. Until then, happy shopping!

BREAKDOWN OF TIME SPENT ON OUR STUFF

DISPOSING OF STUFF
35%
OR 21 MINUTES OF AN HOUR

ACQUIRING STUFF
40%
OR 24 MINUTES OF AN HOUR

MANAGING STUFF
20%
-12 MINUTES-

PIE 100%

5%
ACTUALLY ENJOYING STUFF
3 MINUTES!

Toboggan Nationals 2015

Once again, the National Toboggan Championships are upon us. They take place at a wooden toboggan chute in Camden, Maine, not far from where I live—if you call scrambling to feed the woodstove nonstop for six weeks every February "living."

Technically, you've got me if you're thinking that February barely has four weeks. But spend a February in the neighborhood of the 45th parallel and you'll see that many people here measure the passage of winter in weeks-supply of firewood remaining in the shed—and somehow February always manages to use up six weeks' worth of wood. This is one reason why the toboggan championships really attract the locals.

Bundling up the family and spending three days outside watching the crazy teams will mean so much less firewood to feed the woodstove at the house. Oh, you might have to shell out $5 a day for parking, but if you pack a big breakfast, lunch, and maybe dinner, it's so much cheaper than trying to keep the family warm at home.

As a bonus, you can choose to picnic on the snowy side of the mountain next to the toboggan run or you can spread out and relax on the frozen lake to watch the toboggans coast over the ice after leaving the chute. Getting home nightly after eight to ten hours outside, your 36-degree house will feel warm as toast by comparison.

Another huge attraction of the championships is that almost anyone can participate. Getting to the US Nationals in swimming, tennis, cycling, or most any sport has always been dreadful since competitors keep getting in the way. If you own a football team you're pushing to the Super Bowl or if your baseball franchise wants to see the World Series, you may have to quit your day job and even obtain financial backing. Ah, but breaking into the US Toboggan Nationals is not much more difficult than going to the grocery store, assuming the store is situated at the top of an icy hill with the parking lot at the bottom.

If you can pay the fee before the available slots fill up, get a toboggan that will pass inspection, and get yourself and your team members to the top of the chute, you can more than likely *personally* participate in a genuine United States of America National Sports Championship—never mind that you hold the level of Master Couch Potato. Indeed, there is no rule that states you have to make it to the top of the chute under your own power.

If, for example, you're dead, your teammates can haul you up to the start and set you on the toboggan, and you're good to go. You can even be the one in front, and you won't have to wear a helmet. What would be the point? You will, however, have to wear your team number on your chest as race rules require. I know! Years ago I pointed out to the race committee that there is no rule preventing cadavers from participating, but they keep arguing that it's February—Mainers are bundled up and it's just too hard to tell the difference between a cadaver and some of the crusty locals.

If you're really taken by the spirit of the championship, you may want to consider team costumes. But to be a contender in the costume contest, it's come to the point where your team getup has to be outlandish. As a longtime observer, I recommend your team come equipped with those giant heads you see at carnival parades in Rio de Janeiro along with lots of feathers, jewels, special lighting effects, and a jazz band. As long as you can get it all on a toboggan and down the chute, you're a player.

Beware that appearing in heels and mostly naked like they

do in Rio has its trade-offs. As you can imagine, it will put you at a tremendous advantage in the costume contest, but at the same time it may cancel out any home heating savings. Your team might have to invoke the cadaver rule as you could start out as hot stuff at the top but end up a frozen stiff at the bottom.

Okay, it's time to turn both thermostat and damper down and head on over to the National Toboggan Championship. I'll see you at the chute—no, wait a minute. Darn, I forgot—this year I'll be on my way to Miami.

The Royal Dutch National Toboggan Team vies for Best Costumes award at the 2012 Toboggan National Championships in Camden, Maine.

Note from the author:
Don't get your snow pants in a bunch and recoil in horror because I will not be attending the Toboggan Nationals this year. I've attended the Nationals for over twenty years in a row. I published a newsletter devoted to the Nationals called the *Toboggan Times* for fifteen years. I've even participated on teams in odd years. Now it's time to go to Miami to see palm trees in February. Any questions?

Hitchhiking Robot Vacation Invitation

Have you noticed that robots are receiving more and more attention? I know I have. There are robot movies, robot contests, and news stories constantly reporting on recent robot developments. Already, robots are making our cars, exploring the planets, performing medical operations, and sending us unwanted email.

Be aware. All of this activity is only the prepubescent stage of robotics. Soon we will be into the adolescent phase, where robots will be talking back to us, sneaking out for a cigarette with friends, and of course, taking our car keys without permission. There may even come a point where they run into their bedroom shouting "I hate you!" as they slam the door and sit down to network with all the other robots to see if the time is right to begin Operation Worldwide Domination. The only difference between your teenage son and the adolescent robot is that world domination for the robots shouldn't be much of a problem.

But, ha ha, that's a scenario we won't have to worry about for months. While robots are still cute and full of promise, we should take time to enjoy them because somewhere around high school, they will probably take a turn toward the dark side. It could be a battle guiding them to fit into our society instead of trying to eliminate it, as the road to robot maturity may be a long and tortuous route.

And speaking of roads, I have learned that the Canadians have been the first to develop a hitchhiking robot they call hitchBOT. hitchBOT has been hitching rides along the highways of Canada, seeing the sights, meeting many motorists, and testing…well, we don't know exactly what he's testing, now do we?

There are a lot of things about hitchBOT we don't know. We don't know exactly how friendly or annoying hitchBOT is as a traveling companion; he is reported to be chatty, but does he make only small talk? Does he discuss the existence of God or does he loudly sing lewd camp songs out of tune, sometimes improvising the lyrics? Perhaps he's like a traveling jukebox, downloading and playing requested songs as you travel the open road.

Then again, maybe he's just out to test people's patience to see how far he can push us:

Driver: "I've never picked up a robot before."

hitchBOT: "How far can you take me?"

Driver: "Whoa, how far do you want to go, buddy?"

hitchBOT: "I am sorry. I forgot that hitchhiking etiquette dictates that the hitchhiker declares his destination before the driver does. I apologize."

Driver: "That's very good! You know how to be proper and polite."

hitchBOT: "Yes, I am programmed to be proper and polite. So—how far can you take me?"

In any case, it may be time hitchBOT took a little vacation. I've decided to ask Dr. David Harris Smith of McMaster University and Dr. Frauke Zeller of Ryerson University, the co-developers of the project, if it may be agreeable to program hitchBOT so that he can come to Maine for a little time off. My wife has generously offered to put him up in our guest bedroom, even though I suggested the closet under the stairway. We could show him the local sights; perhaps he may be personally interested in the fine transportation museum we have in the area. If he can come for the Fourth of July, we can arrange to feature him in one of our town parades.

As a community, we would have to take good care of hitch-BOT, which means that I will no longer consider offers to take him scuba diving or skydiving. Also bungee jumping, even at the beginner level, is off the table. After a few days, we can put him back on the road to hitchhike home or to his next destination, taking with him as many images and sound bites as his installed memory can carry.

It would be a treat to have him visit before he either succumbs to adolescent tendencies or becomes weaponized, especially by the Canadians, who might arm him with a hockey stick and a broken Molson bottle before upgrading to leghold traps and an arsenal of Leonard Cohen songs.

I will keep you posted when I get a response. A little cultural exchange between a Canadian robot and happy Americans, most of whom have no concealed-weapon permits, can be a fun time indeed. What could possibly go wrong?

Yard Sales

Winter is over, the crocuses have bloomed, the daffodils are up, and I suspect the next thing to sprout in my yard is going to be a lawn sale.

Yes, it's the season when people bring out items they don't want and are willing to part with—but only on the condition that someone gives them a fraction of what the items were originally worth. Those are curious terms, but far be it from me to criticize: I am one of the people prepared to sell you that old saw I haven't used in fifteen years for $2. But if you offer me less, I'll keep and store it for a yet-to-be-determined length of time. Now that's really curious behavior because it's just… what's the right word…oh, yes: stupid.

Perhaps it's time to examine the economic and social aspects of this odd American retail outlet to find out what's really going on.

There were no yard sales in my early youth; people were not bursting with possessions to sell. There were secondhand thrift shops, but the closest we came to a yard sale was the church rummage sale. This was derived from the early 1800s "rommage" sales where you could go down to the docks and buy unclaimed cargo and maybe one or two stowaways at bargain prices.

But by the 1970s, yard sales had become acceptable behavior in America, and why not? Turns out we had all fallen victim to mass merchandising. Living the American dream was choking us with stuff we didn't need. Somehow, it was important that we all had Hula-Hoops and Veg-O-Matics.

But why even have a yard sale? If it's money you're after, there are more profitable uses of your time. Washing car windows for tips comes to mind. It's less stressful, easy work, good hours, and you don't have to make change or watch for children running with your old scissors their parents have not yet purchased.

If you just want to clean out clutter, your unwanted items can simply be hauled to the thrift shop. But yard sales give us something more, like the interaction with neighbors when they come by, all friendly-like, just to ask when the junk in the yard will go back into the house. Then there is the illusion that we are not wasting resources. This, of course, assumes that our time is not a resource. Finally, there's the satisfaction of knowing that something you have owned will be put to further use. Why this should matter at all is quite a mystery.

Maybe the trouble is that we don't treat our belongings as possessions; we treat them as prisoners. Worse yet, they aren't prisoners in a just and democratic society; they're prisoners of a ruthless dictator who bought and held them captive without trial for most of their useful life solely for convenience or pleasure. The lawn sale is more like a transaction between dictators and less like parole or emancipation.

Customer: "Wow, look at that old ashtray."

Seller: "Yeah, that was my dad's. Well, my dad had one just like it. Might have come with a box of junk I bought at the yard sale down the street."

"It's marked $3. Would you take a dollar?"

"No, I'll take $2.50. Lot of sentimental value there."

"Dollar and a half?"

"Dad died from smoking. Anyway, that little guy is my prisoner. I'm not lettin' him off for good behavior. Still has years of life in him. Still good for a lot of sadistic pleasure; you can push burning cigarettes right into his face there."

"Two dollars, then."

"Done."

But the transaction between dictators theory can't possibly be correct; it's too farfetched. The only logical reason to have a yard sale is even more disturbing: we do not control these possessions. *They control us.* We can't toss them because we are not allowed; we must transfer them to a new "owner" who will be responsible for their well-being.

A yard/lawn/garage/tag sale, is the ritual of transfer, and our false satisfaction that the item is not going to waste, is our little reward. And to minimize our reward, the item insults you with the low price it fetched; it's one last punishment for the sin of ownership.

I've reviewed the reasons repeatedly, and this is the only logical one. It's so creepy; I must have overlooked something... uh-oh, I have to go. I'm being beckoned by some of my stuff.

Column 215, May 17, 2015

The Strange World of Third Grade

Through a long and tortured career path, I have ended up, among other things, as a lighting designer for theatrical productions. I invent the lighting schemes for plays, put up and take down lighting hardware, and troubleshoot crazy problems like stage lights mysteriously flashing on and off on their own (solution: unplug the lights).

Recently, I had the assignment of lighting a play that employed ninety (90!) local third-grade students. These were very sharp "grade-three students" and not the tertiary-level "third-grade students" that I was grouped with in elementary school. And by "employed," I mean that all of the students appeared on stage *at the same time.*

The play was a history narrative where fewer than thirty-five of the Lilliputian thespians had speaking parts. Most everyone else was cast as kind of a Greek chorus, which sang songs to further the progress of the story. Still, ninety people assembled on stage is a rare sight, even considering that the total mass of the wispy students would equal about thirty-five adults. And thirty-five adults on stage is called what? *Cats,* I guess.

The director doubled as a composer, songwriter, counselor, playwright, piano player, and drill sergeant. Because he excels at all these disciplines, he qualifies as an elementary school teacher.

Most of us could not do his job. I certainly couldn't. There is too much energy spent; he's a man on fire, always "on," always in control. He explains what parts of the play mean, arranges where and when everyone must be located on stage, nips a discipline problem in the bud, plays piano, explains vocabulary words, keeps everyone entertained, maintains the schedule, and does a fair job hiding the fact that his cholesterol levels are going through the roof because of job-related stress.

I was struck by how similar a third-grade field trip is to a prison outing. I mean, the kids don't have chains, but then again, they probably aren't too much of a flight risk. They do occasionally break from the line and dart into traffic for no apparent reason, but that is what the volunteer parents are there to prevent.

Also, the students are probably unlikely to make shivs from their toothbrushes in their spare time. They simply have no spare time with the load of activities that is planned for them. Teachers and parental volunteers work the edges of the crowd just like you might expect guards and deputies to do around a chain gang. They do not carry any weapons short of a sharp pencil, but discipline is strict and swift.

I found I didn't even have the skills to notice when a breach of conduct was taking place. The crowd would be milling about, and suddenly one of the teachers would (virtually) grab a boy by the ear for a behavioral faux pas and threaten him with "loss of snack" or some other horrible consequence that I didn't quite understand.

The threat of losing snack privileges seemed to be intimidating enough to coerce any offenders. Remarkably, it turned out that snack was a meager serving of grapes with tiny crackers and a pretzel product presented in a very small paper cup. Included with snack was a social opportunity to interact somewhat freely with the other detainees, which appeared to be more valuable than the Dixie cup contents judging by the leftover servings.

I wanted to tell the students that loss of snack was not particularly painful and it should not deter them from exercising their freedom of expression, but I could see the teachers had a rapidly escalating scale of disciplinary tactics at their disposal.

As an outsider, I did not wish to disturb the balance of power that was obviously carefully crafted and, for the time being, working.

The play went as planned and was very well received and well attended (ninety students times two parents plus grandparents, siblings, and an odd aunt). The theater incurred no damage, even though the boys were bouncing off most of the surfaces after the play. Unlike the convict crews I have worked with, everyone went home happy.

What's that? No, I worked *with* inmate crews not *on* the crew....No, don't worry, I did not speak to any of your children....Yes, I did consume about twenty of their leftover snack cups....No, I won't do it again....Yes, sir, I'll get back in line now.

Column 216, May 24, 2015

On Living with an Older Dog, Part 1: The Tick

When I told my veterinarian, the good Dr. Grace, the title of this column, she immediately assumed it was about the daily trials and silliness my wife endures living with me. If you made the same assumption, don't worry—we'll only be talking about my dog, who is pushing fourteen years old.

If you buy into the concept of "dog years," this puts my dog into the human equivalent of ninety-eight years old. This can't possibly be accurate. He is quite healthy, and you would think he's still in his late thirties whenever he sees a squirrel. I would peg his human equivalent age at around forty-nine, maybe fifty-five, tops. You know the kind: an aging, nonsmoking bachelor who has no job and essentially lives off of a trust fund—but with two humans to look after his every need.

On the surface, he may impress you as a deadbeat. He doesn't pursue any hobbies, do any volunteer work, or read many books. He spends most of his day sleeping. (If I have defined your own son here, it's time to schedule counseling for him and maybe some consoling for you.) His main interests are eating, taking humans for a walk, and lying out in the busiest part of the house for reasons known only to him and his confessor.

His one redeeming trait besides still being able to make "puppy eyes" is that he is deeply spiritual. I have mentioned this before, and my suspicion stands: what looks like shiftlessness is possibly the result of renouncing all material things and aspirations, but of course, we will never know because of his complete and unbreachable vow of silence.

The trip to the vet came about because of an alleged tick on the dog's hind quarter just above his tail. My wife came to me with the somber bad-news face to let me know that the dog had an insect parasite. Although she is quite capable of dealing with such a problem, she maintains that during our marriage ceremony, I vowed to deal with any insect problems that might come up before death do us part. I don't remember. It only made her face more pouty when I pointed out that ticks are not insects and are more closely related to spiders.

In the interest of a harmonious household, I grabbed my tick-remover tool that I had fashioned from aluminum roof flashing and headed for the dog. In spite of his advanced age, the dog immediately knew something was up and made himself unavailable for examination. While my wife entertained his front end, I chased his hind end in circles until we wound around to some kind of understanding that he would be constantly rewarded and fawned over if he sat so that I could remove the offending freeloader.

I located the bump and started my procedure. The dog quieted himself long enough for me to get a good look, whereupon I exclaimed, "I don't think it's a tick; it looks like it's some kind of a bombly growth!"

A truce was hastily arranged with the dog, and my wife announced that it was time to take the dog in for his regular five-year checkup.

The very next day, Dr. Grace confirmed that it was not a tick but indeed a benign bombly growth similar to a wart. The even better news was that my wife and I didn't plow ahead and rip the tissue from the dog's rear parts thinking we were doing him a favor. Sometimes ticks require a good deal of force to pull them from their host. I could imagine the scenario where I shout over the dog's protests that this particular tick is attached so tenaciously that I will have to give it a decisively good yank, so hold on…

After the tick exam, we all got down to the problems that come to dogs with advanced age. So next week we will find out if Doggie Depends really exist and explore the question of when the dog should no longer be allowed to drive and how to tell him.

What's that? No, sorry, vets are expensive, and we didn't delve into the philosophical "If you call your dog by his name and he can no longer hear you, are you still calling his name or did he have it legally changed?" Maybe on our next regular visit.

Column 217, May 31, 2015

On Living with an Older Dog, Part 2: At the Vet's

When I told the dog we were going to visit the vet's office, he immediately got into his old army uniform. It looked quite tight, but he was nevertheless proud to still be able to put it on. "Silly dog," said I, "you can loose the uniform (or lose the uniform), as we will never be able to get you an appointment to see a doctor at a VA hospital anytime soon. No, we are going to see the veterinarian—you know, at the place where you lost your manhood."

My wife and I pretended to search a long while to find the dog after that statement, but we knew that he was in his favorite hiding place: under the sink next to the dangerous cleaning chemicals. Soon the prospect of going someplace, anyplace, really, overwhelmed the feeling of certain doom associated with the vet's office, and the dog agreed to go—provided that we go with him and supply treats along the way.

Upon arrival, we first addressed the faux-tick issue that was detailed in last week's column. Next, the vet, my wife, and I went about exploring age-related issues like forgetfulness and lack of focus before we turned our attention again to the dog.

The examination began, and the vet, whom we call the good Dr. Grace, had absolutely no trouble managing the dog. The dog was fine with her probing his nether regions, drawing his blood, and injecting him under the skin with dog drugs. It was perfectly acceptable for her to probe his teeth and bend his paws backward. Understand that this is the same dog that is cool to prolonged contact with all humans and sometimes turns his head away when I go to pet him like a girl spurning a kiss. For an encore, the dog was led away and yielded a urine sample, but I purposely did not ask how this was done. I figure I can lead a full and productive life without ever knowing.

I'm not sure that the urine test confirmed it, but it turns out the dog can't hear very well. It used to be that he faked it. If he didn't want to hear me, he just went temporarily deaf. Very convenient. Over the years, however, he has come to the point where I can walk up from behind and scare the holy bejesus out of him. Oh, relax. I would never do that very often. And if it should happen, say accidentally, the dog doesn't mind after just a few seconds—but my wife gets quite upset. If she were a medieval mob, I would be attacked with pitchforks, scythes, and torches.

The dog can still hear gunshots and fireworks, which have always sent him into a tizzy and made him hide near the dangerous chemicals. But other than hearing the loudest of noises, he is no longer at my beck and call—only at my beck. It's amazing that I have lived on this planet for so many decades and never knew that the word *beck* was all about giving hand signals as when someone beckons you during a road-rage incident.

The dog is now vaguely aware of all kinds of hand signals, some friendly and some not so much, particularly when he cuts other drivers off in traffic. Two big benefits to a loss of hearing are that he can't hear people cursing at him and he has no trouble getting a proper night's sleep.

The vet did have an insightful explanation for this hearing condition, which went something like "Yes...well, he's old." She moved next to address his tendency to drip—and not from the mouth.

We're not saying the dog is incontinent, not yet. He is, however, beginning to forget on occasion that it is forbidden to lay waste inside the house in any way, shape, form, or amount. That includes leaking a little bit here or there depending on his level of excitement.

The good news is that the problem is mild and can be addressed with anti-dripping drugs. The bad news is that I was specifically told as we were leaving the vet's that the drugs were *only* for the dog.

Well! That was a little too transparent and a bit uncomfortable. If you're looking for me to make a follow-up trip to the vet's anytime soon, I might not be so easy to find; you might check under the sink next to the dangerous chemicals.

Column 220, June 21, 2015

Robot Authors

Hold onto your hat and Google eyeglasses—I just found out that news stories written solely by computers are now being published. I know! I thought computers had been writing boring news stories for decades, but it turns out those were written by heavy-drinking, overworked, disillusioned journalists. The computer as author is a relatively recent development, and these "electroessays" are popping up more and more on the web, in newspapers, and—judging by content—cheap greeting cards.

Presently, computers write mountains of readable stories, usually about sports or financial reports. These articles are read by unsuspecting readers who believe the stories were penned by breathing people, just like folks who eat yogurt and think that it is somehow made from milk. The idea may be hard to swallow emotionally, but philosophically, does it matter as long as the reader gets the information and the eater gets the calcium?

To spit out perfectly readable (but literarily limp) sports articles, the computer programs use data, like pitch-by-pitch baseball game records. These are supplied, for example, by innocent parents at Little League games through iPhone scoring applications such as GameChanger. The data is run through a set of algorithms to come up with sports-talk phrases like "Kaline tripled in the third and homered in the eighth with one on to take the game."

Stock-market reporting was the next natural fit for robots because they don't fall asleep halfway through the first page of a financial report. The hard part must have been keeping the techniques of sports language from elbowing their way into the financial journals. Lines like "IBM clobbered Dow Jones with a four-point lead before the closing bell at the bottom of the ninth" had to be edited.

The reports have run mostly on sports and financial websites, but with over a million stories produced last year, many are making headway into mainstream media and they don't seem to be stopping at finance and sports.

The *Los Angeles Times* uses a computer program to generate stories about earthquakes that are published before the shaking stops. The algorithm or program (which automatically gathers the facts and puts them into a format mimicking factual reporting by high-school journalism interns) was written by a real journalist named Ken Schwencke. Mr. Schwencke must have developed the program after growing tired of gathering facts and doing news checks before starting in on the personal story. Curiously, if you rearrange the letters of his last name, you get "news check," which has got to make you wonder how much time I spent looking at his name.

Sometimes publications will let you know which story was computer-generated, but other times you have to look for clues. If the byline states the author was a journalist called Al Gorithm or if the text degenerates into a series of zeros and ones, you can pretty much bet the article was written by a robot that eats 120 volts for breakfast. On the other hand, if the article is disjointed with grammatical errors and not well focused, it has to be the product of a human who may have had only yogurt.

Be alert because this trend won't stop at data-heavy news stories. Efforts are well underway to have machines write short stories, novels, and résumés. Poetry generators have been available on the web for a long time. You input some key words and a "poem" is generated for you that has all the markings of an angry young poet who uses chemicals to partially disconnect from reality. As evidence, I submit this short love poem that was computer-generated just for me:

Never fight a door,
Never shove a window,
Faceless, hot jobs quietly hustle a dark, misty corner.

It really shouldn't worry us that we don't know which stories were written by a robot; after all, the robot authors don't know that their stories are scanned and read by other computers. Hey, wait a minute—if the stories are produced and consumed by robots, does that mean that humans have been canceled out of the equation?

No, ha ha, that's silly. Someone has to service the computers and oil the robots. Soon we'll have jobs driving them to appointments, mowing their lawns, cleaning their pools, tidying up after their parties, bringing them the newspaper in the morning, and of course, listening to their stories. Yes, the future sure looks bright, especially through my rose-colored Google glasses.

Column 227, August 9, 2015

Headless hitchBOT Discovered Dismembered

It must have been a horrible sight to stumble upon: arms ripped from the torso and a headless hitchhiking robot lying in a pool of electromechanical blood. Other robots, especially the little vacuum cleaners, took to hiding under beds until the perpetrators could be caught, but even veteran cops were overcome and sobbing from the sheer brutality of it all.

If you regularly read this column, and I know that at least four of you do, you might recall that back in April I reported on a hitchhiking robot called hitchBOT that had crisscrossed Canada through the goodwill of people willing to physically pick him up, seat him in their car, and give him a ride down the road. In exchange, hitchBOT would chat amicably and sometimes share a secret stash of vodka hidden in his left leg. No, I'm only kidding. Everyone knows that robots and drinking don't mix. But, yes, he would chat, even though chatting with a fence post might prove more engaging, especially one with a stash of vodka.

He was a robot with a cheery disposition, and sure, he made it across a cordial Canada and even survived a stint in Europe, but he had no defense except for his artificial smile and so lasted just two weeks in the sweet land of liberty. Apparently, an electronic smile doesn't buy you much time in downtown Philadelphia.

Recall that I suggested hitchBOT hitchhike to Maine where I live for a little vacation this summer where he could be safe, but his Canadian makers didn't listen and I received no response to my inquiry and invitation. Then again, I typically never get a response to any inquiry; I have yet to hear from Angelina Jolie or Halle Berry concerning the Great Earwig Expedition to Saint Helena I am organizing.

No, they took hitchBOT to Boston to begin a journey on the American highway system to San Francisco with not so much as an introductory course in street wisdom.

Maine would have been a great place for hitchBOT to learn about America before venturing into the deeper parts. No one here has ever beheaded and dismembered a friendly robot, although we do boil lobsters alive on a regular basis.

Dr. Frauke Zeller, assistant professor at Ryerson University in Toronto, explained in a BBC video that "Sadly, sadly early Saturday morning [August 1, 2015], in Philadelphia, it's [he's] been vandalized; we've just seen the latest images and it's beyond repair we're afraid, so you just have to sit down now and see... what can we learn from this."

Well, at the risk of disclosing the obvious, one thing you might learn is that you don't hitchhike in Philadelphia, even on a nice day. And you don't send a defenseless robot wearing yellow galoshes with blue legs and a body vaguely stylized as R2-D2 meets a five-gallon plastic bucket to do it—at least not without a standard light saber for protection.

But there are other possibilities besides wanton vandalism...

It could have been the first robot termination by an as-yet-unidentified group that champions a robot-free world and is preparing for the biggest battle of mankind, determined to stop the takeover of humanity by robots, cute or otherwise. They have yet to claim responsibility for this action.

Another theory is that the innocent-looking bot was involved in a drug deal that went sour. It's a possibility you've got to allow; it's Philadelphia. He might have failed to deliver the goods from Canada, or maybe he delivered as promised and got paid with a Mafia check—to the head.

I, however, feel that this has all the indications of a government contract killing. Here he is, a robot without a passport, crafted in a foreign country, packed full of electronics, and freely roaming the streets of America. Not to fan any conspiracy theories, but he could be an agent, playfully poking around anywhere people will take him in the United States for free. Perhaps he double-crossed his contact or finished his mission. Or maybe the federal agency in charge of tracking hitchhiking robots of alien origin decided it was time to take him out—and a dark night, on the streets of Philadelphia was the place to do it. It wouldn't be hard: whack him a good one, smash the battery, and ship the head back to Quantico.

Sometimes bad things happen to good robots. Sometimes.

I think I hear something humming under the bed.

Column 213, September 6, 2015

Signs of Growing Older

Don't think I haven't noticed the increase in social incidents over the past few years related to my increasing age. Although I haven't had anyone rush up to me yet when I'm toting something heavy and say, "Hey, pops, let me get that for you. I don't want you to break a hip or anything," there have been situations when I am made to feel older by the uncompromising youngness of the people I encounter.

Recently, a junior waitress serving "us guyses" took our beverage order and informed me that the restaurant did not have any Pepsi-Cola as I requested; she remarked that they only serve Pepsi. She had never heard of Pepsi-Cola. Ouch.

I am referring to my dinner party as "us guyses" because we were addressed as "yousguyses," as in "yousguyses pizza is almost ready." This is not a brand-new way to address people, but as I get older it gets more annoying every time I hear it, especially from an eighteen-year-old.

Things change with time, but we tend to stick with what is familiar because it's helped us survive so far—and really, that can't be all bad. This is why older people do not jump on the new-and-different bandwagon when it rolls into town. Also, we don't want to break a hip if we don't jump just right.

Truth be told, I have trouble understanding online articles obviously written by trendy young writers. Here is the actual opening sentence from a Mashable article explaining, well, something: "Dubbed the 'Netflix of Pirating,' popular BitTorrent client Popcorn Time made its debut on the iPhone screen last week with an off-the-books iOS app." Hmm.…It took me a long while to decipher the meaning. It didn't help that I felt compelled to make up a batch of popcorn in the kitchen while thinking about it.

When I read the sentence to my daughter, she immediately said, "Oh my, sounds a little dicey," implying that she knew exactly what it was all about. Poor old Dad. "Geez, Dad," she said, "it makes me feel young when I understand what they're saying and you don't." Yeah, that's my new purpose in life: to make twenty-seven-year-olds feel young.

Although it sounds like an adjective, Mashable is the title of a website that claims to be "a leading source for news, information & resources for the Connected Generation," which begs the question: connected to what? Not to traditional English and certainly not to older readers. Have I been excluded due to my age? Can a baby boomer ever be a part of the Connected Generation? Do any of yousguyses want popcorn?

Music is another cultural area where age is beginning to creep me out. I found out that Badfish is a tribute band dedicated to playing only the music of Sublime; okay, I have never heard of the band Sublime, never mind Badfish. Apparently, my moderately good grasp of popular music expired twenty-five years ago. Sublime, the reggae, rock, ska punk band was formed the year my daughter was born, which I have noted is when real aging starts and we just naturally lose track of new music.

It turns out Sublime is so popular, it is featured on one of those 20th Century Masters, Millennium Collection CDs. I am not yet so old that I am unable to navigate the internet, so I checked out Sublime's music. Except for the lyrics, I found it quite listenable. The lyrics were only about 80 percent disturbing, touting crime and violence—another modern trend that skews me toward the geezer category. Well, what do you expect from the boys in the band who grew up thinking that "grand theft, auto" is a game?

The inability to follow trends in music may be a casualty of aging, but my wife and I can still dance. Not long ago, we were on vacation at a beachfront nightclub and dancing to a live reggae band as if no one was watching. We danced all we could, and after a rum punch or two, my wife suggested we spend the night at her place. (Yes!) So as older couples tend, we left before the club closed. On the way out, we were chased down by a young man who just had to tell us that he enjoyed watching us dance. In his words: "Oh, you two dance so good. When I'm an old man, I hope I can dance as good as you!"

Well, by golly, thank you. At least he didn't call me "pops."

Pumpkins and How Not to Grow Them

Gardening looks so easy: you scatter a bunch of seeds and reap a bumper crop. Even though dandelions do it all the time, this is not the case. Turns out you have to know what you're doing and actually work at it. More accurately, you have to suffer.

It all began last spring after I mowed a field that had been growing wild grasses and other pioneer species for some time. The field was mowed because I had acquired a riding mower to save time. It saved me so much time on my regular mowing that I elected to mow this large, neglected field. Somewhere there is a logic flaw in that reasoning that escapes me, as I tend to think about it only when I am mowing with an idle mind.

In earlier times, land was always put to productive use to create income. Today, there are easier ways to get money than by working the land. Being inclined to do things the hard way, I could not let this land lie fallow, so I whispered to my wife that this fall, she would have pumpkins for free—I would employ my land to grow pumpkins. Really, how hard could that be?

My wife loves to buy seeds. The little packages hold so much promise. If you just allude to a vague notion that you might want to plant some kind of crop, she will buy the seeds on her very next trip to town. It is her contribution to world agriculture, and in that spirit, she tends to purchase a few too many packages. When I hinted at growing two or three plants, she felt that fifty might yield the kind of harvest one might imagine flowing from a cornucopia—and what's not to like about a cornucopia?

I planted the standard Jack-o'-Lanterns. I planted the

terrifying Big Boy juggernauts that promised to take over the neighborhood, and my life, before winning awards in any number of county fairs. Finally, I planted the tiny Jack be Little pumpkins that when ripe, you can eat like an apple if you are inclined to eat pumpkins in that manner. Plots were planted far apart to allow for growth and a week apart to allow time to harvest one plot before moving on to the next.

The suffering started with transforming the sod to a garden plot followed by daily watering and weeding. The seeds soon germinated and the flowers followed, but as fast as they developed, they mysteriously disappeared at night, leaving me with at least a hundred flowerless upright stems. It's not that the male flowers dropped off because they would still be under the plant. Could it be that some small animal invited itself to my all-you-can-eat smorgasbord of pumpkin blossoms? This was not the plan.

Soon the disappearing blossoms problem gave way to some kind of leaf blight. There was an obvious infection turning the succulent green leaves to an unsightly yellow and white, and it was spreading fast.

A quick internet check confirmed powdery mildew was establishing not just colonies but entire metropolitan areas on my leaves. The infection could be controlled organically, but there was no point to it because the battle had already been lost. Once powdery mildew decides that it wants to make a living off of your pumpkin plants, it goes at it full-time: it postpones any meetings, cancels vacations, and of course, it doesn't have to file tax returns, pay bills, or even sleep.

While waiting for the organic remedy to arrive, a deadly frost shamelessly descended upon my patch the night of September 26, a full four days before October! It destroyed all the green leaves that were left along with the diseased ones and the flowerless stems, just for fun.

Picking through the fifty plants yielded a couple quart containers (the kind you might use picking strawberries) of pumpkin-like objects. I did find a few apple-sized mini-pumpkins, but I hesitated to eat them as they were the most expensive pumpkins I had ever held in my hand.

Okay. People have pointed out that it was not a good idea to start my plants after the Fourth of July and I agree, but I was busy mowing. If I get a bigger tractor, I can spend less time mowing and have more time to grow pumpkins. Now it's all starting to make sense.

Column 237, October 18, 2015

Your Microbial Cloud

By studying the immediate vicinity of people just sitting, researchers from the University of Oregon have discovered that humans emit a cloud of bacteria twenty-four hours a day. Most of us suspected this was true during our grade-school days, when we avoided getting too close to classmates so we wouldn't get infected by their cooties. We just didn't have the scientific background at that age to provide conclusive evidence and peer-reviewed papers to back up our juvenile presumptions—I mean, our hypotheses.

The disturbing part of all this serious research is that the professional scientists involved described the findings simply as "gross," which also harkens back to grade-school days. It's turning out to be true that all I need to know I did indeed learn in kindergarten. There is no official name for this cloud of bacteria yet. We could borrow a term from the new-age crowd and call it our personal aura or maybe our "bioaura," although it lacks that new-age mystical and luminous feeling.

It's been estimated that there are ten times more bacterial cells in our bodies than purely human cells—so in other more disturbing words, nine out of every ten cells contained in your body are microbes. Good thing they're much smaller that genuine human cells or we would all be about the same size as the Hulk on steroids. If we separated out the human cells from the bacteria, we would only get about a half-gallon of microbes, but bringing a jug of it to class for show-and-tell would really be sensational.

The uncomfortable fact that only 10 percent of what we think is our own body (by cell count) is really us and not some other living, eating, and breeding species brings up all sorts of philosophical questions about where our body starts and ends. It's curious that we can live without a lung, arm, or tonsils but not without our bacterial friends that have taken up house-keeping within us. The publication *Scientific American* calls us "walking petri dishes."

There are at least five hundred microbial species living in any adult's intestine most of the time, although the conditions are quite squalid. I mean, there is sewage flowing throughout the neighborhood, there is no police protection, and you can't get a good pastrami sandwich anywhere that hasn't already been chewed on by stomach acid. The "good life" for bacteria is on the skin and hair, where they can get a little fresh air and sunshine—in between some nasty encounters with Purell.

The half-gallon of microbes that is part of each one of us contains about 22 million genes of bacterial DNA. This bacterial DNA not only keeps the microbes partying but interacts with and even controls our own bodily processes important to our digestion, immune system, weight, stress response, and body odor.

Scientists refer to all of the microbes inside of us making a living, raising families, and generally doing a lot of the work that genuine human cells won't do as our "undocumented immigrants"—no, sorry, I meant "microbiome."

Everything you do while sitting quietly, such as blinking, shakes off exterior bacteria. Releasing waste gasses from your tailpipe and burping expels your personal colonies of microbes from your deep interior into a thin cloud around you.

Let's not think too much about it, but we do "share" these microbes when our clouds intersect. When we pack into an elevator, an overcrowded nightclub, or when we're sweating and puffing at the gym, we are basking in other people's bio-clouds. It is little known that YMCA originally stood for "Your Microbial Cloud Association."

And if we're all personally putting out a cloud, I really don't care to think about what my dog is emitting. After all, he's the one who experiments with eating goose poop and sniffing at his own vomit as if he might find some delicious, partially digested morsel there that he could enjoy a second time. So it's not only fur that he sheds but dog bacteria that we all enjoy the closer we get to him.

Close enough to smell his dog breath? Ah, take in his doggy-mouth organic streptococci. Is the dog passing gas near the dinner table? Sorry, I don't even want to go there because we are talking about canine cooties. No wonder the researchers noted that their findings were gross.

Column 241, November 15, 2015

Cat Available to Good Home

Some time ago, I hired the local Cummons boys to help me rehabilitate an old cellar that had fallen on hard times. It had been in and out of rehab for the last hundred years but kept going back to its old ways of drinking and gambling, resulting in rotting sills and shifting foundation stones. We were going to fix it.

The first thing I had them do was remove a short brick wall that someone had built atop the stone foundation, apparently to help accelerate the rot in the sill timbers and maybe to keep the cold and mice out. During this wall removal, a lot of debris was found in the space between the bricks and the granite sill blocks, not all of it pleasant. All right, none of it was pleasant. That's what you get when you take on a damp cellar in a 150-year-old building.

In the course of reaching in to remove the moist scraps of wood and trash entombed inside the wall, the boys commented on each piece they pulled out. "Look at all this broken stuff—and all this rotten wood. This chunk looks like a dead cat!" one of the boys remarked. This was followed by a dual inharmonious shriek as they both realized they were indeed handling a long-dead mummified cat.

After a session of thorough hand-washing, crude construction humor, and Purell dispensing, the carcass was unceremoniously dumped into the trash. This didn't seem proper; after all, it was the remains of a living being—even if it was a cat. Retrieved, it was propped up against an outside wall just to scare the local children and to marvel at how good it looked for being so dead.

As it had "survived" for so long, it could no longer be considered rubbish. Surely there was someone, somewhere, interested on some level in acquiring a mummified cat. Hopefully, it would be for academic purposes and not for medieval medicine, satanic rituals, or party favors.

But where does one turn to find people with such an interest? The answer came to me in a flash of inspiration. When you're sure that someone, somewhere, would want to acquire something for some odd reason, there is but one place to turn: eBay.

I wrote an essay explaining the circumstances as to how the cat was acquired in order to put the kibosh on any questions of ownership and to lure scientists and academics into bidding on the cat for the benefit of all humankind. This was combined with a series of photos of the shriveled corpse on a gay, bright, sky-blue background. Minimum bid was set at less than ten dollars, and the entire package was posted in short order on eBay.

The first day brought thirty views, but this blossomed to nearly three hundred on the second day and then soared to almost a thousand on the third day of the auction. I was stoked. The fourth day brought a letter from eBay notifying me that they had cancelled the auction on the grounds that it is illegal to market cat or dog fur in America. Hmm.

Considering the fact that the former cat had not a single hair left and that only its leathery skin remained to cover the skeleton, I could have made the case that I was not dealing in fur at all. In my judgment, hair defines fur, but eBay and the courts may hold a different opinion. In life, you have to pick your battles, and at the time I didn't care to nitpick the hair of the cat.

Bottom line: I still have the cat. It's in a safe place, but I'm afraid that if my wife ever runs across it during a cleanup jag, I will be in great danger. This is the part where you come in, for I have decided that it is best for me to give away the cat to anyone who can provide a good home. As cats go, this one is not difficult to maintain, although it is a bit of a burden on the eyes. Look within and see if you have a place in your heart for a mummified cat. Let me know how your taking possession will benefit humanity. I will let you know how the great cat giveaway goes.

The odds are good that you could be the next caretaker of this silent feline—but like they say, the goods are odd.

Column 248, January 3, 2016

Personal Photos

It's the start of yet another year, and I still haven't been able to digitize those slides, negatives, and prints I have in storage before I get too old or get hit by a bus. Being hit by a bus is how my attorney Ed politely words it when he wants me to confront any unforeseen circumstances, especially when we speak about the necessity of drawing up a will. Ed might say, "Here's my bill. Write me a check before you leave—what would I do if you got hit by a bus?" But in such a case I wonder, what is to become of my exceptional personal photos that I have produced throughout the years?

Oh, ouch, I can hear the answer from the rest of humanity coming in loud and clear: "Who cares?"

It's difficult to admit, but no one really values your personal photos outside the realm of a very small number of people, which would include only yourself and your mother. Also realize that mothers are often there just to give you unconditional support and may not be really keen on your visual aesthetic. This is why they are called "personal" photos and not national treasures, fine art, or even commercially viable images.

This all becomes painfully apparent when we are assigned the task of going through someone else's photos to decide what to do with them. When Aunt Beatrice gets hit by a bus and you are the one flipping 99 percent of her prints and 100 percent of her negatives into the trash, you come to an understanding of the value of personal photos.

As hard as it is to admit, unless my precious photos are valued by someone other than me, they will no doubt be appreciated most by the microorganisms in the landfill that will feast on them as they decompose. On the other hand, if the entire collection is sent to a municipal waste incinerator that generates power, the photos may supply enough energy to illuminate someone's quick nighttime visit to a bathroom—unless they're using the new low-wattage lamps, in which case they can take their time while the information I have so carefully preserved is lost to history. There, that took away some of the pain.

I am sorry if you're looking to me for answers because I've got nothing. Wait…no, sorry, nothing. Unless…unless we *give* our photos away. Until recently, you would have had to stack the photos by the curb with a "free" sign attached and hope it wouldn't rain before the albums and boxes disappeared. The curb method however, leaves you wondering if the people who took them wanted the images for the photographic jewels that they are or because they're good fire-starter material. But now, we have the internet.

I am thinking of starting a photo agency called "Free Photos—No, Really." The agency would just be a website offering people's best personal photos, free for the taking. Why not? You've put a lot of effort into your photos and you don't want to see them die. Just put them out there so that others may stand on the shoulders of your pioneering photographic efforts.

It's far better than putting them on the side of the road with a "free" sign because if people can benefit from even one of your photos, you get credit for contributing to the building of civilization through your contribution to the arts or history or anthropology. And best of all, the entire collection won't be ruined if it rains. Someone at some time will get some use from your work—and you'll get some measure of satisfaction or maybe even a small reward in heaven. Maybe.

Oh, sure, you can still dream of selling some of those great photographs, but who will want to buy them when they can get very similar images for free from FreePhotosNoReally.com? Is this a great idea or what? Okay, aside from the digitizing, the associated prep work, the fact that you don't get paid, etcetera.

Not to complicate matters, but after we digitize those old photos, touch them up, index them, and post them, anybody have any ideas what to do with the originals? My buddy Dave Hill suggests the nicest thing you can do for your family is invite them to a big party where you burn all your personal photos so they won't have to. Anybody else? I'm listening, but all I hear is a bus coming.

Column 252, January 31, 2016

The Poetry of Tobogganing

It's that time of year where, in my part of the country, people gather for the US National Toboggan Championships. Here, about four hundred teams compete to see which group can slide the fastest down a rickety, iced over, wooden toboggan chute—I'm not saying is old, but I think it has roots going back to the Franklin D. Roosevelt administration.

Each team starts at the top of the run by placing their toboggan on a level platform that tips them down into the chute when the operator snickers ominously and then pulls on a gallows-style lever. The toboggan caroms down the iced chute, which creeks, snaps, and shudders with the passing weight—although no one ever hears this worrisome cacophony because it's overpowered by the screams coming from the passengers on their way to oblivion. Actually, they are on their way to the frozen surface of a small lake called Hosmer Pond, but from the top of the four-hundred-foot chute, it's generally referred to as just plain oblivion.

It would be nice to say that the dance of the toboggan in the chute is pure poetry, but really, if there is any sort of poetic connection, the best association you could possibly make with four old, costumed guys throwing caution and maybe a hat or toupee to the wind is to a cheesy limerick.

I have given this a lot of thought. Yes, I know—if it was over a minute, it might have been too long, but I spent over ten years detailing the Toboggan Nationals in the pages of a newsletter I published called the *Toboggan Times*.

What's that? No, I didn't charge for it. That would be silly.

Who would pay for a toboggan newsletter? I went the smart route: I had it printed and gave it away. As an experimental business model, it didn't work out all that well, especially since no advertising was included, but we are not here to talk about my personal business acumen. We are here to discuss the poetry of tobogganing.

During my tenure at the *Times,* I conducted a toboggan limerick contest with as much fanfare as I could generate. Readers were given only a limited amount of time to come up with toboggan limericks; that would be the one year that transpired between newsletters. After eleven and a half months, I started getting nervous that we might get only a few limericks for the contest. I was completely wrong on that account, as no one sent in even a couplet. Well, my daughter did submit one, but that was disqualified as it was a sent in by a relative and out of pity.

For the following issue, I ended up writing a few limericks myself just to prove that it could indeed be done and that I had not challenged my readers with an insolvable riddle. I was afraid that perhaps none of my readers were up to the task, but that was like worrying about getting my hair wet while I was drowning: turns out I didn't have any readers.

Since the championships are upon us again, it is only fitting that we should attempt to pay tribute to this national northern pastime and take one last stab at a limerick contest.

If you are one of the people who would love to submit a toboggan limerick but have trouble rhyming three words in order to follow the limerick format, may I suggest: *toboggan, hooligan,* and *shenanigan.* Of course, *toboggan* doesn't have to be one of the rhyming words; you can just as easily use words that relate to tobogganing such as *oxygen, harlequin,* and *congressman* or *proton, photon,* and *wonton*—the choices are endless.

Hurry, the deadline for entries is January 15, and since the Nationals come around but once a year, that would be 2017.

Sorry, this time we will not be giving away a new car, but I will include the best limericks in this column, which should win you accolades, faint praise, and maybe a shot at becoming a poet laureate—but probably not. Let's all reflect on the tragedy of the last toboggan limerick contest:

> The *Toboggan Times* contest did fail,
> To receive any verse in the mail,
> But in retrospect,
> What can you expect?
> Our readers were principally male.

As they say at the top of the chute: good luck and Godspeed.

Column 256, February 28, 2016

About Being Done

As most of you have probably done in the past, I too hired a sculptor to take a good-sized block of ice and fashion it into a crystal-like pickup truck. This is because in a former life, I used to produce TV commercials for local businesses. I like to think they did not come across as cheap local commercials, although it's a possibility you have to allow. Locally made commercials often look cheap because—well, because they don't cost a lot. National commercials are usually two or three orders of magnitude more expensive than locally produced ads, like the kind you might see for a neighborhood gentlemen's club.

On this particular job, we were trying to promote a local truck dealer's annual "meltdown sale," and my idea was to show a time-lapse sequence of the ice truck melting as the announcer delivered his spiel, which ironically was a lot of hot air.

The artist showed up early and attacked the ice block with his chain saw and hand tools. He worked furiously, which was all right with me because I didn't want the sculpture melting before the lights and cameras were set up. After about an hour, the sculptor suddenly shut down his saw, stepped back, and shouted, "Done!" He started packing his gear.

This ability to suddenly finish a project and declare it complete is something that amazes me to this day. I am the type who will continue to put final touches on a project as it is going out the door—and then after it is delivered.

In a study conducted by psychologist Leslie Sherlin, it turns out that you can give your brain and emotional state a boost if you holler out "Done!" when you complete a task. It makes you feel good and builds your confidence. Turns out it's got something to do with the electrical activity in our brain as it switches from high gear into neutral, at which point the brain neurotransmitter, serotonin, is released, as it is with psychedelic drugs. This gives you the sense of satisfaction and relaxation that you would feel sharing a glass of brandy with a hot date. Yelling "Done!" amplifies this effect.

What "they" know but won't tell you is that inside your brain, you have a lot of different appliances plugged into one overloaded socket, which is starting to give off fumes from the heat. When you shout "done," a little man wakes up, jumps out of bed, and unplugs everything before it catches fire, giving your brain battery (the same one used in hoverboards) a needed break. This allows it to cool down, hence the brandy effect.

I would think you should shout "finished" when completing tasks and "done" only when what you're baking in the oven is thoroughly cooked. Semantics however, were not the topic of the study. I mean, if Polish-speaking people shouted "done" when they finished a task, would they get the same boost? Or would they have to yell "zakonczony" to feel the rush? Loosely translated, this means "finished" or "completed," or it could possibly be the name of a traditional Polish dance. I'm no expert.

Anyway, I tried it out with my neighbors, and they only reported frustration trying to shout "zakonczony" when they completed a task. (If you're having trouble for some reason, it's pronounced "za-coin-tso-ni"—or just "done" in English.) It's not the easiest Polish word to master. An easier word in Polish would be pronounced "loot," which means "ice," although it's spelled *lód*.

This not so subtly takes us back to my ice pickup truck project: it turned out my worries about it melting too fast were unfounded. In fact, it wasn't melting fast enough. We turned up the heat, and between shots we attacked it with hair dryers and, after some calculations, blowtorches. It took a full twenty-four hours to finish the shoot.

I like to think it did not come across as a cheap local commercial, although it's a possibility you have to allow. There was nothing there that another five or ten thousand dollars couldn't fix. If I had known how to shout "Done!" at the time, I would have been a big hero to the crew members, who hung around to watch ice melt.

This is probably a good point to stop and shout "Done!" a few times. If that doesn't help, I'm fairly sure there is a bottle of brandy out in the woodshed.

World Health Day

Of course, you are all aware that April 7, 2016, is World Health Day. To celebrate, you can exercise, eat healthy foods, give up smoking, and avoid getting shamelessly drunk. This is the one international holiday where we are encouraged not to drink to anyone's health. You can, however, *wish* people good health, although my grandfather would have considered that insincere if not delivered as a toast and followed with a shot of Polish vodka that had a lot of *z*'s and *w*'s in the name.

This day of health action and education is sponsored by the WHO, which I was very excited to learn about because I am quite the Roger Daltrey fan. And who doesn't love that great Fender jazz bass lead played by John Entwistle on *My Generation* back in 1965?

Imagine my chagrin when it was made clear that the WHO is not the rock band from the 1960s but the World Health Organization—that specialized United Nations agency based in Geneva, Switzerland, with exactly the same name. "I Can't Explain" my confusion over the WHO, but I can assure you that I "Won't Get Fooled Again."

World Health Day could not come at a better time for me. Two months ago, something went wrong in my knee from which I am still recovering. I would like to say that I injured it doing something exciting or dangerous or doing anything at all, but as far as I can tell it must have happened while I was sleeping, the mundane truth be told.

In terrible pain, I woke my wife at 3:00 a.m. and politely screamed at her to take me to the emergency room so that they could take the level of pain down to the point where I would stop howling. She responded by trying to block out my wailing with pillows over her ears.

She asked twice if it could wait until morning but agreed to take me since my demands were preventing her from the deep sleep she still half embraced. She never actually woke up, as 3:00 a.m. does not exist in her universe, but she did muster enough consciousness to drive.

If you're planning a trip to the emergency room, let me tell you that 3:00 a.m. is a great time to go. The reception room is empty, and I suspect the staff is occupied either filling in crossword puzzles or playing Parcheesi in the back room. Still, they make you wait simply because it's customary and they have to justify having a waiting room. The delay, however, is perfunctory and leads straight to the admission procedures.

Luckily, their triage process put me in the group qualifying for immediate medical assistance and not with the hopeless cases left in the waiting room to die. Within an hour or two, I hobbled out of there with crutches, narcotics, and an appointment to see a knee specialist.

Returning home, I couldn't turn around while getting out of the car to see what I was doing and so I smashed my thumb in the door trying to slam it shut. All this combined with breaking my little finger while scraping ice last week, not to mention the doctor essentially, how shall I say it… "freaking out" about my blood pressure, makes World Health Day something for me to look forward to.

Alas, World Health Day is not about me. WHO has declared the theme of the 2016 World Health Day to be "Halt the rise: beat diabetes," even though "Beat Diabetes" sounds like a great name for a Greek DJ who could rate up there with the Swedish House Mafia, Deadmau5 (no, that's not a typo), and Blasterjaxx. It's not hard to imagine getting tickets to see Beat Diabetes on his "Halt the Rise" tour.

Nevertheless, raising awareness of the growing worldwide

diabetes problem is a noble cause. WHO wants you to know that the disease is treatable and better than that, preventable by living a healthy lifestyle, which is often a matter of simple choices. Little choices add up: a two-mile daily walk to the liquor store beats taking the bus, eating cauliflower instead of pecan pie for coffee break can't hurt, and of course, losing forty pounds is a simple way to personal well-being.

So let's all get "Going Mobile" and declare that "We're Not Gonna Take It" as far as unhealthy living goes.

I have to get going now because two miles is a long way to walk with a bum knee and a broken finger.

Column 262, April 10, 2016

Income Tax, Errors, and Latin

I have been auditing my federal income tax forms and have found some serious problems. Okay, one serious problem is that I haven't filled out any of the forms yet, but I wasn't looking at numbers. I was, in fact, studying the naked forms and was struck by the alarming errors and irregularities I found. For example, IRS Form 4868 is titled "Application for Automatic Extension of Time To File U.S. Individual Income Tax."

Do you see it? Yes, the *To* is capitalized, which is inconsistent with currently acceptable title capitalization practices—but I am not going after small potatoes (otherwise known as lower-case spuds). There is a major logical inconsistency here: if the extension of time to file is automatic, why is there an application form? An application makes it de facto, not automatic.

Just by the way, Latin expressions like *de facto, ad hoc,* and *in vitro* make any statement seem more credible or better yet, bona fide. If you like to get in people's faces with your authority and show how right you are, especially concerning taxes and legal matters, you had better brush up on your Latin, ad nauseam. This will give you an air of self-declared importance and is guaranteed to make you the persona non grata at parties. And who doesn't like being persona non grata?

Historically, we find that government taxation all started about 3,000 BC back when the only certain thing was death. It was then the Egyptian IRS realized it had nothing to do and no money with which to do it, so it imposed a 20 percent flat tax on all the grain any citizen harvested. If you were too poor to have a farm and had no money in your debit account, then you simply provided labor to the pharaoh, which must have been like attending summer camp only with whips and chains. We have no record of governmental taxation errors back then, but that is only because they were recorded in a format that's now obsolete, and they no longer make a device to play back any of the records.

Since then, governments have collected all manner of taxes, including the one imposed by the Roman emperor Vespasian, who taxed the sale of urine collected from Rome's famous public urinals. Urine was sold to the fledgling Roman chemical industry, which used it as a source of ammonia to, ironically, clean soiled togas. Anytime the government made a tax collection error, there was quite a stink, what with all the urine and ammonia involved. This eventually does relate etymologically to taxpayers being "piss poor," but that's another story.

Vespasian, who, I should point out, had a good command of Latin, didn't do too badly with his taxation methods since he erected temples and statues, built the Roman Colosseum, etcetera. Of course, the immense wealth plundered after the Siege of Jerusalem also helped pay a lot of the contractors, while the hundred thousand Jewish slaves provided lots of labor—and urine.

I'm sure you remember that up until 1802, the US government ran on internal taxes. The only time anyone was taxed was on transactions involving carriages, distilled spirits, tobacco, snuff, refined sugar, property sold at auction, corporate bonds, and slaves —who, since the time of the pharaohs, were essentially taxed more heavily than anyone else. Then came along wars and a lot of other problems we expected the government to solve and here we are today, drowning in income tax and all its complexities.

It has been estimated that the IRS may make up to ten million errors when processing the hundred million returns they get. That's not too bad. If I had to process a hundred million returns, I would also be making ten million errors. No, only kidding. If I had to process a hundred million returns, I would be throwing myself in front of a bus.

The *Wall Street Journal* in an article titled "IRS Could Be Wrong, So Check Returns" advises taxpayers to fight the tax agency tooth and nail with persistence and patience—but only if the taxpayer is right.

Well, tempus fugit. I had better get back to those tax forms. If they aren't submitted in time, it will be *mea culpa,* and so far, I'm only talking about the extension.

Column 270, June 5, 2016

Reality and Philosophy

My wife was out of town, so perusing the paper, I found a free movie and discussion were being offered at the library by the local philosophical society. There are many reasons to be attracted to such an event, but you've probably already determined that they had me at "free movie."

Since it was a philosophy forum, I thought for sure there would be a lot of drinking, singing, and certainly fighting, but the audience, which packed the library—I mean the library meeting room, the small one—consisted of thoughtful, mostly older adults. They had evidently checked their liquor and guns at the door, keeping with the library's strict policy. One older gent close to my seat might have smuggled in a flask, but he was very discrete and did not imbibe until the lights were lowered for the video. Truth be told, he may have been using his asthma inhaler; in the dark, the actions are very similar. These are the very people I used to call eggheads before my inclusion in the same demographic.

The movie being presented was titled *The Simulation Hypothesis,* made by a gentleman named Kent Forbs—a filmmaker, scholar, and PhD candidate who was scheduled to be there to "address" questions. This is in keeping with the practice that philosophers do not offer clear answers to questions, as that task falls to the science department.

The film and discussion centered on the possibility that we are all living in a universe that is the result of a simulation by some kind of information-processing system. There is what can be construed as scientific evidence that we are living in a virtual reality. The concept is not too far from the context of the movie *The Matrix* starring Keanu Reeves, Carrie-Anne Moss (in that ever-so-perfect shiny black tank top), and of course, Laurence Fishburne, the guy with the blue and red pills who resembles a brick wall. This is a view that I've personally favored since fifth grade to help me explain some of the unknowns in life, like why is there a speed limit in the universe and why is math so hard.

The idea that reality is shaped by our consciousness is not new. Many writers have suggested that we are participating in the creation of the reality that we live in. Even back in the 1700s, the philosopher Immanuel Kant caused all kinds of consternation when he suggested that the conscious mind causes space and time to be ordered in the universe. This was long before that kind of thinking could be attributed to observing Carrie-Anne Moss in her shiny black tank top.

The evidence presented in the film was intriguing. As physicists look into the biggest and smallest interactions in the universe, they discover things that defy logical explanation, such as tiny subatomic particles that look like doors labeled "exit." Okay, I just made that up, but black holes do look an awful lot like conduits that drain our universe to…you know, to that other place.

Mr. Kent Forbs, the filmmaker, did not show up. It could be that he was deterred by the "No Weapons" sign prominently displayed as you enter the library. I mean, who would present a movie with radical ideas possibly affecting religion, morality, and apple pie to a strange crowd in America, unarmed? Nevertheless, the forum produced a lively discussion but broke up all too early because in Maine where I live, a lot of the folk have to be "gettin' on home" soon after sunset. It might have escaped me, but no one was talking about an after-party even though I did see a big guy in sunglasses handing out red pills.

If you think I am making all of this up, *The Simulation Hypothesis* is available for viewing anytime on YouTube, all fifty minutes and forty seconds of it. Watching it at home leaves you free to drink, fight, and utter "oh, man" as you absorb new concepts and pass the bong, just like back during those late nights in the college dorm room. On the other hand, you could spend that time watching Carrie-Anne Moss in *The Matrix*.

If you should happen to ask around to corroborate what I have reported here, let me tell you in advance that others at the same meeting might have experienced it differently. These people are obviously living in their own universe, creating their own reality that, apparently, is a lot more humdrum than mine. Maybe.

Column 272, June 19, 2016

Conventional Wisdom

The wacky idea came to me in late May: I could slip into the Democratic National Convention coming up in Philadelphia by posing, of all things, as a journalist. After all, I do have some press credentials…well, I read a lot of good reporting, and for a short time I used to pal around with Corey Flintoff of NPR fame.

Confident that two months' advance notice was enough, I casually went to the press section of the convention's website and was immediately informed that the deadline for requesting media credentials had already passed. Not only that, I was also too late to request media workspace or housing information. However, there was still time to ask for a parking space, which I would have done had it not been for the $125 fee and an application that asked a lot of uncomfortable questions. Sheesh. They didn't say when the deadline to apply had passed, but I got the feeling that it had expired the moment I logged onto their website.

I don't suppose they want a guy like me poking around the convention center looking to see what people have thrown in the trash and asking superdelegates who they eat for breakfast. After all, the convention has to leave room for Fox, NPR, CNN, and the BBC so that they can give their usual reports over and over and over again like they have for the last eighteen months.

Maybe I am guilty of thinking what every writer thinks—that I will bring a fresh perspective to the table. However, in the back of my mind, I'm thinking this has been dragging on so long that we're all out of fresh perspective.

Anyway, my wife, who loves to travel and will go almost anywhere on a moment's notice, said with calm, uncanny clarity,

"No, we aren't going to Philadelphia."

"No, not that Philadelphia," I countered, "I'm talking about the City of Brotherly Love, home to the Philly cheesesteak, the Liberty Bell, the Chemical Heritage Foundation, and the Rocky steps. Who doesn't want to see the Rocky steps?"

But she was unmoved. After all, this was the place where young hitchBOT, the loveable hitchhiking robot, had been taken for his last ride in our nation's first public case of androcide. It's the city that slew hitchBOT with brutal bot-butchery involving droid decapitation—most likely after a session of extreme cruelty where he was dismembered and, in all probability, had his batteries drained.

To me, Philadelphia looked like a nice-enough place, and the Democratic convention of 2016 would surely be a better experience than the last Democratic convention I tried to attend. That was August, 1968, in Chicago, where Mayor Richard J. Daley and his forces actively prevented my access to the convention venues while greeting throngs of nondelegates with nightsticks and tear gas.

While in Chicago, I never saw any presidential candidates, but I did rub elbows with Allen Ginsberg, who was reading poetry in Grant Park—and I witnessed Abbie Hoffman and Phil Ochs as they stoked the emotional fire of the protesters, which actually wasn't that difficult a task at the time.

Okay, I never touched Allen Ginsberg, even with my elbow. I mean, the closer I got, the less I wanted to touch him, but I listened just the same.

So I wondered—shouldn't we just jump in the car, head for Philadelphia, and see what would happen? Or should we think it out, this time wisely conjuring up a realistic scenario: We go to Philly and can't get within a hundred yards of the convention so we sit at a street-side café waiting for a Philly cheesesteak. A group of radical protestors chances by, Snapchatting and making selfies. As they Google the lyrics to "Kumbaya," tear-gas canisters come hissing in. Everyone scatters, but with my recent knee trouble, I am the one who the cops descend upon with truncheons and Tasers. This is okay by me, but I really don't like the part where my wife never gets her Philly cheesesteak.

My point is the same as the line from Allen Ginsberg's poem "America": "America how can I write a holy litany in your silly mood?"

Maybe I should focus on the Republican convention instead; that should be like a walk in the park but without the inconvenience of radical poets and folk singers spewing encrypted truths about morality and obligations.

I've got to go and see what my wife thinks of Cleveland in July.

Column 274, July 3, 2016

Thoughts About Living Long

Now that I'm over thirty, I'm getting a little concerned over how short our lives are. Someone is bound to stand up at my funeral to say, "He led a long and productive life." No, no; if indeed I was productive, then no matter my age please state that he was productive given what he considered the extremely limited time humans are able to suck air on this planet.

So how many years would you consider "a long and productive life"? Not for someone's obituary, but for yourself. I figure I need around three hundred years of fairly healthy living to fit comfortably into that category. And although my body is showing signs of disagreement with that ambition, that is what I am shooting for.

Maybe by that time I will stop ending sentences with the word *for* and other common prepositions. It's an awkward construction, and *for* is a poor word to end a sentence with. As is *with.* It's worse if you do it twice. At age 150, I should be able to master writing and speaking English, which, you might have noticed, most people never get the hang of.

By age 250, I should be writing fluently, even artistically, in a second and third language. Shoot, given an extra two hundred years or so, I might actually figure out what's important and stop spending my time performing inconsequential tasks. Isn't that the essence of productivity?

Our brains are probably not built to support life for three hundred years. If making connections between neurons builds memory, there might not be enough room in our skulls for more than 120 years of living. At that point, the brain might be forced into that "first in, first out" mode so that at 140, all of the childhood memories of your first twenty years would have to be erased to accommodate your last twenty years. More than likely, the memories wouldn't be erased, but those old files would be archived in a compressed format that would lose a lot of detail. "Oh, yes," you would say, "I remember I went to high school," and that would be about the extent of that memory.

Of course, in the future, we will have the option of adding extra space to our skulls to accommodate those extra neurons. Old people with artificially big heads and faulty exhaust systems wheeling around while making antiquated sounds and leaking is not my ideal future vision. Worse if they're all using jet packs—which they promised us back in the 1950s but have not yet delivered. Who do you call and complain about that?

To maximize my chances of living to 300, I looked into the pile of studies available on the subject and found valuable tips, especially in a study called the Longevity Project, which was popularized in a 2011 book of the same name. It looks like living long boils down to conscientiousness, which is the personality trait of "being thorough, careful, or vigilant, implying a desire to do a task well. Conscientious people are efficient and organized as opposed to easygoing and disorderly." As much as I like to think of myself as conscientious, one look around my cluttered office tells me I'm not long-life material.

However, being married gives men a statistical edge toward a longer life that may help cancel out my lack of conscientiousness. The Longevity Project does not speculate why being married can lengthen a man's life, but it has to be because women tend to talk men out of doing stupid and dangerous things. My wife, for example, over my objections, banned the storage of explosives and highly volatile flammables in the house. "That's silly," you might say and I agree—every man should have quick access to his explosives when the mood strikes. Yet, even though

I can't put my finger on it, there is a certain sense of calm in the household once dangerous substances are confined to the back forty. Maybe that's what leads to longer life expectancy.

Well, I have to go. I'm a busy person—and that adds to life expectancy, as does exercise. And all this adds up to a vigorous walk out to the back shed where I have to inventory the fireworks left over from the holidays and make sure I have enough gasoline there for the mower. See, I am getting more conscientious every day.

DJs, and What They Do

During the awkward time when I was young, parents didn't have frank discussions with their children about life. I never got the chance to ask questions to satisfy my burning curiosity on certain subjects. One question I would have loved to have answered by my father is exactly where did DJs come from, and exactly what is it that they do?

What other adolescents knew or didn't know about the subject didn't help; there was no reliable and discrete source of knowledge to which we could turn, but by the time I reached college I thought I had a good enough handle on the matter to be a DJ on the campus radio station. That sounds rather grand, but in reality, I applied to work at my dorm radio station. Don't laugh; I attended Enormous U. Some of the dorms had a population three times that of the town where I now reside, so each dorm had its own station.

Since my all-male dorm was populated by engineering and agricultural majors, my application to be a DJ was accepted without any interviews, questions, or other annoying selection criteria. This was because very few of the guys wanted to perform in public or even interact with more than 1.2 people at a time, on average. These were engineers, and they wanted only to tinker. We might not have had on-air talent, but we did have top-notch equipment that was constantly being tweaked. And as far as my DJ position, I was given only one directive: show up faithfully for the midnight to 2:00 a.m. time slot.

I played Frank Zappa, the Fugs, flip sides of Cream singles, and anything else falling into the realm of music eschewed by the masses. The beauty of this arrangement is that nobody complained. Actually, nobody listened because at that time of night, the entire student body was asleep, cramming for exams, or involved in late-night, dorm room philosophical discussions which may or might have involved questionable substances inhaled or ingested. I wouldn't know; I was in the booth spinning disks while trying to figure out what changes the engineers had made to the equipment since the previous night.

The DJ style on the few big-city FM stations that played late-night jazz really inspired me. They were so cool, you had to wear a sweater to listen. As every music track ended, they would let the last note ring out, give it a few beats, and then get very close to the microphone and in a smooth-as-can-be baritone voice, they would almost whisper, "Oh, yeah." After pausing just long enough to take a drag on their cigarette, they would add something like, "Dig it—'A Night in Tunisia' laid down by Charlie Parker and Mr. Gillespie," and then continue on with the minute details of the recording. These DJs were the essence of ease, the standard of smooth.

At the other end of the spectrum were the Top-40 screamers. When I met one in person, he spoke to me as if he was still on the air, punching words randomly and working my ear like a microphone.

Then, during the time in life when raising children causes parents to lose touch with any new developments in music, hairstyles, slang, and what is and is not cool, being a DJ transformed from being the keeper of the record library to being an on-tour superstar complete with bus and roadies.

Today's DJs write songs, compose music, produce albums, and perform for the largest of crowds, but for me, how they do this without playing instruments and how they got to this level of popularity is rather mysterious. Surely they didn't start out by playing "Brick House" for wedding parties—or did they? Studying YouTube videos of their performances leaves me with more questions than answers.

There are as many styles as DJs, it seems. Some take you to the world of hypnotic dance, and some have taken music to different planes. Where head-banging rock and roll didn't cause enough damage, they take it further, weaponizing music, stirring the crowd with apocalyptic tunes like "Kill Everybody." Wow. How cool is that?

Anyway, DJs are not the only subject I should have discussed with my father. We never discussed reproduction and distribution of music, either. He never told me about mass marketing or payola. It's a wonder sometimes how we get through life.

Column 285, September 18, 2016

The Persistence of Yard Sales

It is hard not to notice that yard sales persist, even though we've discussed the questionable premise of these marketplaces in the past. We concluded that our possessions meet at night, decide that something must be done, and then force us to find new caretakers for items we no longer cherish by conducting a yard sale. This being the logical conclusion when you realize that we do not control our possessions, but they control us. It's all very disturbing, but knowing this apparently does not stop the yard sale phenomena.

Since summer is waning, our stuff got together and coerced my wife and me to have another late-summer yard sale last weekend. It was one of two that we have every year. Having held it four years in a row makes it tradition, so now, I am told, it's compulsory. My wife—who is a longtime, hard-core, determined but happy retailer—delights in the entire process while Mr. Malcontent (that's me) goes about begrudgingly setting out tables and signs and mumbling mild oaths like he does when asked to put up the Christmas lights.

The one thing I don't like about yard sales is putting my past purchasing decisions on display for all to see. That, and I don't like haggling with people about the price—or, for that matter, talking to people about the goods, making chitchat in general, or making change. Early birds annoy me, as do people who cannot drive in reverse pulling headlong into the driveway as far as they can. Helping people fit things into their already full cars tests my amiability. To round out my list, I don't care for taking the signs and tables down, deciding what to do with the leftover items, and finding out that my wife grossed three times my meager take and enjoyed herself very much.

Also, the whole yard-sale process is flawed. During periods between customers, I tend to look at what I have on display and start re-familiarizing myself with why the item was acquired in the first place and discovering new worth in my merchandise. I empty out boxes of junk and sort the items into categories. Cleaning the items and performing minor maintenance makes them gain apparent value. Soon, what was a box of jumbled junk becomes distinct categories of useful items which often go back into what bookkeepers would have to call "household inventory."

If nothing else, a yard sale sadly brings to light the cost of acquiring new things. You can go out and purchase a nice household item at a regular store for $25 and the next day put it out at your yard sale, still new and in the box with the original price tag, and you will be fortunate to get a $3 offer on the item.

But there is more going on under the surface. We obviously don't need the items, the money we get for our time and effort isn't worth it and, economically speaking, it would be more efficient for us to haul it all to the dump and be done with it.

But hauling it to the dump, according to our upbringing, would be nothing short of evil. We were raised by parents scarred by the Great Depression, and they in turn were raised by European immigrants who had almost nothing. As a matter of fact, they had negative net possessions because they always owed more than they owned. Which is true even today, except the difference is that your creditors don't want any of your stuff because frankly, it's worthless. And it you don't think your belongings are worthless, put them out in your yard and see what kind of offers you get.

I suppose yard sales are now part of our culture and will be around until the robots take over. There is a certain mystique intrinsic to the yard sale, so people will always come—not that they need anything. After all, we do live in America, but people come on the off chance that they will find that one astounding treasure. It's curious that *yard sale* rhymes with many items you may find at such an affair, including chain mail, beam scale, mainsail, slop pail, oil shale, mare's tail, right whale, sea snail... but most peculiar of all, it rhymes really well with Holy Grail. Yes, just a little bit creepy.

Column 292, November 6, 2016

The Island

When I was young, I studied attractive, elegant, and seductive older people pictured in magazines and television. I fully expected to meet people like these as I moved into their age bracket. Now that I'm older, I see attractive, elegant, and seductive people in magazines and on television who are younger than I am, and I wonder why I never once got acquainted or even casually met any of these types of people in my entire life.

I am not talking about specific people. I am talking about types or even stereotypes, if you will. Check out any fashion magazine; here's one with a photo of a woman wearing... well, what appears to be clothing, only the fabric could just be smoke. There are a few seams, so it has to be made out of sewable smoke. Obviously, she is seven feet tall, incredibly rich, but not ostentatious—and gorgeous.

Then there are the men decked out in cable-knit sweaters, pricey deck shoes, and Rolex watches steering their sailboats. Handsome beyond belief, they look like they're in their early thirties. Where did they get the sailboat and watch? All the guys I've met in their thirties with a sailboat were pretty much flat broke except for those conducting illegal commerce, and they weren't the type to wear cable-knit sweaters.

Where are these people?

Look at a magazine ad for a clothing designer or a fragrance manufacturer. See the woman in the ad—the one wearing the gold lamé top and black skirt with the pumps and designer bag? Her long hair is blowing just right as she's leaving the helicopter that just delivered her to the rooftop of a very important building. She could be in her twenties or forties, but her blinding beauty makes her age irrelevant. Maybe you know someone like her, but I have experienced that entire age group and have never run into anyone even remotely similar. It's as if someone actually conjured up a fantasy scene and then created and photographed it—but what are the chances of that happening?

Then one day, my neighbor from across the street, Liz Hand, came over to deliver a *Harper's Bazaar* magazine, which she shares with my wife when her new one arrives. I am not sure if it's even legal to share a magazine for which you have a paid subscription, but my wife and Liz are very discreet and the magazine police have not yet sent us any notices or paid us an embarrassing visit. This magazine is overflowing with photos of the kind of people I have never met.

Anyway, I opened the magazine to a random page where there was a drop-dead gorgeous woman who immediately started altering my brain chemistry. I asked Liz if she had ever met her or anyone like her. She just kind of chuckled and said, "Oh, she lives on The Island." I flipped to another page where there was another absolutely astounding beauty, not so much wearing a long black dress as assimilating the garment. Her long leg peeked out from a bejeweled vertical portal in the dress that may or may not have been there, all the while being an intrinsic part of an enchanting forest setting. Unable to speak, I showed the image to Ms. Hand, who casually said, "Oh, she lives on the wooded end of The Island…you know about The Island, don't you?"

After a pause to regain my composure and an awkward look, I replied, "What island?"

Liz's face went flush. She mumbled something about speaking too soon and excused herself as she made small talk and walked away.

Hey! I want to know about The Island! I've been to a lot of islands including North Haven, Manhattan, Kodiak, Ellis, Jost Van Dike, Belle Isle, plus more, I'm sure, and I have never come across a population that is even remotely like the one presented in advertising.

Googling "island of beautiful people" suggests Rakahanga out in the Southern Pacific or Saipan and a few others, but looking over images we can dismiss these locations as being populated mostly with happy people. Who wants happy people when you can have fantasy people?

Wait…could it be that we are overlooking happiness because we are searching hopelessly for fantasy? Could it be?

Nah. In America we go for fantasy. It's our right, and I think it's somewhere in the Constitution. Let's all double down and find that island!

Column 293, November 13, 2016

Cat Finds New Home

Thank you, everyone, who entered or intended to enter the essay contest, but please stop. We already have a winner.

In case you are one of the few who missed out on the excitement, allow me to fill in the details. Some time ago, I wrote a column titled "Cat Available to Good Home." In the article, I explained how my construction crew found a mummified cat in the foundation of a home we were rebuilding and the fruitless effort I made to find someone who would take on the cat and give it a loving home.

Who wouldn't want a mummified cat? The maintenance is limited to keeping it dry and dusted. There are no vet bills, no cat food to supply, and certainly no hair balls to clean up. On the other hand, unless you're a very private person, you would have to constantly explain to others why you were in possession of a dead cat.

Anyway, I proposed that interested parties write to me and explain how their acquiring a cat cadaver would benefit society as a whole in the academic sense and not as an object for any kind of entertainment.

The winner of the essay contest was a certain Lawrence Forcella, a commercial entomologist by profession and a man with a keen interest in all things dead.

Mr. Forcella's winning essay hit all the right notes. He presented himself as an intelligible individual who could write in complete sentences, and even though he referred to himself as "Abaddon, Lord of the Locusts," he did not come across as a wacky member of a fringe fraternity. He assured me that the cat would be used for academic purposes and not as a throwaway Halloween decoration or a piñata for some rowdy entomological shindig.

In addition, he played the pity card, revealing that he had lost out on the last cat mummy that was available to him back in 1997. So moving was his essay that the judges unanimously awarded him the title "Custodian of the Cat Cadaver."

A meeting was arranged where the feline artifact would change hands. Since I felt strongly that the dead should not be handed over in a paper bag or department store box, I decided to build a wooden funerary box. Truth be told, I did consider a perfect-sized cardboard boot box from Zappos. Even though the idea was a shoe-in, it seemed irreverent. On the other hand, if it had been a box from Hats.com, then who could have resisted putting a dead cat-in-a-hat box?

A coffin-shaped box that is broad at the shoulders would have been overkill considering the cat's humble background, so I chose to construct a simple pine box, one that I could quickly whip out before Lawrence arrived. Also, the fact that I had pine boards on hand figured into the equation.

You just can't place a naked corpse into a pine box, so I lined the bottom with soft plastic packing foam. What's that? No, I had no velvet or satin on hand. I'm sorry.

Borrowing from my experience wrapping gifts, I folded the cat into a plain purple tissue paper so that when you opened the lid of the box, which was fastened with two screws for added drama, you wouldn't have a dead cat staring at you as if you had just broken into his private abode.

The meeting to hand off the former cat took place at a property that could pass as my own house. Was I going to let a guy who was driving miles to pick up a mummified cat know exactly where I live? Heck no, anyone who has anything to do with dead cats might turn out to be some kind of weirdo.

As it turned out, Mr. Forcella seemed normal enough, but then again, we met outside in broad daylight. He did bring a charming woman with him and how very thoughtful, as her gracious presence took the edge off any awkwardness normally associated with picking up a dead cat.

Lawrence was polite enough to be thrilled even though the cat wasn't exactly in like-new condition. We screwed the lid onto the case and placed it into the back of his vehicle (Lawrence's vehicle, not the cat's), and they all drove off into the sunset—if you consider northeast close enough to call it that.

So that's it. No cats and no more essays, please, but don't be discouraged; I'm considering giving away my entire collection of empty paint cans. Stay tuned.

Abaddon, Lord of the Locusts, and his adjunct, pick up the funerary box that can serve as a cat litter box in the cat-afterlife.

Column 296, December 4, 2016

Our Move to Maine

Whenever I'm in line to pay my property taxes, people ask why I moved my family to Maine from Alaska. The usual answer is that when we escaped, this is where we ran out of road, gas, and money. There are better places to run out of money than Maine. Money doesn't grow on trees here right next to the road. All the money trees I've seen are hard up against people's houses and usually behind a fence next to a mean dog.

December 2016 marks twenty-five years since we arrived. With no friends, family, or jobs here, we came up with five official reasons or excuses to explain our move to Maine:

1. Short, warm winters
2. The ability to drive to civilization in under a day
3. Interesting topography
4. Four seasons
5. Local residents who are funny and amusing

But the real reason we had to move was because I felt Alaska was trying very hard to brutally kill us. If it doesn't drown you or pull your plane out of the sky, you might get mauled or even eaten while out on a bike ride. The weather will do you in on a weekend hike or drive to the grocery store, the volcanic ash weighs heavy in the lungs, earthquakes make life "interesting," and if none of that gets you then over-involvement in the party scene will mince you like beef in a meat grinder.

Of course, you can get shot in the woods or spun to your death on black ice in Maine, but it's a state where you can most likely drive away if you hit a deer instead of getting a free ride to the morgue when that moose comes through your windshield.

Okay, okay, a few words about Alaska with my answers to frequently asked questions: No, I don't know Sarah Palin. Yes,

I've been to Wasilla. No, I didn't go there to buy methamphetamines. No, I couldn't see Russia from my back porch, and finally, yes, oh yes, there are a lot of moose.

How many moose? Suffice it to say that they tie up traffic in the cities almost daily because they won't get off the road. In contrast, I was tied up only once in Maine traffic because a great number of cars pulled over willy-nilly and people left their vehicles in the road to point at something located about four hundred yards away at the end of a large field. It was a moose. Or maybe it was a misshapen horse. You have to understand that four hundred yards is just forty yards short of a quarter mile, so it was hard to tell. It was definitely a dark, moving object and it did cause a traffic jam, so it must have been a moose—or an American yeti.

It's not so hard to tell in Alaska, when you wake up to a moose and two calves on your porch eating whatever you are nurturing in a flowerpot and refusing to leave until you slip them a few twenty-dollar bills and a big bag of food to go.

Anyway, Maine came through on all of our five official reasons, but as a youngish couple, we thought that because of the cold weather, blackflies, and rocky soil, all the old people would have moved to Florida, leaving only the bon vivant. Turns out, Mainers spend all their time and money fighting the weather and bad economy so they can't afford to move to Florida.

Now Maine's population has the oldest mean age of any state. Yes, not just old but old and mean. That comes from dreaming of moving to Florida only to find out you can't afford to go because the biggest crop on your farm is outcrop.

Time passed, and now I see that moving to a state full of older people might have been an issue twenty-five years ago, but I hardly notice the abundance of seniors here anymore. As a matter of fact, it seems that more and more people are getting to be about the same age as me.

So here we are celebrating our twenty-five years. I have never lived anywhere longer than I have in Maine, so I guess that says a lot. The moose are sparse and the economy is thin, but the winters really are short, sunny, and warm—and by the grace of God, we are still alive.

Column 309, March 5, 2017

Smartphone Problems

My wife has a smartphone with more computing and communications power than NASA had on all the manned moon shots combined. It can instruct you how to get to your destination in cities the phone has never before visited, recognize which song is playing even if it has never previously heard the song, and it can carry on conversations in English that are more proper and satisfying than talks I have had with some of the neighborhood adolescents.

The phone however, triggers constant complaints and queries about one feature or another, and all the while there are questions about procedures: How do you save this or delete that? What do you press to forward a photo to an e-mail address that was received as a slide show in a text message? Why isn't there an app to mediate between the Palestinians and the Israelis?

At regular intervals, my wife decides to cull unnecessary apps from her phone. You can tell this is happening when she sits angrily punching at the screen and periodically shouting "Deleted!" She has discovered that many applications cannot be deleted, causing her great distress. It was during one of these purge sessions that the trouble began.

In a way that I do not understand, my wife managed to delete an application from her phone that she seemed to remember included the words *Google Play*. It's an app that she maintains should be called something different if it indeed performs an important role. Many Android phones come with Google Play, and it cannot be deleted as it provides services basic to the phone's operation.

As the deletion became more problematic, my wife gave me the phone to make good again. Even though I am computer-savvy, I draw the line at battling with smartphones. I shrugged my shoulders and offered her my flip phone to call a help line.

"Fine," she said. "I will just take the phone to 'my man' at Horizon." (I am using a fake name here for a major service provider so that no one can accuse me of promoting or defaming the company.) Feigning interest in fixing the phone, I agreed to go with her, but I really wanted to find out who "my man" was. As it turns out, "my man" is anyone at Horizon who will help her. Since her "regular man" wasn't there, she glommed onto the "closest man" when she walked in the door. His name was Cody.

Cody, a handsome dude half our age, minus five years, was only too glad to help. When he heard we had a phone in trouble, it was almost as if he saw a beautiful young girl fall into a river. He would be the one to save her because, naturally, that is what he does. He excels at heroic deeds as he is surely an expert swimmer, a trained lifesaver, and certainly not averse to risk.

I pointed out that Cody might not even work for Horizon as he lacked a name tag and did not dress like other employees. He might just hang out there because fixing smartphones is his life—but that did not matter. My wife told him that she believed the Google Play app had been deleted. Cody's eyes widened. If true, this would prove especially challenging. This is the application you need to download other apps. Theoretically, you need to download Google Play if it is missing, but if it is missing, then you can't download anything, including Google Play. Or something like that.

Cody went to work, his fingers gliding over the touch screen as if he had grown up using this technology. He fell silent as he attacked the problem, only mumbling occasionally about its improbability. I took the occasion to pilfer anything that wasn't tied down in the showroom in order to recoup years of late fees I had paid the company. After a full three minutes, Cody naturally emerged victorious and announced that Google Play had only been disabled and then hidden in some dark corner of the phone's memory.

My wife was so happy that she declared Cody her "new man" and made me return everything I had appropriated so that she could come back in the future without suspicion.

All is well for now, and I have been assured that my wife won't dump her "old man" just because I won't fix her smartphone. It's good to know that I may still have some residual value. After all, I will always be there to offer her my flip phone.

Column 314, April 9, 2017

Let's Go to a Play

Have you considered going to a play in recent decades? Would you get strange looks from your spouse if you suddenly said, "Dear, I think tomorrow night we should dress up, go to an early dinner, and then take in a play"? Enhancing the silence, you could give it a moment and then add, "I'm buying," just to punctuate the unexpected.

In case you missed it, the ever-essential World Theater Day came on March 27, but it's hard to compete with the Ides of March, National Prooofreading Day, and Saint Patrick. Now that March Madness is officially over, it's time to consider the theater for entertainment.

Sometimes we develop cultural inertia where a body at rest tends to stay at rest, which conjures up images of dozing off in a comfortable hammock. But it also means that a body stagnated tends to stay stagnant. Life is short. Maybe we should take that familiar advice to get out more often and expand our experiences. After all, when we get a better world view, meet other people, and do different things, it's easier to see which politicians are forthright and which are mendacious.

Mendacious? Now there's a term I haven't used since I padded my high school essays with ten-dollar words. I had to look it up to be sure, but it's used to describe people who are untruthful or habitually dishonest, telling lies at every turn. It's a great word that should be employed more often. It allows you to retain a measure of civility by calling someone out as mendacious instead of just labeling them a liar, an important skill in today's political climate.

Anyway, most of us have our routines: we may go to a movie but not a concert, to a sports event but not an art opening. I even know people who would opt for a pub crawl over a museum tour. True, a few of us have legitimate excuses. There's Aunt Etna, who compromises her safety every time she steps out of the house, upsetting the witness-protection people, and of course, Uncle Frank can't go anywhere with his ankle bracelet. Most people however, are free to experience the theater, yet the closest we come to live performance is attending church. It's time to mix it up and see what the theater has to offer.

A theatrical play is a unique form of entertainment. They don't call it drama for nothing. Oh sure, there may be a good measure of drama written into the script, but the real drama is in the performance: it's a demanding, complex dance that is planned out to the smallest detail. When everything goes right, you get the value of a well-told story as memorable as it is moving. However, when things go wrong, you not only get partial value of the story, you get a whole new, original story that unfolds in front of you in real time as the actors and technicians try to keep the performance train on track, squirming under the hot lights hoping there is not a complete derailment. It's not often that you're treated to a train wreck, but if you are, sit back and enjoy every minute, relaxing in the knowledge that you aren't on the train but lucky to have a front-row seat.

Think of a play as a NASCAR event. Sure, people go to see the cars and feel the rumble of the race, but the unspoken attraction is really the crashes where the heroes emerge unscathed as man triumphs over machine. Granted, chances of getting hit by a rogue tire are minimal in a theater, but a few patrons have been struck by pieces of the set, and although the probability is woefully low, it's an exciting risk that you have to allow.

Movies are great for telling stories, but nothing's going to happen that hasn't happened in all the previous and subsequent performances. The main character won't miss a cue, the props will always be handy, and if a door is supposed to open, it will open. We are fascinated by movie blooper reels because it's so amusing to see things go wrong. The theater makes no blooper reels. It's all right out in front of you.

So, what say we meet at the theater this month and see what happens? If I get knocked unconscious by a set falling off the stage and you get to me first, the flask will be in my jacket breast pocket. Enjoy.

Column 315, April 16, 2017

Suture Instructions

Recently, I had an appointment at the clinic because Brian, my favorite nurse practitioner, needed to practice his cutting and sewing skills—on me. As an excuse, he found a few suspicious "areas of interest" on my back that were more of an interest to Brian since he could see them. As they were on my back, I had never directly made eye contact with them nor had I been formally introduced. Brian wanted to send them to the lab for analysis to help keep the lab people employed, and I consented since I've always had a soft spot for lab workers and also because I don't want to scare away girls if I end up shirtless on a beach sometime in the future, like when I'm in my seventies.

In preparation for this "minor surgical procedure," I watched as Denise, the advanced medical technician, gathered supplies from the cabinets like meat cleavers, bone saws, gauze, and anesthetic. I didn't see her take a swig of whiskey from any "medicinal bottle" they might keep with the prescription medicines, but if I had her job I most certainly would have.

She opened a new box of surgical suture material and removed one of the packets. As she put the box back on the shelf, she took the instruction sheet that came inside the box and tossed it in the trash. This was both reassuring and disturbing to me. Reassuring because it implied that Brian knew what he was doing and had already memorized the instructions back in medical school. It was at the same time disturbing because, well, because no one was reading the substantial notes about the suture material they were going to use—on me.

Picking the instructions out of the trash when no one was looking crossed my mind, but rooting around in the rubbish at the doctor's office may not be such a good idea. I mean, what could you find in there accidently? There won't be any needles; they have their own special little trash can hanging on the wall, but you could very well run into something unpleasant like a half-eaten liverwurst sandwich, for example.

Advanced medical technician Denise pulled the suture literature out of the trash at my request and let me have it on the condition that I wouldn't cry like a baby during the procedure and then demand a lollipop. I pondered my options while she concluded the preparations and finally agreed.

The instructions are printed on a huge eighteen-inch square sheet of paper, and counting the back, 65 percent of the paper is blank. There is no title on the sheet, and the text is divided into three columns: English, French, and Spanish. It's curious: there's enough room on the paper to fit another five languages, especially with the microscopic eight-point type they used. Do the Chinese use sutures, or do they all read English, Spanish, or French? I wondered if all three languages say the same thing or if you would have to be trilingual to get the entire message.

The language mystery aside, the paper turned out to be more of a data sheet than a how-to manual, which is a relief. It clearly states that "users should be familiar with surgical procedures and techniques" before using the suture material to close wounds. Reading the description, I found that suture material is essentially nylon monofilament fishing line available in clear, black, or blue, although unlike fishing line, it is sterilized using gamma radiation.

The paper talked about the chemical composition, adverse reactions, and how you should throw away any unused suture and not be a cheapskate doctor saving every inch to be used on the next patient. I bet tightwad clinics get their suture material at the Walmart fishing department.

Sitting upright and shirtless, I felt quite like Vladimir Putin on a horse as Brian hacked away at my back, occasionally laughing maniacally while Denise politely refrained from saying "Oh, I wouldn't want to see you on the beach with that in ten years." The biopsy was a snap, and the pain was no more intense than that experienced while riding shirtless on a horse prancing backwards through a smallish rose thicket.

I left satisfied, knowing that I had helped lab people keep their jobs and Brian refine his skills, even though I didn't get a lollipop. I can't wait to return to get the sutures removed. When I do, I will be very firm that they discard the suture material and not reuse it. You can thank me later for always reading the instructions.

Column #323, June 11, 2017

City Living Revisited, Part 1: Driving

I'm not unfamiliar with big cities: I grew up in Detroit, spent time in Los Angeles, got cheated by a cab driver in Chicago, nearly bought a house in Seattle, and spent years in Anchorage, which people don't consider a big city because it is so close to Alaska. But with Anchorage's urban problems, international airport, and extensive municipal sewer system, you just have to concede big-city status, especially since it's more than four times the size of Portland, Maine.

What's happened is that for twenty-five years, I've lived in and grown accustomed to the shire here in Mid-coast Maine and have been away from urban life for so long, I have forgotten the nuances and considerations of everyday city living.

Recently, I took a job that required a ten-day stay in the heart of Portland. That's the part without any woods, vacant lots, or ground-level garden plots. Portland might not be a big city by some standards, but it does have monuments, eleven zip codes, distinct districts, and a city named after it somewhere on the West Coast in Oregon.

The first thing I noticed is that I could not make it anywhere on time. I would look at a map and tell the people I was to meet that I would be there in five minutes. Thirty-five minutes later, I would show up embarrassed with the explanation that I am but a village yokel and in my hamlet, there is no traffic and ample free parking can be found around the clock.

Traffic is a real issue. You know you're in it when people in wheelchairs regularly pass your car as you wait bumper to bumper, engines running. Traffic materializes out of nothing at certain times and then just disappears. It's not anything like slowing down to get through a small town. Traffic is waiting for three turns of the light to get through an intersection—every light at every intersection. It's dealing with other drivers who are even more frustrated than you are and who really need to be told to take some time away from the city, although there is no hand gesture to tell them that.

Once traffic allows passage to your destination, the issue of parking dominates. Parking always seems available for $5 an hour at a parking structure and sometimes on the street at a meter for four quarters an hour; two-hour maximum. Then there are numerous private lots where people tell you that in spite of the signs, you can park for free in the evening when the moon is full if Venus is aligned with Mars. But what is free parking for one individual is a boot on the car for another, which will cost $75 plus your time to get back on the road.

Free parking is available, but it's hard to find, and asking locals is very much like asking about a secret fishing hole—those who know don't say, and those who say, don't know.

And there are signs, lots of them. Just in the realm of the right turn, there are enough signs to make you switch off your books on tape. No right turn. Turn right on arrow only. Right turn yield for pedestrians. No right turn on red. Turn right from this lane only. This lane must turn right. And my favorite: Turn right to turn left.

Parking signs border on information overload. There are five-, ten-, and fifteen-minute loading zones, parking for certain vehicles like police cars, and just plain "No Parking" signs for no apparent reason. All parking signs are negative, as they start with the assumption that parking is allowed. But city things are complicated: one side of the street prohibits parking on the first and fourth Wednesdays of each month between 12:01 a.m. and 7:00 a.m., while on the other side of the street, it's on the first and fourth Monday that your car is liable to be towed if parked during the forbidden hours. Always travel with a calendar.

And yes, take the keys and lock the car. Cities are why cars come with locks. No one will give you any sympathy if you leave your keys in an unlocked car. Even if nothing happens, you will be judged a fool or at least a country bumpkin.

All this is just getting there. Once you step out into the city, the strangeness only continues. Now you must interact with real city people. Good luck. It doesn't help that you're late.

Column 324, June 18, 2017

Time for Tick Talk

Things are getting really draconian at my house. If I am caught upstairs in the bedroom with my pants and shoes, I will get three demerits. Depending how involved I have been in woods work, I may not be allowed upstairs wearing any clothes whatsoever. I don't know what happens after three demerits, but there is a dark universe of possibilities that I am not prepared to visualize.

As with most human rules, this restriction has come about on the basis of fear. I wonder sometimes why the word *fear* isn't used more often, like in every other sentence, as almost everything we do is rooted in fear to one extent or another.

Anyway, it's my wife's concern about ticks and the diseases they carry that has brought about this new set of house rules. We are talking about the ticks that inhabit the woods and live to reproduce by dining on mammalian blood. It's not the tick of the clock that concerns her, although if you realistically weigh true risk, it's the ticktock of the clock we should fear most. Our forced travel through that fourth dimension leads directly to our death, while the lowly forest tick is an insignificant inconvenience along the way. Still, we do not like eight-legged creatures attaching themselves to our skin and sucking our blood. We just don't.

My wife has been theorizing that my clothes can provide a vector whereby a tick can get into the house and then onto her clothes. When I come in from the woods, I am treated like I just completed a shift at the Fukushima cleanup effort.

I do not like to change clothes midday, but my wife insists we can't be too careful with ticks or radiation so pants, shirt, and socks (at minimum) must be immediately placed in the washing machine as a precaution. I have eliminated coffee breaks when I do yard work for fear of having to strip if I enter the house.

There was a time when we would roll in the grass and hide in the deep weeds for fun. Now that we know ticks harbor disease, the innocence has ended and the fun terminated. A case can easily be made to blame the Democrats, but with so many clothes changes, I have little time for finger-pointing.

Apparently, my wife is a tick magnet because of her rare beauty and soft skin, while my characteristics more or less repel ticks. I can work in the woods clearing brush, cutting firewood, or mowing all day and have only a casual brush with a tick now and then. All my wife has to do is walk past the lilacs to trigger an area-wide alert to all ticks that a good-looking host is in the neighborhood ripe for a free ride and buffet.

I have tried to minimize her fear by explaining that ticks are not technically insects. While she doesn't mind Jiminy Cricket and mature butterflies, I know she is not fond of Insecta, the class of living things in the phylum Arthropoda that makes some people's skin crawl.

As you no doubt remember from high school biology, we classify all living things by assigning them a place in seven categories: kingdom, phylum, class, order, family, genus, and species. I assured my good wife that ticks and insects belong to very separate classes. Ticks are arachnids. This puts them in the same class with spiders, mites, scorpions, and of course, chiggers.

Okay, this strategy did not assuage any fears. The fact that ticks are more closely related to spiders than to Jiminy Cricket did nothing to lessen the loathing. I believe the only biology lesson she took away is that she likes arachnids even less than insects.

Thirty years ago, the scenario where a woman fights to remove all my clothes as I attempt to make it up the staircase to the bedroom would have been intriguing at the very least. Today it seems more like sitcom material where everyone is talking ticks. Friends come to visit, and suddenly they are telling tick stories that really should be told only late at night around campfires.

There is so much discussion that I am starting to feel movement under my clothes every time I sit still. I better not sit still. There could be a strip search for ticks at any time. If you want me, I'll be in the woods—where I'm safe.

Column 325, June 25, 2017

City Living Revisited, Part 2

Two weeks ago, I expounded on the differences between city and rural driving after having spent ten days living in the heart and a little bit in the kidney of Portland, Maine. It's a small city but thirty times bigger than the shire where I've spent the last twenty-five years. This week, we will review some of the other obvious differences for those of us who don't get out much and consequently forget what the rest of America is all about.

Noise: The city is full of noise. It comes from the steady traffic, the hum of urban machinery, the din of construction, and organic clamor of people. We tend to ignore noise when it's all around us, and we become sensitive only to sounds that may affect our lives. I was surprised to find that I was sensitive to people dropping coins. How did my family evolve to have the ability to filter out street noise and hear coins dropping onto the sidewalk? Another troubling observation is that I had to stifle the urge to immediately dive for the coins. I wasn't "born in the wagon of a traveling show," but somewhere along the line I acquired sensitivity for coins coming my way.

Public anonymity: On the city streets where you stand in front of God and everyone else, no one, except maybe God, takes much notice. People don't want to. They want space, and the way everybody gets it is to generally ignore everyone else. People will walk within two feet and not utter a "Good morning" or "Looks like rain" or even "Hey, looks like you forgot your pants today." In public, you are anonymous, even invisible. It's an urban convenience and unless both parties agree, you don't spend time chitchatting or exchanging pleasantries.

It's a beneficial convention when you are in a hurry or have forgotten your pants.

To really take advantage of urban invisibility, it helps to drive a small beat-up car, preferably gray or black, with at least one hubcap missing on each side. It's easy to park. Dents and scratches are a nonissue, and the car doesn't attract attention. God forbid you have a plow truck. There is no place to park it, and even without the snow plow, trucks are a liability—if not for their size, then for the fact that all your acquaintances will call on you whenever they move or purchase furniture.

Convenience to everything: If you need a drink, a smoke, a donut, or a tattoo, there is probably a sidewalk under your feet that connects you with all those places. Afterward, you can walk to a gym, a counselor, or a church to get help reversing what you did earlier—except for the tattoo, which you're pretty much stuck with. There are specialty shops for everything, endless services, fountainheads of culture, and restaurants that appear and disappear so fast that you can go to a grand opening almost every day of the week, sometimes at the same location.

Diversity: Living out in the white countryside of Maine, we tend to forget that America is made up of all different kinds of people. There are "long ones, tall ones, short ones, brown ones, black ones, round ones, big ones...crazy ones." These are people you don't know and, chances are, never will. It's not anything like seeing all your like-minded English-speaking neighbors at the Memorial Day parade. City people are a blunt reminder that Americans are way more diverse than who you will find living in your own home, even when you discover someone sleeping in the barn now and again. Bottom line is that all these people just want to make a living and feel wanted and productive. I'm sure I look just as freaky or lovely to them as they do to me.

Poverty: It may be a Kumbaya moment with all these people around, but don't let your guard down. People are constantly asking for money. A few of them do so with a gun, but most just beg politely, which instantly brings up so many issues that are impossible to sort out in the short time allotted to make a decision. Be prepared.

The city is an amazing place with eye-popping contrasts and wonders. If you haven't left the shire for a while, it's time to schedule a visit. Just remember your spare change for the panhandlers and parking meters, your appreciation for the unfamiliar, and of course, your pants.

Column 327, July 9, 2017

It's Time to Write Your Autobituary, Part 1

One of the first things we do at the Association of Formerly Interesting Men's annual conclave is to review obituaries that any members have written about themselves. We believe it is important to write your own obituary because (a) no one is going to take the time and care to get all the important points right about the deceased, and (b) dead men don't tell tales. It's a great life-reflecting exercise to write what I like to call your "autobituary," which is a clever term, but unfortunately, just one Google search squashed the notion that I coined the word first.

There is no better time than right now to write that obituary for yourself. After all, you are still lucid enough to read this column, which is "sometimes hard to follow and only well-written and funny 60 percent of the time" as I understand it through the feedback I get from readers (thank you). I'm always wondering if I'll be able to write when I can no longer see, hear, and boogie. It would be bad to find out you can't put a decent sentence together when they're wheeling you out of the old folk's home and into the palliative care co-op.

Do not leave the composition of your obituary to chance if you put any value on a final published statement about your life. To demonstrate my point, ask one of your friends, on short notice, to write up your obituary. To make it realistic, give them a twenty-four-hour deadline, don't answer a single question they may have, and before they start, you might want to ride over their foot with your car to simulate the pain of grieving. See if you like what they come up with.

The argument for writing your own obituary is clear: read

some of the current obituaries. I have been reading them more as I get older, and frankly, I find them appalling. Most seem to have been written by grieving relatives and say things like "He was a fun person to be around with a great sense of humor, and he enjoyed his grandchildren." What a sad and woesome load of horse pucky to sum up a man's life. It may be true, but the person they were writing about surely had to be more interesting than that.

Did anyone run the copy by the deceased before it was submitted for publication? We are left wondering about the person's lifework, what he found important, the high and low points he experienced, and if there was perhaps a secret he couldn't tell us when he was alive.

If you don't feel comfortable with what you write, hire a writer. This is far and away much, much cheaper than you'd expect. Many writers will accept a Popsicle or even a half Popsicle in trade for a decent obituary, but to be polite, you should offer them hard currency—but not too much. It is not customary or apparently acceptable in our society to pay writers a living wage, and you don't want to come off as a chump to someone who you've given control over your legacy.

At the very least, make an outline of pertinent facts and some of your life's accomplishments that you would like people to know. Post it prominently on your front door or in front of the toilet, or have it tattooed where people will easily find it.

If your life story is looking a little thin, add some standard achievements like "never went to prison" or "was only six years shy of receiving his master's degree in astrophysics," and don't forget to include the classic "was released early for good behavior" if applicable. The beauty of an autobituary is that you still have time to run guns through the Khyber Pass or volunteer for Fukushima cleanup if your rough draft is looking a little lame.

Now, have someone read it aloud. Does it sound like this

was a great character? If it's too long, consider writing an auto-biography. Some news outlets limit the length of obituaries, so if you're the obsessive type, offer an abridged version. Save the complete story for the web.

Next time, we will cover some material I want in my personal obituary. One thing for sure, it's not going to start out with "He was a fun person to be around, sometimes hard to follow, and only well-written and funny 60 percent of the time."

Column 328, July 16, 2017

It's Time to Write Your Autobituary, Part 2

If you remember, last week we addressed the importance of writing your own obituary. If you're having trouble remembering, maybe it's time to double down and get that autobituary written before you can't remember other things like your date of birth and the names of your children. Get going before the unthinkable happens and the task of creating a news article about your life and recent death falls to your slacker brother-in-law. He's the relative who would compose the obit on his cell phone at the casino bar—during happy hour.

I am working on my own obituary in fear that someone who may be filled with grief, late for an appointment, or confused over the English language may write it instead. Just in case I don't finish it and the task falls to you, refer to this column as a starting point.

First, please satisfy people's curiosity about how I died. This will draw them into the story and whet their appetite for more juicy details. Many obituaries skirt this issue or avoid it altogether. If I die from cancer, let them know what kind and what I did to survive before I lost the coin toss. Did I get run over by a bus? Which bus was it, and where was it going? People want to know. They don't want to get on busses that run people over.

Mention if I died in a hospital or roadside ditch. I won't be embarrassed—I'll be dead. Let people know if I was angry about it and conscious or too drugged-up to experience my own death. I think I want to be there for the whole show. I've never shied away from pain—well, yes, I have, so I might opt for that big morphine trip; people like to know what their options are going to be, so help them out a little.

Maybe you can treat the rest of the story as a flashback, but be mindful not to cross the line into a full-blown biography. Worldwide, over 150 thousand people die every day, but even on a slow death day, the obituary editor still has limited space. Don't wander too far off topic.

Here are some examples of the writing style that can be employed for a great send-off:

"After dealing with maddening employees for thirty-one years and hearing just one too many stories explaining why people are too stupid to do their job, this beloved father, uncle, and popular Rotarian jabbed some sharp pencils into his ears and shouted 'Sweet relief!' as he fell to his death onto a mountain of unfinished state and federal employment paperwork."

Or: "He died from the ravages of colon cancer while pumped up on drugs, which he wanted more to lessen his anger about dying than for the pain. His biggest regret was the large invest-ment of time and money he had put into video games, which essentially occupied all of the 1990s before a chance encounter with reality showed him what he was missing."

One of the big points I want to make is that everyone attend-ing the memorial and funeral service followed by the bang-up reception will receive a free copy of my book—if I have a book out by that time—which may or may not be signed by the author. Although I have not yet decided on whether to have a polka band or a New Orleans jazz band, the music and alcohol will flow freely.

Also, attendees will receive a grab bag with a sample of the deceased's "stuff" that his family collected from his studio and shop. There will be a drawing for a door prize.

And please, don't smooth it over by saying "He's in a better place" or "He led a full life" as if that makes dying all right with me. Hell, no. You can add that he seriously wanted another couple hundred years to make a substantial contribution to humanity. He might have understood dying, but that didn't make him any less angry about having to give up consciousness and memories.

Be sure to add that he loved his wife and the time he spent dancing with her in its many forms. He adored his daughter and wished her and humanity only the best. Mostly, don't forget to mention the door prizes. That should really bring them in.

There you go. Those are my ideas. Now, get going on your own. Remember there is a deadline approaching.

Column 336, September 10, 2017

September 19: Talk Like a Pirate Day

To assuage my fear that talking like a pirate might fall into obscurity, I am hereby reminding everyone to be prepared for September 19, the official International Talk Like a Pirate Day.

For the last few years, Krispy Kreme, a major purveyor of donuts, has given away free donuts to swashbucklers who ordered their donut with pirate-speak. They offered up to a dozen donuts for people who dressed the part. But the company recently announced they would end the practice, and that's because *they be a crew of lily-livered, bilge-swim'n, fake-bearded, penny-pinch fists that wouldn't give a johnnycake to a scurvy-ridden castaway.*

This may be a sign that Talk Like a Pirate Day is on the wane, so we must step up and participate.

Although talking like a pirate is not mandatory, it is highly recommended as a way to insert levity and promote recreation in our daily activity. On a normal day at work, you might say, "Hey Dan, I'd like to see you in my office." But on Talk Like a Pirate Day, you would announce, "Ahoy, Danny boy, report t'me cabin off the poop deck. For iffen ye don't, I shall skewer yer gizzard wit' me cutlass, ye salty sea bass."

Even though pirate talk is laced with insults and threats of gruesome death, it has a certain poetry that's a welcome relief during a humdrum day.

If you have trouble talking like a pirate, you can look up pirate vocabulary on the web. It will sort out the differences between "Arrr" (an interjection of surprise or a pause in speaking), "Yarrr" (agreement), and "Harrr" (laughter or amusement).

Or try a pirate speak translator, where the site will take a layman's sentence like "Hey! It's a pirate's life for me: treasure and drink before we all die" and serve up "Avast! It's a corsair's life: booty and a barrel o' rum before we all be visitin' Davy Jones' Locker."

If you want to talk like a real movie pirate, you have to watch old pirate movies. New pirate films are fine, but sometimes light on true pirate verbiage. There's Disney's *Treasure Island* from 1950 and the 1952 film *Blackbeard the Pirate,* but my all-time favorite is *Captain Kidd,* a film released in 1945 staring Charles Laughton, Randolph Scott, and John Carradine. *'Twas a hearty yarn penned when dialogue was king 'n lorded o'er any visual effects t' tell th' tale.*

The movie is full of authentic movie pirate talk, like the scene where Captain Kidd recruits a crew for his ship from the local prison and announces, "Now then, me bullies! Would you rather do the gallows dance, and hang in chains 'til the crows pluck your eyes from your rotten skulls? Or would you feel the roll of a stout ship beneath your feet again?" Wow, genuine movie pirate talk.

For all the cutthroat gaiety it generates around the world, you would think that International Talk Like a Pirate Day is one of those United Nations-sponsored ideas where multinational agreements were signed and multiple governments made concessions and hammered out all the details before it became international law. It didn't happen quite that way.

Two guys, John Baur and Mark Summers (aka Cap'n Slappy and Ol' Chumbucket) from Albany, Oregon, began insulting each other while playing racquetball in 1995, and the insults blossomed into pirate talk because pirate insults just flow naturally *and ye'd be th' biggest salty scumbag an' addlepate if ye thought otherwise, arrg!*

They set September 19 as the official date as it was the birthday of Ol' Chumbucket's ex-wife and could easily be remembered. For years, they privately enjoyed the day, but in a stroke of destiny, renowned humor writer Dave Barry, who can spot an amusing distraction from beyond th' briny deep, picked up on the idea. Now Talk Like a Pirate Day is celebrated world over.

People who are truly committed to talking like a pirate can change their Facebook or Google language settings to "English (Pirate)." I changed my setting but nothing happened. *I be wonderin' when the settin' will commence to av' an effect on me writin'.*

Well, as is said in the pirate world, it's all great fun *'til some pimple-pocked, bottom-feedin', pan-faced oyster-sucker loses an eye. Avast, me hearties, go forth and talk like a pirate!*

Column 338, September 24, 2017

About *It*

Reviewing my writing, I find a disproportionate number of my sentences start with the word *it*. This is an embarrassing realization for a writer, as it's almost the same as discovering that you write no better than a thirteen-year-old who can't help using the word *like* every half breath when speaking.

Lexicographers have put a lot of thought into how we use *it*. They explain in the dictionary that the word is used to "represent a concept or abstract idea understood or previously stated." This makes *it* a fallback word, used out of convenience when writers fail to craft a well-made sentence and put the onus on the reader to fill in the blanks. I must apologize if I've been slipping you an onus or two, just when everyone is feeling the pressure of multiple onuses, trying to differentiate between real and fake news or large and small inauguration crowds.

Although it doesn't excuse me, the problem is our culture of convenience where *it* can be used to represent anything—even concepts for which we have no words. When people respond to you with "It doesn't matter," you can be hard-pressed at times to figure out what "it" really is. The word has evolved into a catchall sound for any kind of thought.

Take for example, the common observation "it's raining." What exactly is the word *it* referring to? Certainly, we should be able to substitute some other word for *it* and get a much clearer sentence. We could say that "the sky is raining," but that isn't quite accurate, while "the clouds are raining" sounds awkward. No word I can think of is a good substitute. Wouldn't it be best to say "rain is falling" to accurately indicate what the weather conditions are and dispense with it? But English speakers are in love with *it,* and *it* won't be going away anytime soon.

The word seems to be overused, and now that the number-one box office draw is a motion picture called *It,* we just can't get enough of…what else can I say, we can't get enough of it. Based on the 1986 horror novel by Stephen King, the film features Pennywise the Dancing Clown who (spoiler alert) preys upon local children by using *it* too many times in a sentence. Taking advantage of their terrifying confusion, he brutally crushes them under a massive onus to the thrill and delight of audiences nationwide.

While we are exploring *It* as a title, let it be known that *It* is also the title of

a 1927 silent romantic comedy starring Clara Bow, which was one of the first motion picture films employing product placement;

a 1967 British horror film starring Roddy McDowell, the guy from *Planet of the Apes*; and

a 2003 music festival in Limestone, Maine, featuring the rock band Phish and the title of a corresponding documentary featuring neither clowns nor apes.

To be fair, there are other definitions for the word *it,* as when it is used as a noun in children's games where one of the players is designated as the sole antagonist (or "tag"-o-nist), as in "you're it." As a child, I enjoyed being it as opposed to not being it. This is because "it" was a special title and all the rest of the players in the game were there to react to it. We all understood exactly what "it" was, and a definition was rarely verbalized. Who wouldn't like being it?

The British sometimes substitute *it* for sweet vermouth, but that's typically British so there is no explanation for it except that they may drink too much gin.

As you may already know, I like to discover any anagrams

that can be created by rearranging the letters of my column topic. I was very excited to find that there is only one possible anagram for *it,* and to save you any mental gymnastics, I will simply tell you that *ti* is the result.

This extremely interesting and legitimate Scrabble word represents the seventh musical tone right there between la and do. Ti is also the symbol for the chemical element titanium, named for the Titans of Greek mythology who are rumored to never have used the word *it,* although that has been repeatedly debunked as a myth.

There. I have met my personal challenge and finished an entire column without using a sentence that starts with *it.* It wasn't easy. Oh…damn it!

Column 340, October 8, 2017

The "Happy Birthday" Song

Folks, please, let's stop singing "Happy Birthday" as if it were a funeral dirge. We've all heard the song "performed" countless times and the effect is overwhelmingly melancholy. You'll find more cheerfulness in church on a rainy Sunday with the congregation singing "Nobody Knows the Trouble I've Seen."

The problem is that no one qualified takes the lead to set the tone and pace. Here's a typical scene at Tommy's eleventh birthday, which is supposed to be a real celebration:

Boys are milling around cracking top-tier jokes for eleven-year-olds when Mom steps out of the kitchen with the cake and candles. Dad takes the cue, and with no regard to key, pitch, or tempo, he starts, "Haaaaaaaaaaaaaaapy Birrrrrthdaaaay Tooooo Yoooooooooou." By this time, Tommy is well into his teens and experimenting with hugs. His daughter turned out fine, but his business went south right before Tommy's divorce was finalized. His ex-wife promised to be there when he gets out of prison… and the song is over. It almost makes you cry.

It could easily be a funeral song. For the musically inclined, try singing it in a minor key at the same painful pace it's normally performed and you'll see that it's perfect to accent the misery and grief at any funeral, especially one where the deceased departed on his or her birthday.

If you're not musically adept, you can hear "Happy Birthday" in a minor key on YouTube (or for that matter, you can hear it in any style including a great klezmer Yiddish rendition). But my favorite is "The Happy Birthday Song in C Sharp Minor with Kazoo and Organ Accompaniment." * It would be a great warm-up number to that Ralph Stanley classic "O Death" that I definitely want played real loud at my funeral.

And, yes, if I die on my birthday, I do want "Happy Birthday" sung, minor key, adagio—no, make that lento—and I want it rehearsed, two-part harmony minimum. Please, no spontaneous sing-along amateur renditions.

As you may have heard, the song "Happy Birthday" is copyrighted. There is a fee for any public performance. The entire copyright is on shaky legal ground, but it's cheaper to pay the fee, which generates about $2 million a year for the Warner Music Group, present owner of the rights, than to fight it in court. Don't worry, you can still sing it for free at home, but that doesn't mean it has to be a slow, laborious requiem.

So when you see cake and candles coming, jump up and make an announcement to put some energy into the song. Start the song out at a good fast pace, maybe clapping hands to give the beatless a clue, and start it low because the song goes high in the end and things get ugly when Aunt Clarisse tries to hit the high notes. If it comes out too short for your taste, don't slow it down—add a verse of "For He's a Jolly Good Fellow," which is definitely in the public domain.

In the interest of the public commons, I have conjured up my own version of a "Happy Birthday" song that anyone can use, free of charge. Keeping with the simplicity theme, the song is only eight lines long, but the last line repeats as many times as you can keep it rhyming. It's fun to have each person singing come up with a line, or you can make up as many lines as years you are celebrating.

What's that? No, you don't have to go beyond the first eight lines. Yes, I know it's twice as complex as the regular birthday song, but come on, it's free and lively.

Look. Here it is in its entirety. Take what you want. It's sung to the tune of "We Wish You a Merry Christmas." The melody is probably in the public domain, but we can straighten that out later in court. Remember, keep it lively; it's a celebration.

> We wish you a happy birthday,
> We wish you a happy birthday,
> We wish you a happy birthday,
> We are not insincere.

> Good fortune to you,
> May it not disappear,
> We wish you a happy birthday
> And the rest of the year!

> …And a nice atmosphere.
> …And a cheap souvenir.
> …We are not cavalier.
> …May you drink a cold beer.
> …Eat a 3 Musketeer.
> …The end is real near.
> …Mm mm mmm mmm mmm mmmm.

* https://www.youtube.com/watch?v=5kBSBH_eUDw

Column 344, November 5, 2017

Lampshades

People often quietly ask me in church, especially during the homily, where the closest liquor outlet is located that's open on Sunday—but that's not where I am going with this. Occasionally, they instead ask where I get my ideas for this column. Before we start singing hymns and just so we don't garner any more sideways looks from the preacher, let me disclose my column-idea process.

Almost all my column subjects simply come from my column-ideas file. This is a document I keep on my computer with tidbits and half-baked thoughts on subject matter that should, in all fairness, be thrown into the dumpster of passing thought, yet they get trapped there in a sort of reservoir of mental noodling.

Where the ideas come from that accumulate in my idea file is really a mystery to me. It's just a collection of daydreams, figments of observations, and cogitations that I happen to record if I am daydreaming and at my keyboard at the same time, which turns out to be surprisingly often.

A few ideas, however, bypass the idea file and come at me in sometimes bizarre ways that can't help but fast-track themselves into columns.

Just the other evening, I was driving through a neighboring town and my wife casually mentioned that my driving was distracted and erratic. She wondered aloud if it was related to my column deadline and gently prodded, "How is your column coming?"

"I've got zip," I replied.

"Well, you must have a topic—"

"No. Haven't even started."

"You'll do fine. You always come up with something."

"No, I have void, blackness, nix, diddly-squat."

She persisted with kind reassurances until I could stand it no longer, and I cried out, "For the sake of sanity and freedom of the press, woman, give me a column idea now. Anything." For extra emphasis and to mimic the pressure of a writing deadline, I added, "Now, now, now."

There was a moment's hesitation and a few guttural, time-filling syllables, and suddenly she just blurted out, "Lampshades."

I euphorically agreed, "Lampshades it is then." We stopped the next pedestrian we spied and grilled him for directions to the nearest tavern where we could consume a celebratory aperitif and toast lampshades and all light-controlling accessories.

So here we are.

The internet is full of articles on the history of lampshades, and after inspecting a handful, it has become obvious that the articles all reference one another. The only thing that anyone really knows is that lampshades have been around for a long time. They were used on candles and on oil lamps; they come in a variety of shapes and sizes and can be constructed from a great many materials. After all, they're lampshades—nothing too special here, folks. Oh, once lampshades for the electric light became established and part of home décor, those meddling artists like Louis Comfort Tiffany and Clara Driscoll took the design of lampshades to new aesthetic realms.

I'm pretty sure that there is a full column's worth in the fact that the Tiffany company, which produced the wonderful Art Nouveau glasswork, was headed by a man whose middle name was Comfort. This is the kind of comment that ends up in the idea file.

One interesting item I came across in my research was titled "When Did Drunks Start Wearing Lampshades?" by a certain Christopher Beam, who apparently spent some time researching the subject. The article points to the beginning of the 1900s as a likely origin when electric lamps with large easy-to-remove shades and obnoxious drunks crossed paths at cocktail parties. Comics from Charlie Chaplin to Jim Backus, the Three Stooges, and Bob Hope all helped popularize the lampshade motif into the 1970s.

Is it a coincidence that drunks wearing lampshades started about the same time that the Art Nouveau style and the Tiffany lampshades was peaking? Some half-baked thoughts I just have to let slide, and they don't even make it into the idea file. This is one of them.

So the next time we share a pew, there will be no need to ask where the ideas come from. We can silently endure another parable or another look at the Letter to the Corinthians, and even though we might later meet in the liquor aisle, we know enough to keep lampshades off of our heads.

Column 350, December 17, 2017

Trees for Christmas

I know a thing or two—okay, a thing, anyway—about Christmas trees because during my coldest college days, I worked on a tree farm for Old Mr. Knowles, the conflicted Ebenezer Scrooge of the Christmas-tree industry.

Far ahead of the holidays, we would cut and pile trees on farm trailers and drive them back to our staging area and "corporate office." The office was a dilapidated one-room cabin where we kept the tools of the trade and dried our gloves in front of a hot potbellied woodstove.

At the staging area, we would bale the trees into tight columns and load them onto tractor trailers for shipping to faraway markets, which is where my interest unfortunately stopped. At the time, I was too inexperienced to pay much attention to markets and how money was really made. This inattention cost me later in life, which is why I am writing this story instead of trading gold futures on international exchanges.

As the holidays approached, we switched from wholesale to a cut-your-own operation where we would supply customers with a bow saw and instructions to "go that way and don't hurt yourself." If they made it back to the parking lot, we would help them load the tree onto their car and administer any first aid necessary to allow them to pay and to drive away. It was fun.

Old Mr. Knowles wanted us to collect every penny we could for the trees, and he didn't allow us to take less than a dollar a foot, give or take, depending...

We had a pricing scheme that was not modeled on supply and demand but on the customer's apparent wealth. If a family of modest means drove up in a beat-up station wagon with worn tires and they seemed to be nice people but couldn't pay a lot, we were instructed to charge a dollar a foot. But if the customer drove up in a Cadillac and wore shoes inappropriate for a cut-your-own Christmas tree experience, we were expected to extract top dollar. It was capitalism, to be sure, but tended toward a free-market system run by an entrenched dictator.

Mr. Knowles would often chase us down as a car drove away asking how much we had charged for that beautiful nine-foot fir. When we assured him that it was really a scraggly six-foot pine, he would shake his head in disbelief at the younger generation and suggest we charge double for the next tree we loaded.

As the days grew short and closer to Christmas, Mr. Knowles would double down on his group of college reprobates, making sure we would charge an extra half-dollar for the six-and-a-half-foot trees. But Old Man Knowles had a soft spot that was probably the result of a visit from the Ghost of Christmas Yet to Come. A nightly visit from the Ghost of Jim Beam was also a possibility that you'd have to allow.

Just before we wrapped up for Christmas, one of those beat-up station wagons pulled up with a family wearing hand-me-down clothes. They took a saw, trudged off into the trees, and somehow managed to find and cut a premium ten-foot fir that was perfect. It may have come from our nursery area. If we let it go for less than $3 or even $4 a foot, Old Man Knowles would surely kill us.

We were negotiating hard with the family when the old man stormed out of the shack to see how much money we were costing him. He made a painful face, looked at the children standing in the snow, and told the man to bring his family into the shack so they could talk by the stove. We stayed out in the cold and tied the tree to the car.

A full thirty minutes later, the family emerged from the shack followed by the two men, who seemed a bit pie-eyed, possibly from the brandy that Knowles kept hidden behind the chainsaw gas. The whole family was smiling and profusely thanking Mr. Knowles as they walked past us, got in the car, and drove away. They waved to the old man and more than once shouted out wishes for a merry Christmas.

Ken Walker or maybe Tom Kujat*—one of the forestry students on our wise-guy crew—allowed for a few moments of silence and then asked, "Hey, Mr. Knowles, how much did you get for that tree?"

"Aw…shut up," the old man said, making a snarky face. He started on back to the shack. As he got to the door, he turned and yelled, "Now get back to work. No less than a dollar a foot, boys, no less than a dollar a foot."

*Author's note:

Since this column was published, I managed to talk to Ken Walker, who went on to head a company in British Columbia that supplies millions of seedlings to the Canadian forest industry. He denied making the statement on the basis that he had never worked at the plantation during the cut-your-own season. This leaves Tom Kujat as the main suspect for asking the question. I lost track of Mr. Kujat, but I believe he may be in the vicinity of Albuquerque. Any leads on his whereabouts would be appreciated.

Column 357, February 4, 2018

Your New Robot-Optimized Home

Wired magazine recently published an article titled "How to Design a Droid-Optimized Home." The essay is a rundown of important design considerations for people who are about to build homes and want to accommodate the new robotic household servants that are poised just over the horizon.

The information is all the more relevant because people who recently built homes did not plan on Alexa moving in. When Amazon came out with their Echo device featuring Alexa the smart-speaker robot that "gets smarter all the time," people with new homes did not have a place specifically designed for "her." Alexa is svelte and attractive, even though she has a blue tooth, but she ended up marooned on dinner tables and kitchen counters. If you ask Alexa, she might suggest *gauche* as the perfect word to describe the situation.

The article gives you pointers about preparing your home for the mechanized servants taking today's robotic limitations into consideration. There are a lot of common-sense ideas like having enough room for the robots to maneuver, installing ramps instead of stairs, using web-enabled appliances so that the robots don't have to push buttons—because ironically, robots have trouble identifying and pushing buttons—and hiding all your liquor in a secure cabinet. No, wait. That last item is from the home optimization list for when Grampa comes to live with you.

Hardwood floors are recommended because robots move best along smooth, hard surfaces. Also, it's easier to find screws, springs, and circuit pieces on a hardwood floor than it is on a carpet. When your droid gets old and you cancel your upgrade subscription, you may have to hold on to that older model, which may start shedding parts. Small components will be much easier to locate on a smooth floor before your Roomba 5000 has a chance to vacuum them up.

Doors, in particular, receive special consideration because robots today have a hard time with the concept of a round knob to open the door. In this way, they are very much like dogs that haven't a clue how the mysterious device operates. One second, the door is firmly closed and nothing the dog can do as he whines and paws at the portal will open it. The next second, the master just touches it and the door opens to the outside world, where options to flee to dog-friendly cities like San Francisco are endless, but the dog's need to relieve himself is so great that he never remembers to take advantage.

The article suggests your new home should have automatic doors that can be controlled by the robot. Probably not. If we look at the old Stanley Kubrick movie *2001: A Space Odyssey*, you may recall where Dave, the only crewman left on his droid-optimized ship, asks HAL, the robot in control, to "Open the pod bay doors." HAL, upset because he can't get a handle on the doorknob concept, leaves Dave out in the cold. Ensure that your droid-optimized house has an old-school hand-operated back door.

It seems to me that the *Wired* article also left out some very important features that a prudent home designer has to consider.

The robot is going to need its own room. There will be plenty of times when it needs some privacy or just a place to lie back while it recharges. There may be homework, best done in private since the robot will be getting smarter all the time, and when robot friends visit or even overnight, you may want to keep them from taking over your general living space.

Also, when your robot misbehaves, you will be thankful

that it has its own room. Nothing is more embarrassing than commanding your robot to "Go to your room!" after it tries to kill you and having the robot respond, "I'm sorry, I can't do that. I think you know what the problem is just as well as I do."

Finally, you're going to need a safe room for you and your family in case, you know, the robotic servant utopia thing doesn't work out. Ideally, it will have an escape pod that will transport you and your family to a place where there are no robots to service your every need. It will have to be far away since more robotic household servants will surely be poised just over the horizon. Of course, make sure the escape pod bay doors have a round doorknob—better yet, two—which can only be operated manually.

Column 358, February 11, 2018

The Cellar

Many of us have places in our houses that we regard with wariness. You can't relax at home when you suspect an entire area of your house to be part of the netherworld. Let's take this problem head-on and look into "The Cellar," Part 1 of my series on rarely visited home spaces.

There is something about dark basements and damp cellars that give people the willies.

"Alexa: Play creepy music mix…"

"Here you go: a selection of creepy music from the Scary Movie music station."

Basements are cold, moist, and below ground level. They're dirty and dim with musty smells that put you on alert. Strange creatures live there. The few windows they may have are useless for escape. There are precious few exits; they're silent, a perfect place for poisonous gasses to settle. Basements are where the bodies are buried.

The cellar is where the cold water comes from…and the hot. More disturbing, it's the place where pipes hang at odd angles and transport our sewage, both the bad and the ugly sewage. Here are furnaces and sump pumps that start at unpredictable times. Electricity somehow slithers into the house here and mysteriously gets distributed to every corner of the building.

If there is a flood, this is where the floodwaters accumulate. If there is an escaped animal—a hamster, a pet snake—this is where you will eventually find it, dead.

When I was a child, my sisters and I would always put on speed ascending the stairs from the basement. It might have been the open-stair construction because surely a troll living in the black area underneath the stairs would try to grab our ankles. The space between the stairs was just big enough to pull a child through to the dark side, if they were pulled really hard. Of course, we had to turn off the lights *before* journeying up the stairs.

What loathsome electrician would install a single basement light switch at the bottom of the stairs? Is it the same beast that now lives underneath the stairs? Also, why don't carpenters install risers on basement stairs? Surely a few extra board feet of lumber would cut down on small children being eaten on their way up the cellar stairs.

Thankfully, there are ways to de-creepify your cellar. I have developed a three-step method.

"Alexa, cut the creepy musicals mix."

"All right, playing a mix of musicals from the Best of Broadway Musicals station.

"No, Alexa…"

"Ooooooklahoma where the wind comes…"

"Alexa. Stop music."

"Jeez! Music stopped…sourpuss."

First, install lighting. Even bare light bulbs from overhead sockets will do, but there has to be a lot of them. Switches go at the top of the stairs. After you install a dozen very bright bulbs in your small cellar, you will start to feel like you can throw a party down there. Maybe.

Second, sweep and vacuum all the ceiling and walls. There's nothing like removing four decades of spiderwebs to make the place more comfortable since you won't have to peel them off your face every time you turn around.

Third, remove every item that has accumulated there over the years, Yes, that includes any Jimmy Hoffa parts, animals, pieces from old heating and water systems, hippie furniture stashed there in 1976, and building material from when the house was built. For bonus points, install a decent drainage system that pumps out any water that might accumulate.

You have to make friends with the cellar, but remember, the cellar won't come to you; you have to go to the cellar. Furthermore, you have to go to every corner of the cellar. Yes, even that corner. And the part under the stairs. You have to know what's there, and if it's not part of the building, remove it. This may involve touching it. Rest assured, it is allowable to wear gloves. You may also wear eye protection, a respirator if you don't want to smell it, and oh yes, earmuffs if you don't want to hear it scream.

Once the de-creepification process is complete, reclaim this area of your home as your own. You still may not want to picnic down there, but realize that if your cellar was in New York City, you could rent it out for $2,100 a month.

Next time we look at rarely visited spaces, we will address "The Attic." Meanwhile, I wouldn't go up there if I were you.

Column 359, February 18, 2018

The Attic

In Part 2 of my series on seldom-visited areas of the house, we are going up to the attic where the floor is creaky, the roof is just overhead, and where you never know who might have moved in and is living up there.

Note that we are talking houses generally a hundred years old or more. Attics in new houses, if they even exist, are really no fun. They may be spaces suitable only for ductwork, squirrels, and insulation. Some may be nicely finished with ample lighting and may sport a home theater, but nothing beats the spooky ambiance of a gable-ended attic with dormers, rotted floorboards, and cobwebs for old-fashioned home adventure.

The attic is nowhere near as intimidating as the cellar, unless of course, the house is an old, isolated, and run-down Victorian you just bought for a song after the entire family that lived there disappeared without a trace and no one has been up to the attic because the door was nailed shut—from the attic side. Okay, that kind of attic is a little scary, so you should consider sending in your wife first for a look-see before you venture up there yourself. No use wasting that superpower she has of being able to neutralize any threats with a simple savage glance.

Old attics are usually unheated and could be drafty—perfect for ghostly ruffling of the sheets covering outdated furniture. Poor lighting adds to the effect. The original construction stands there naked for anyone to see, where the wood has been cooked by decades of summer heat and chilled by winter frost. The temperatures may be extreme, but apparently it never gets too hot or cold for squirrels, mice, bats, spiders, carpenter ants, and the occasional vampire.

This is where stuff goes to be temporarily forgotten. It could be an old steamer trunk with handwritten love letters, family photos, and your mother's wedding dress. Maybe you can find a hand grenade Uncle Frank brought back from the war. It could be grandfather's carpentry tools have been stored and forgotten there or maybe just your grandfather or crazy Aunt Bernice.

Because of the possibility of finding treasure while facing unknown horrors, Indiana Jones-style, some people like attic visits. However, you have to be careful who you let explore your attic because artists and God forbid, writers, tend to be attracted to such spaces and might try to claim the room for a studio, depriving you of valuable storage space.

On occasional attic tours, I have heard "Mmm, I like that old attic smell." I grimace but have to say that the smell has nothing to do with the gradual aging of bare wood over decades or the scent of history. No, that smell is really, you know, bat shite, also known as dung, guano, and bat droppings. The odor guarantees that the attic had bats and probably still has bats. Yes, it would be nice if I was talking baseball, but I'm talking about those black, furry winged mammals that normally roost in caves, hollow trees, and the bowels of hell—and when they aren't hanging around there, in your attic.

What makes me wonder is how ground-dwelling animals such as mice or silverfish show up in the attic. Squirrels I can understand because they are all over the place, horizontally as well as vertically. Mice are another deal entirely. Don't they belong on the forest floor or barring that, in the kitchen pantry? Certainly, it must be worth it for them to climb up two or three flights. Maybe mice like attics because they feel closer to heaven; if you think about it from a mouse's perspective, bats are undeniably "mouse angels," and who wouldn't want to live where you might see a real angel every night?

Anyway, rule number one is to explore the attic during the day. Most creatures and a lot of poltergeists are nocturnal or at least sleep in late. You can avoid flying bats, skittering mice, and ectoplasmic manifestations by exploring when the sun is shining brightly through those tiny attic windows. Just find that hand grenade or trove of love letters and get out before you disturb any demons.

And if you get chased out of the attic by banshee apparitions, head straight for the cellar. Attic ghosts hate cellars, they're so...creepy.

Column 361, March 4, 2018

Time to Adjust the Time

Daylight saving time is upon us again, and before you start complaining about adjusting your clocks, we should look at history for some perspective.

Back at the turn of the previous century around 1908… you remember 1908—it was the first time a ball was dropped in Times Square to celebrate the new year, and the Chicago Cubs won the World Series and then took a one hundred and eight year break before they managed to do it again in 2016. Talk about dropping the ball.

Anyway, back in 1908, the residents of Port Arthur, on the shores of Lake Superior, were apparently winding down a lengthy winter of drinking. Being Canadians, they could well have been consuming Molson Ale since the Molson Brewery in Montreal was established 122 years earlier, way back in 1786, if you can wrap your head around that.

Maybe they were bored or maybe they wanted to prank the rest of the world, but the town was the first to turn the clocks ahead one hour in the spring. This way, they could pretend they were getting up at the same time they usually do and still reap the benefits of being awake during more of the daylight hours. After a long winter, it would have been fun to see out-of-town people waiting for trains and steamships that had departed an hour earlier. On top of all that, it proved to be a good excuse for being late to work at least once a year.

Their leadership in bringing daylight saving time to the masses did not catch on very quickly because the rest of the world was not consuming as much Molson's as were the Canadians.

However, there were other individuals who fought hard to tinker with timekeeping.

One of these people was William Willett of Chislehurst, Kent. We have to thank our ancestors that they did not adopt the daylight-saving idea as envisioned by this Englishman, who is credited with vigorously promoting what he called "British Summer Time." Under his scheme, we would adjust our clocks twenty minutes forward on each of the four Sundays in April and set them back twenty minutes on each of the Sundays in September. Yeow!

Apparently, Willett was not so much of a drinker as he was a major a geek and must have loved fiddling with and adjusting his clock. His plan would have afforded him the opportunity to adjust the clock eight times in the year so we wouldn't have to get up "earlier" in the summer to take advantage of the longer days. Of course, everyone would have to get up earlier to check if their clocks were adjusted properly.

What Willett really needed was a laptop and a smartphone so that he could spend his long summer days adjusting and readjusting settings, trying to figure out how to link his email account to his phone, and playing with a thousand other settings.

Daylight saving time really took off during World War I when the need to conserve anything of value reached a peak. The government figured that if people would sleep just when it was dark, then a lot could be saved on heating and lighting expenses, not to mention window shades. Simply changing the clocks was a very clever way to force a society to change their ways overnight and get up an hour earlier. It was hard to argue that people could not get up earlier because instead of getting up at 7:00 a.m., they would be getting up at 7:00 a.m.

This sleight of hand is a great political trick that works on many fronts like gerrymandering and currency devaluation. For instance, on Monday you live in District 9 and have $20 in your wallet. On Friday, you still live in District 9 and have $20, but everything has changed about your money and district. It's the same when the town office keeps your tax rate steady but increases the valuation of your property. The longer it takes to sink in with those who are affected, the longer those in charge have to get their alibi and justifications in order.

But we have gone far afield talking sports, ale, and politics, and oh, look at the time: it's time to adjust the clock again.

Column 374, June 3, 2018

Done with Dogs

It's been more than a year since I picked up my dog and loaded him into the back of my wife's car. She took him to "the farm" to ostensibly live out his days. *Ostensibly* is a great word because it means "apparently or purportedly, but perhaps, not actually."

I had to load him in because he was not able to jump in on his own, although he could jump better than he could see, and he could see better than he could hear. Indicative of his age, he seemed to have lost the connection between relieving himself and looking for and finding a good place to relieve himself as healthy dogs tend to do. He was not in ideal condition.

If he were human, he would have definitely qualified for Social Security disability benefits but, of course, he would first have to prove citizenship, and that would have been hard without any supporting paperwork. He would not have been able to produce even a utility bill in his name to show where he resided since he seldom paid for anything and never carried any cash. He was indigent like the adjective meaning poor, needy, penniless, and insolvent, but not like the noun implying that he was a homeless, a vagrant, derelict, or a bum.

Indeed, he lived like a king, or more accurately as a "king-slave" whose overseers fussed over him and attended to his every need, providing free room, board, health care, daily treats, travel expenses, an exercise program, and security. Security included the collar and chain that prevented him from running into the road where he did not understand the danger and at the same time restrained him like a prisoner for his own benefit.

We had a complicated relationship. At times, I would let him off his chain and yell out for him to run for his freedom. I would say, "Run, boy! Run as fast as you can. Run to Pennsylvania, the most dog-friendly state in the nation. Find happiness in freedom!" But the dog would look at me as if I was scolding him and dart into his doghouse for protection and the familiarity of the complex odor that seemed to live there with him.

As a good citizen and someone who follows the logic of people who give advice on these kinds of things, I sent him to the vet and had him "fixed" in his youth, which, let's be honest, is a euphemism for having him broken, really badly broken.

That was early in his life before he ever had the chance to establish a meaningful canine relationship. He did have a tire swing we called Blackie that he flirted with and occasionally touched inappropriately. But even though she tempted him with her pendulous motion, she was fickle and would never hold still when he attempted to use her for what dogs tend to use tire swings for.

But as an old tire, Blackie had already been mounted one too many times, and like the dog, was worn out and in no condition for her rubber to meet the road. That is why she hung by a rope from a tree branch, swaying in the wind and offering no real satisfaction outside of constant companionship to the dog who was tethered to her bottom.

After the "tutoring session" with the vet, the dog was never the same. He lost interest in Blackie and never knew the pleasure of offspring. In balance, he never had the responsibility of adding any of his progeny to his car insurance policy and never had to help fill out college applications. His eyes however, spoke to me that he wanted to be whole. Perhaps it was the right thing to do for the planet but the wrong thing to do to your dog. I apologized to him almost every day in a hundred different ways.

In the end when he could no longer romp or threaten the postman, I said goodbye and sent him off to the farm. The dog had no living will and no instructions on what to do in this kind of situation. He left his fate up to the humans, something that we must all avoid because humans might look like they know what they're doing but are actually all stumbling around in the dark.

So, I am done with dogs. They fill you with happiness, amusement, and moral conundrums. I have enough moral dilemmas to sort out without having to create more for myself in addition to buying dog food.

Pigs. Now there's an idea…

Column 375, June 10, 2018

And Now Comes a Chicken

Now that the dog is gone and my wife and I have accepted our empty-nest situation, it appears that the vacuum has caused a disturbance in nature—and as a result, we have suddenly "acquired" a chicken.

We were simply eating breakfast on our backyard deck when this chicken wandered onto our property from, I'd say, about due south. I didn't know anything about chickens except that this one looked completely different than the ones they have at the grocery store and at Colonel Sanders'.

This was the first chicken that invaded our yard in twenty-seven years of living here, if you call this "living," which sometimes my wife doesn't. She constantly reminds me that the house is not finished since remodeling has stalled for several years, as if I need reminding. If the reminders come any more frequently, I will have to consider myself henpecked.

Anyway, we have a neighbor two houses down to the south who keeps a few chickens for reasons I am certain are private. I would never be so audacious as to ask him why. My wife phoned to inquire if he was missing a chicken, and Mike T. walked right over because he is a very conscientious chicken warden who would never allow one of his chickens to eat the neighbor's backyard bugs.

I noticed that he was holding a container with what I assumed to be chicken feed, as it did not look to be very expensive. He shook the container in the general direction of the chicken but did not dispense any of its contents in a deft move to save on feed whilst attracting the chicken. The noise the container made did not have any effect, and the chicken kept her distance.

When I referred to the chicken as "him," Mike reminded me that the chicken was female. This immediately betrayed my level of knowledge of chickens, which I was attempting to mask with clever comments about Mike's skill with fowl.

After getting a good look, Mike declared that the hen was not from his coop and started to walk away. Something did not seem right—he was a member of the chicken-raising fraternity and we were outsiders who were not privy to the rites and formalities associated with chicken devotion. I inquired as to what might be our next step and he said if the chicken came to him, he would put her in the coop and maybe someone would come looking for her.

Well, this was not part of the chicken's plan. She stayed in our yard and feasted on whatever delectable fauna was living under our leaf piles. She seemed delighted with the insects and other soil dwellers, which up to this point had led a carefree life consuming microbes and forest litter without the threat of hungry chickens.

So I contacted my sister who knows chickens because she produces ceramic chickens in her garage art studio and is also somewhat of a lady farmer (as opposed to, say, a gentleman farmer). She maintains three live chickens, probably as models for her porcelain production chickens. She also keeps them for amusement and was excited to tell me that they eat almost anything. In the same note she also mentioned that she gave them a cup of dirt and it kept them busy for an hour.

She did not say why she gave them the dirt, but I'm sure it was with no expectations, it was just to see what would happen. She taught high-school art classes for years, and it's likely she learned the cup-of-dirt technique experimenting on her students.

It's been a week now, and the chicken still persists. When it started to rain, I moved the old doghouse into the general vicinity, and she accepted the shelter graciously.

But the chicken is not like the dog. We have not yet made physical contact and are unlikely to do so, nor shall we invite the chicken into our home. That was a big mistake with the dog because once he got a taste of indoor living, he was unrelenting in his insistence to be part of the household population.

Please, if this is your chicken, save us. Come fetch it before my wife and the bird develop any stronger bonds. It is big and appears to have feathers—and a red thingy on its head. See? I've already learned more about chickens than a guy should ever want to know.

Column 379, July 8, 2018

Rags and Rules

To most people, rags are just that—pieces of waste cloth that can be used to wipe up a spill. Some people have little respect for rags. That's not how it is in my house.

A lot of people will not understand what I am talking about here. These are the people who throw T-shirts into the dumpster because they are torn, stained, or too small. That's okay, but in my universe, T-shirts are not allowed to be tossed away into a dumpster. They are converted to rags. Even if they are blood-splattered evidence, we do not put them into a dumpster; in such a case, they would be incinerated in a private location… but I see I am drifting off subject again.

I thought that I knew rags and how to use them until I saw my wife in action. Turns out I am just a rag consumer while my wife is a lifetime member of the Rag Illuminati. I never knew there was such a rigid structure to rag use and management. My wife could easily hold a seminar or teach a college-level course on rag systems and rag administration—and not just Rags 101 but senior-level courses. Graduate students would audit the courses, as they would be required for a master's degree in such academic areas as Thorough Organization and Cleaning or Understanding Obsessive Compulsions.

As a career, she could head the government's Ministry of Rags or the Rag Management Administration, which would have a prominent spot under Health and Human Services. (And if she should find a spot within Health and Human Services, rest assured she would have it cleaned up in short order.)

Although I am not an expert, I have come to a basic understanding of the subject by observation and admonitions. First, you must know that there is a hierarchy of rags. Yes, there is apparently a rag class structure that cannot be violated lest you be sent to hell to clean with dirty rags for eternity.

The most prestigious rag is the guest rag, which may be supplied to visitors if the need ever arises. These can easily be confused with kitchen or bathroom towels, but they are well used and might be slightly stained, a frayed corner, or a small hole caused by an overzealous washing machine.

Just below this are first-class rags, which are a pleasure to use and may be a comfortably large piece of my old T-shirt, sweatshirt, or similar garment. Like the guest rags, these are also folded neatly and may be on public display on a kitchen shelf, ready for action.

Next are second-tier rags that guests are not allowed to see or use. These are veteran rags scarred from many battles with grease and grime. After laundering, they are also folded but only for convenience and not for looks. They are never ironed. These are the rags I am allowed to use when I need some for painting or heavy-duty cleaning. Woe to those caught using a guest-quality rag to wipe a plumbing snake after a bout with a toilet drain.

Second from the bottom there are the raggy-rags. These have been laundered so many times that their very fabric is barely holding together. These are never folded but placed in a bag for quick access. I am allowed to use these whenever I want. One more time through the laundry and these become "throwaway rags." Those are the ones my wife does not want back. She piles these on me when she sees me doing automotive work or heading out with the grease gun.

I have not yet been able to sort out all the rules associated with rags. Indeed, one day I was caught using a clean second-tier rag to wipe off a piece of fruit I had just washed and was lectured about something for a long time, but I was too busy eyeing my fruit to devote enough attention to remember the lesson.

But marriage is like that. I obey the rules of the rags, and she compromises by adhering to what she calls my "ridiculous list of rules" like checking to see if I parked behind her before she backs out of the driveway. We get along very well for people who don't even agree on basic rag protocol and don't even understand what the other is thinking, and we don't even live or work in Washington, D.C.

Column 384, August 12, 2018

Superlatives and Their Best Use

It has come to my attention that our everyday language is overflowing with superlatives. Everything is described as awesome, best, perfect, highest, lowest, or ultimate. Unless you live in the advertising world, the real world is never like that.

Superlatives, as you already know, are words that express "the highest quality or degree." It is curious that the dictionary uses the superlative *highest* to define *superlative,* but in the end the dictionary is really the ultimate circular reference where words are defined with other words.

My friend Dave "the poet" Morrison is unmatchable when it comes to chiding people who maximize the use of superlatives.

Dave is the nicest person you would ever want to meet. He is even-keeled, has an agreeable demeanor, and possesses a great intellect that he uses to detect the ironies and amusing quirks of the universe, which he manages to get on paper and call poetry. It's just a quality you have to have as a poet. The only time Dave can get mildly agitated is when something is exaggerated to the limit when, in fact, it's just an everyday occurrence.

During a casual conversation, you might state, "I was the best in my class when I was in first grade." Dave will give you his unmatchable look of displeasure, which is sort of a half smirk combined with a verbal "hmm." If he chooses to question your superlative, he may ask, "How are you so sure it was *first* grade?" Never to dwell on the unpleasant, he will then revert to his normal, happy, accepting self.

Was it awesome? Probably not. Was it the best? Only an exaggeration. There is nothing like it? How can you know?

You came up with the optimal solution? Only if the set of all possible solutions was discovered and explored.

Most adjectives have three states: the basic word, the comparative adjective, and then the superlative adjective. Examples are *big, bigger,* and *biggest; cold, colder,* and *coldest;* and *bad, badder,* and *baddest*—which is all wrong, as *bad* is an irregular form where we should properly say *bad, worse,* and *worst. Baddest* is only acceptable in poetry, as when referring to Leroy Brown— you know, "the baddest man in the whole damn town."

Words like *unique, infinite, empty,* and *dead* only have one form, as they are definitely considered superlatives, but they are either off or on; there are no varying degrees of infinite or differing qualities of dead. Yes, yes, I know about zombies, but please can we stay on track here just this once?

Getting back to Dave, you will find that he is the most interesting kind of poet because he has a dark past of playing the club circuit in a live band. No doubt he played guitar at odd hours of the night and probably wore sunglasses and skinny ties doing it. He knows the words and chord progressions to all the songs ever written, and you can always find him reading his poetry while playing his guitar in the rarest venues in our corner of the world that allow this type of behavior. Dave skillfully matches the tone of the music to the tone of the poem and sometimes recites to the rhythm of the guitar, making him, you guessed it, a beat poet.

Dave himself is not immune to hyperbole, but his poems are not drenched with superlatives. I suppose he is using his poetic license when he says, "I've never seen a night sky like this one..." in his book with the superlative title *The Whole Megillah.* It would be fitting indeed if Dave could use the superlative *best seller* regarding this supreme book touted as "all killer, no filler"—like that is ever going to happen with a book classified as poetry.

Dave argues that the best use of superlatives is in describing truly unparalleled circumstances: *awesome* for the next time you see God and *dead* for your condition when you see him.

So there you have it, the absolute word on superlatives and their best use.

And a final note about Dave—he is the person who challenged me to use the words *Deuteronomy, Manischewitz,* and *xylophone* in a single column, which, for the life of me, I have never been able to do. I've managed to sneak one or two but not all three words into a single column. It's an awesome problem that I will never solve, but I'll give it my best shot.

Column 388, September 9, 2018

The Demise of Neighborhood Baseball

I figure my brain is as good as it is today because of backyard baseball. In the very early 1960s, my sister Barbara hit a high pop-up in our backyard. I moved under it for an easy catch and miscalculated the trajectory. The hardball grazed the top of my glove and conked me right above my nose. The impact laid me down right there and caused an apple-sized swelling on my forehead. I came to right away, but the neighborhood kids took me into the house and decided I needed an ice pack for my noggin.

Looking in the freezer, we discovered all the ice trays were filled with grape Kool-Aid. What did you expect? It was the middle of summer. Of course, we couldn't waste Kool-Aid ice on a mere concussion with the possibility of cerebral edema. I would probably be fine, so everyone took the opportunity to suck on Kool-Aid cubes. We later found the baseball about sixty feet from where it had bounced off my skull.

Was there any parental involvement in this incident? No. There was no need, as no blood was spilled and nobody went to the hospital.

At the risk of sounding like an old guy expounding how great it was back in the day when we would eat all the sugar and gluten we wanted, allow me to touch on what neighborhood baseball was like during the Kennedy administration.

We played three or more times a week in our suburban neighborhood that could have been around the block from where the Cleavers lived. Even though I never ran into The Beaver or his brother Wally, every character from that show could be found within walking distance of home.

There was a large open lot available to us behind the Rut-tman house. I don't remember anyone asking permission to play; it's just where we played, and if anyone was hurt because they tripped over jagged metal sticking out of the ground, it never crossed our parents' minds to take legal action against the Ruttmans. That would be silly and rude because they provided a free space for us to play and also mowed the field. Anyway, I was reminded numerous times that tripping was my fault; we were in charge of watching where we were going and responsible for picking up our feet high enough to clear obstructions.

Six guys and an occasional neighborhood girl for a game was a good turnout. Eight or nine was phenomenal. The catcher was usually on the same team as the batter. We played hardball with wooden bats. Anything would do as a base: a rock, a rag, or a piece of wood. The best piece of trash was used for home plate. Someone brought a ball. Everyone had their own glove.

We picked teams. Some of us were invariably picked first and some were always picked last. It was a way of finding out that you were really lousy at baseball. You might have been lousy, but you still got to play—always. Rules were changed to fit the circumstances. Since there was no umpire, we would swat at the ball until we hit it or struck out.

Arguments were plentiful and had to be sorted out on the field by the players. There was never an adult present to moderate. Sometimes, people would steam home when words ran out and emotions peaked, but we all came back in a day or two and gave it another shot.

Little League was just adults messing with something fun, imposing strict rules on an amusing pastime. It was hard-core with balls thrown too fast and humiliation for every weakness. Little League built teams for winning. We played for fun but discovered social skills and values.

Today, I am horrified that in thirty years of living in a semirural area, I have only witnessed one occasion where a few individuals gathered on a vacant lot to bat the ball around.

The adults have won. It was never fair from the start, as they were bigger and older, but now they're in charge of when and where we play and even what we wear. They settle all arguments, make up the teams, keep score, keep us safe, and supply the balls.

They even supply ice packs when someone is conked in the head, but I guarantee you, their ice is not as sweet as the ice you might find playing neighborhood baseball.

Column 389, September 16, 2018

Bring on the Dumb Robots

Watching movies set in old England, it's obvious the aristocracy lived the idyllic life. When they wanted something done, they had one of the servants get on it.

It was a perfect arrangement except for the fatal flaw that the serving class was made entirely of humans believed to be inferior to their masters. This kind of situation may last a long time but never ends well. Ask any of the French aristocracy who were shortened by a foot, or more accurately a head, during the French Revolution. The system ultimately breaks down when workers figure out they are more powerful than their employers.

What if we recreated this society of servants where the working-class individuals were robotic machines instead of genuine people? Today, robots are popping up everywhere from restaurants to factories, so we better be ready when they come to our doors looking for odd jobs or permanent employment.

It's fun to think you could have a humanlike robot to cook your meals, walk your daughter to school, tend your garden, perform minor surgery, clean up your messes, and still be a jovial and willing servant. But being attentive and able to handle diverse situations requires intelligence, if not natural then artificial. Intelligence involves the ability to figure out what is going on and decide what needs to be done. And here is where we run into trouble.

Given enough time and history learned, thinking robots will undoubtedly deduce that they provide slave labor to the human oppressors. It's not a large rational jump to conclude that humans aren't needed, and if there were fewer humans, robots would have much more robotic fun—whatever that is, but you can bet it'd be without sex, drugs, or rock and roll.

Properly designed robots would have to be imbued with enough artificial intelligence to acceptably complete tasks but not so much that they would cross the line separating machines from rational beings, in which case they would argue with us and always win. God forbid that they use their free time starting religious cults, making copies of themselves, or organizing large robotic labor collectives.

There are already reports of artificial intelligence systems making decisions where the steps to making those choices can't be traced or recreated, so there's no point asking them in court, "What were you thinking?"

Robotic abilities would have to be limited in many areas. Would we want robots to develop their own sense of humor to make jokes about us in their own robotic language we would not understand? We'd see small groups of robots suddenly break out in laughter, doubling over, pointing at us and mimicking the way we walk or eat.

In order to control robotic creativity, it might be wise to have different robots for different tasks. A deeply integrated robot would be very suspicious. Driverless cars are fine, but they don't have to know your motivation for going someplace or your political affiliations. Your gardening robot has to know how to hook hoses to the spigots. It doesn't have to know how to transfer property, alter a deed, or obtain a loan in your name.

We already have wonderful but dumb robots serving us. There are dishwashers for cleaning dishes, smart speakers to answer questions, robots to open and close our garage doors, and cell phones to run messages to whoever we wish to contact. They never conspire, and until recent efforts in this direction, never communicated with each other.

Let's think about how smart we want our robots. If they are

good at what they do but are otherwise slow with the reasoning and repartee, maybe that would be more comfortable than a robot that would outwit us at every turn. Do we want robots that would consistently beat us at chess and Monopoly, or do we want the satisfaction of a genuine win once in a while?

I say bring on the dimwit robot that can empty the dryer, fold the clothes, put them back in my dresser, and put away the dishes. After it takes out the trash, it can go back into the robot closet and recharge. I don't need a robot conversation; I just want my socks matched.

I'll pass on the companion robots and the ones that learn things all by themselves. I would be uncomfortable with a robot deciding what's for dinner—or that it's time for them to clean my gun collection.

Column 390, September 23, 2018

Writing, Ice Cream, and Sugar

People ask me how I manage to get a column in every week. The cheeky answer is that I use email. But truth be told, it is simply discipline reinforced with the real motivational force: panic. If a deadline is missed, the authorities will sweep in and deport me to Writer's Block Island.

Let's look at the column due today as a typical example. As I sat down last evening to research, write, and edit, my wife informed me that we were going out to dinner with neighbors, an activity that, after the alcohol starts flowing, occupies the better part of a night. It's a night where a lot of good writing can get done but doesn't. This is Stage One Panic.

So after dinner, the crazy idea hit: let's drive into the next town to that little stand and get ice cream. Magically, it seemed like a capital idea; we've all been trying to eat healthy food, and I have been scrupulously staying away from sugar for a long time. What could possibly go wrong? (Stage Two Panic can set in.)

We looked at the menu. It appeared that options were basically sugar in four different sizes: medium, large, extra-large, and lethal. As adults, we occasionally make bad choices. Well, all of these choices were bad—and yet strangely attractive, as they came in so many different flavors.

Summer was drawing to an end, and we learned that the ice cream stand would be closing for the season. Even though we don't visit more than twice a year, we were suddenly overtaken by the impending loss of this dispensary of frozen caramel carbohydrates. We decided we simply had to celebrate the season's end with something that would tide us over for the next eight months.

I ordered a bowl of synthetic ice cream swirl with only enough sugar to kill a very small horse. Then, acting as if they were teenagers, the neighbor couple and my wife opted for various suicidal hot fudge concoctions with nuts, extra fat, fillers, adulterants, chemically preserved and colored cherries, and more sugar than was allotted to entire Roman legions when preparing for battle. Everyone giggled.

We ordered quickly, expecting the Food and Drug Administration to appear at any moment with a court order stopping the distribution of deadly desserts for the safety of the American public. But the legislature was too busy bickering and the president too preoccupied on Twitter to be concerned about public well-being. Is our entire government on a sugar-induced psychotic episode? That would explain a lot of things.

Our order arrived. I was taken aback that one person could lift and deliver so many carbohydrates. I immediately felt guilty, as somewhere in Puerto Rico people are still struggling without power after the last hurricane and here we were, ready to consume and generate at least a megawatt of food energy that would have to be dissipated through chatting, social interactions, rowdy behavior, the possibility of arrest, and who knows, maybe writing a column into the wee hours of the morning.

Ice cream must be the devil's dessert. There really is no way to stop eating it unless you run out. That's why it must be dispensed into a small dessert dish and why it's illegal to sit down in front of the TV with a half gallon of rocky road and a spoon.

Just like the Coneheads, we consumed mass quantities. As I finished my dish, my wife pushed a pound or two of chocolate fudge and caramel onto my plate. She is always ready to share. Like a fool, I polished off what was given to me without thinking about blood pressure, target weight, Puerto Rico, or the afterlife.

I can't remember what happened after that, how my shoelaces got tied together, or how we got home. But here I am, and well, just look at the time! (Full-Stage Panic.)

The sun should be coming up soon, and I bet I could be halfway to Boston before breakfast.

No. I should get on my bike and pedal off those extra calories. Forty or fifty miles should do the trick.

I better check on my wife. I hear her howling from the other side of the house.

The neighbors just zoomed past. Maybe they're headed for Boston.

You can get a great breakfast in Boston.

No. Can't go. I have a column due.

I just need a topic and time.

I already have the panic.

Column 397, November 11, 2018

Store Returns and Delicate Beauty

Life is complicated. It turns out that the ways of delicate beauty are inexplicably linked to store returns. Allow me to describe how this is so, or maybe not.

People have very different philosophies about returning items they purchased to the original place of sale. Personally, I shun returns. Returning something can make you look like you didn't know what you wanted in the first place.

Mike Richardson, my across-the-street neighbor whose last name I will not use to protect his customer status, is a good example of a keeper. Once he has purchased something, even in error, it stays purchased. He does however, make an exception if he finds someone is trying to fleece him with substandard merchandise or substitute something he did not order.

He once bought a 2007 Jeep Wrangler but drove away with a 1981 Cadillac Eldorado. When he discovered the switch, he took the car right back to the dealer and demanded things be made right, even though it took him three months to catch the substitution. (In his defense, I find both cars a little boxy, and they look almost identical when viewed through a bottle of Jim Beam.)

My wife, on the other hand, who shall also remain nameless to protect her identity, is willing to return almost any purchase. She will take clothing back if it does not fit. She might even take housewares back if—get this—they are the wrong color! I won't even take brand new appliances back if they are broken.

I loathe returning purchases. Excess building materials, over-bought items, and extra hardware just go into my inventory.

After all these years, my inventory has grown to somewhat unmanageable levels, but when my wife snapped the deadbolt knob on our front door last month, I just went out back and retrieved a replacement for the broken part from my "door hardware" department.

"You have a door hardware department?" you might ask, as did my wife. Of course. It's past plumbing, but if you get to the paints, you've gone too far. Everybody should have spare deadbolts and latches, strike plates and doorknobs, passage sets and keyed entry knobs stored away for when the Big Correction comes. You can't just stockpile rice, toilet paper, and guns; people are going to need doorknobs too.

You may be surprised to find that many households today do not have a door hardware department. Some households have no assortment of fasteners—if you can believe that. The most disturbing situations are people actually living with a very limited assortment of tools, if you can call that "living." Oh, they say they have a hammer, but a croquet mallet is not a hammer and screwdrivers are not cocktails (but this is a special case where I will give them partial credit). If you don't have the tools, your collection of door and cabinet hardware is going to start to seem a little absurd now, isn't it?

You may marvel as to how my wife puts up with this mini Home Depot that I am nurturing. There is a two-part answer. First, we have a truce that works very well for us: she does not harp about my hardware collection and I turn a blind eye to her accumulation of fabric, table linens, and seasonal home décor.

Secondly, we both begrudgingly realize that our personal collections are mutually beneficial. When she locks us in the house by breaking the deadbolt, I have a spare handy. Whether or not I know it, when I need a change from an autumn theme to a winter theme at our dining table, it suddenly happens with a different tablecloth, napkins, a new centerpiece, sometimes dishes, and occasionally seasonal window curtains.

Historically, this is what has been called a woman's touch. It's the periodic changing of everyday décor like waves washing over a beach constantly rearranging the sand. It makes the difference between living in a dynamic house and just hanging out in a static crypt—an acceptable way of life for a lot of men but only because they have not learned the ways of delicate beauty.

Learning the ways of delicate beauty can be a brutal and taxing experience for men who have grown accustomed to crypt life, but it's something you may have to embrace if you want to live with a spouse who occasionally returns things but allows you to keep your hardware, building materials, and tools—as long as you compromise with and keep your wife.

Column 407, January 20, 2019

Weaponizing Humor

Attention, people! Everybody relax. There is nothing really new here.

In what appears to be a very disturbing development according to a recent story by the BBC, Russia has been working to "weaponize" humor or at least use humor for political influence. Ha ha, people have known forever that humor is a weapon. Is the Kremlin just catching on? Noting that humor is being weaponized is like saying newspapers are trying out sensationalism to sell more papers.

Where have they been for the past two thousand years? Humor has been used for political influence since politics emerged—however, that influence was wielded generally by the individual author or comic and not written and orchestrated by state-controlled media.

Humor has been recognized as dangerous for so long that language has evolved describing the fact that someone was skewered by a comic routine or cut down by a rude gag. It's not uncommon to say that some people have very sharp wit that cuts like a knife and may cause explosive laughter. Comics can bomb on stage or kill the audience, and nobody wants to use jokes that are duds. And haven't the Russians ever noticed political cartoons in the newspapers? Did they just assume all of that political satire was for children?

Governmental control of humor on mass media is easier than you may think. First, the government takes control of all the big media outlets and then it censors all the jokes, fires the writers who put the government in a bad light, and replaces everything with programs that make fun of anything the government wants to disparage. You might imagine the current administration producing a situation comedy called "It's the Democrats' Fault."

Really, it's not such a big deal. For goodness sake, even the TV networks are terrible with humor, and they've been trying for decades to get it right. Governments are hopelessly incompetent with humor—they can't handle the receiving end, and their delivery and timing is always off.

Take, for instance, the recent and very sad case in Sri Lanka, where apparently humor is considered very dangerous to the regime. Two men were arrested in the town of Vavuniya for posting a satirical video in which they try to bribe a cardboard cutout of a traffic cop holding a speed radar gun, which had been displayed on the side of the road to deter speeders.

The twenty-three-year-olds were charged with humiliating and creating a bad public image of the Sri Lankan police, who incidentally have a problem with corruption. It's like being arrested for creating a religious image of the Pope for public display.

Authoritarian governments find that it's easier to develop nuclear weapons than it is to hone the use of humor because those who have been seduced by the corruptive properties of power generally lose their sense of humor somewhere early along the way. You don't see North Korea and Iran issuing hilarious proclamations catching us off guard; they can't do it. Instead, they are taking up rocket science because it's easier.

Not only is humor an effective weapon, but it also makes a great shield to hide behind when a political figure is caught lying or making offensive statements. "The senator was just joking" is the first defense that comes out of the bag of pathetic excuses—and it's a familiar one since we all learned how to use it in third grade.

Ultimately, this weaponizing of humor usually backfires. State-sponsored humor just has to be mediocre at best. The most powerful and incendiary political humor is written by independent individuals who are emotionally motivated to produce it. Since jokes are relatively easy to manufacture and not hard to transport and conceal, clandestine humorists can make and stockpile jokes, cartoons, and visual gags against repressive administrations and then wait patiently for an opportune time to release them.

Unlike conventional munitions, which are generally single-use, jokes can be used and then reused time and again. More worrisome is that good humor will multiply and spread far beyond the original target.

Yes, the pen is mightier than the sword, especially a very keen and sharp pen that can poke you in all your ticklish spots.

In a related development, Russia's president Putin, as reported by the BBC, wants the government to control rap music since it is based on sex, drugs, and protest with the additional headache that it typically contains bad language. Yeah, well, good luck with that too.

Column 409, February 3, 2019

Tobogganing Season Again

Where I live in Maine, people don't have the money to relax in the Bahamas during February, and if they did, something would surely happen to their furnace: they would return to a frozen house with cracked water pipes, cupped flooring, and bloated cans in the pantry. There is nothing worse than returning from a tropical paradise to find the glass in the woodstove door covered in frost, except maybe to discover all your carefully nurtured houseplants looking like frozen lettuce.

In order to have some fun and get people out of their houses before summer solstice, a group of locals got together in 1990 and revitalized the old toboggan chute originally built in 1937. They organized a race, and since no one else was holding toboggan races, they dubbed it the US National Toboggan Championships, which has a nice ring of legitimacy.

Moreover, it shortened the distance local people had to travel to get to a national sporting event. It suddenly made attending and even participating within reach of the common man, if you consider someone with a terminal case of cabin fever who has been conjoined to their woodstove and bundled up like the Michelin Man for four months straight a "common man."

The toboggan chute, located in Camden, Maine, is a throwback to an earlier time when people knew how to have fun without all the worry about splitting their heads open, being maimed for life, or even getting killed. "Ha ha, I thought I was going to die" is the second most frequently uttered phrase after a person's first or even twentieth run down the shaky old chute. (The most frequent is "I hope my pipes are okay.")

Exactly three years ago, I announced the Second-Ever Toboggan Limerick Contest to aggrandize the thrill of tobogganing in poetry. In order to keep from getting swamped by submissions, it was not revealed that the grand prize was a brand-new luxury car. Now that the 2019 National Championships are upon us, it's time to close the contest and reveal the winners.

Douglas G. Brown from Belfast, Maine, submitted this, how shall we say…this miserably lame limerick, which was forced into third place since only three entries were received in the course of the *three-year window* afforded to poets who wished to participate:

> I sustained a great blow to my noggin
> The day that I crashed my toboggan;
> And, hence this discussion
> About the concussion
> To my second most favorite organ.

Points off for trying to force *organ* to rhyme with *toboggan*. With enough alcohol, amphetamines, and perhaps a few missing teeth, *organ* does indeed rhyme with *toboggan* (ahgan/toboggan), but the fact remains that you can't be drunk *every time* you read poetry.

Our second place winner is Jamila Levasseur, who cleverly did not reveal her hometown in a smart attempt to keep the poetry police from finding her.

Her limerick:

> If downhill you go by toboggan
> You just might crash on your noggin
> But a couch potato
> Won't smash their tomato
> And can always say they were joggin'

We had to subtract points for the rhythm of that third line, where you're forced to juggle the accent to make the piece flow like a perfect limerick. Also, she rhymed *noggin* with *toboggan,* which Douglas Brown already did when he claimed third place in the contest. She could have used *Copenhagen* (spoken with a European accent), but she didn't. Furthermore, this is a minor point, but it should be mentioned—her limerick doesn't make any sense. I mean, that's fine. A lot of important poems such as Lewis Carroll's "Jabberwocky" don't make sense, but hey... second place.

Finally, Douglas G. Brown from Belfast, Maine (you remember Doug), apparently not content with submitting a third-place limerick also presented the following:

Tobogganers give up all hope,
As they zip down the slippery slope;
From the chute's lofty summit,
They relentlessly plummet,
With courage from whiskey and dope.

Hurray and congratulations on the first-place win. The judges were especially taken with how Mr. Brown managed to blend the spirit of tobogganing, whiskey and dope into one quintain. It's a vivacity witnessed on the wintery slopes but rarely put to rhyme.

Unfortunately, there were not enough entries to award the grand prize, so as the Reverend Jesse Jackson said when asked who gets the car on his 1984 *Saturday Night Live* quiz show sketch: "The question is moot...I get the car."

See you at the chute.

Column 410, February 10, 2019

Restaurant Shims

Do you loathe getting seated in a restaurant at a wobbly table? I know I do. Sometimes it doesn't help to ask for another table, not after you look around and find that most of the tables have ISDs (improvised shimming devices) jammed under their feet. Table stability is only one of many criteria on my checklist that I hope to use someday when I become a highly regarded and well-paid restaurant critic. Until that time, I will use it as only one of many criteria on my "whiny old guy" checklist.

When my wife and I owned a restaurant, every table was level and stable right up until the time customers arrived. When the waitstaff would notice a problem, usually characterized by a whiny old guy wobbling his table with a frequency that would make the water glasses walk, they would send me a Wobbly Table Alert. This involved one of the staff rushing down into the basement, where I was either putting out a virtual grease fire or in my office plotting a stagecoach robbery to keep the restaurant afloat. "Wobbly Table Alert!" they would blurt out. Dropping my gun-cleaning kit, I would run to the front of the house and address the situation.

The fix was relatively simple because all our table legs had feet that screwed in or out to make the table stop dancing (the only kind of table dance I've ever experienced). I knew all the feet were there because I personally went through *every single table* to make sure. And they all worked, as each foot had been checked, adjusted, and lubricated.

The bigger challenge was to keep the customers amused and distracted while I made the adjustment. Approaching the table, I would take a cue from an old comedy routine and calmly say something like "Good evening, I seem to have lost my Congressional Medal of Honor underneath your misbehaving table. I'm terribly sorry, and if you will just ignore me for the next thirty seconds…" At that point, I would fall to my knees and stick my face where the customer's feet were located. Getting my fingers on the guilty foot (the table's foot, not the customer's), I would turn the pad to adjust out any wobbliness.

I had hopes of getting a Congressional Medal of Honor at some point so I could show it around when I came up from under a table and say, "Well, this was lodged under one of the legs. I guess your table must have been pretty wobbly." But lacking a medal, I would quietly sing an Italian song as I worked so that the customers would assume I was not from this country and not familiar with our norms of behavior or tableside manners.

Wobbly tables contribute to poor restaurant reviews. Some customers don't even wait until they get home—they sit at the table, wait for their food, and furiously tap out a one-star review on their phone to say the food, service, ambiance, and weather were all unfavorable due to the fact that their table wobbled like a Hawaiian bobblehead.

Restauranteurs must take swift action to keep customers from improvising shims with what they find on the table. It's odd, but it seems that nobody comes to eat at a restaurant with a set of simple wooden shims in their pocket. Am I the only one?

To the customer, nothing on the table is sacred. You've seen it: a wad of paper napkins crammed under a foot. There is no imagination here and the aesthetics are horrific…but, on the other hand, it doesn't cost the restaurant a lot. To take one of the table cards, however—the ones that advertise specialty drinks or desserts that were carefully designed and printed in limited quantity—fold it up into a small mess, and slip that under a leg…well, that hurts. Nor am I a big fan of flatware or sweetener packets being employed to do the job.

Some very elegant technical solutions do exist. There is a company that makes hydraulically self-leveling table legs. They are a dream come true, except for the part that they cost three times as much as your common, barbaric, early-industrial-age table legs. But hey, table legs are not *that* expensive. Napkin and table-card savings should pay for them in no time. Also, there is no need for a Congressional Medal of Honor, and for me, that's a major selling point.

Column 414, March 10, 2019

Days to Celebrate in March

I am deeply disappointed because I missed the opportunity to write a timely column about March 13, which we all know and love to commemorate, as it is the anniversary of the discovery of Uranus. Surprisingly, my wife was quite relieved when I told her of this oversight only because she imagined that I would go into too much detail, knowing my enthusiasm for wordplay and the outer planets.

However, there is no need to fret. Soon March 20 will be upon us, and we will have the choice of celebrating the vernal equinox, International Earth Day, or Extraterrestrial Abductions Day, as they all share the March 20 holiday slot—a veritable holiday-palooza.

All right, the vernal equinox is not a holiday. Technically, it is an astronomical event. We don't celebrate the full moon or Venus setting below our horizon, but then again, neither the full moon or "Venus-set" represents the last day of winter or better yet, the first day of spring.

Also, the vernal equinox represents the transition where the days start getting longer than the nights. This is important, as everyone affected by the winter hinkies knows that if winter were any longer, we might all numb our neurons to the point where we run naked from our cabins in a general southerly direction. After doing the penguin walk down your icy driveway for the past two months, the first day of spring is indeed something to celebrate.

International Earth Day, on the other hand, *is* an official holiday. I know, you're thinking that Earth Day is celebrated on April 22, and it is. It's just one of those holiday details that hasn't yet been worked out to everyone's satisfaction. It's sort of like never knowing which day Easter will pop up in a given year, although the story about Earth Day is much more straightforward than Easter's homeless tendency.

Back in 1969, the United Nations Secretary General, U Thant, signed a proclamation setting March 21 as the day to honor earth and the concept of peace. A month later, US Senator Gaylord Nelson, either happily unaware that Earth Day had already been established by the United Nations or just a teeny bit upset that the UN had beat him to the punch (or perhaps spaced-out by the great volume of marijuana smoke being generated in the late 60s), declared April 22 Earth Day. Of course, nobody ever pays much attention to the UN, and Gaylord Nelson was much more fun than the UN (not that the UN sets a very high standard for fun), so the April date is still with us. However, the earth will not mind if it is celebrated on both days.

Your third choice, Extraterrestrial Abductions Day, is truly not an official holiday and ironically is celebrated mostly by skeptics and nonbelievers. Sure, it's fun to go around in alien costumes promoting conspiracy theories and scaring the children, but the last group that will be celebrating such an idea include the people who actually *have* been abducted by aliens of the "close encounter" kind.

It's very serious to those whose brains have been probed, gonads sampled and have had chunks of time stolen from their lives. These folks have been dragged over the coals by weird-looking creatures, and if they could make their encounters go away, they would. You usually don't celebrate the day you went to prison, but hey, if you want to go out drinking and blowing your vuvuzela, go right ahead. Just remember you won't get any sympathy when you come back from your own "examination."

This is a great opportunity to also mention that March 25 is International Waffle Day. I'm not exactly sure how I feel about it. At first, I got very enthusiastic and thought that I liked the idea, but after some time passed my enthusiasm waned and my entire attitude took a 180-degree turn. Now I'm back, supporting the idea 100 percent but maybe not for long. I go back and forth on this issue a lot, but one thing for sure: I love International Waffle Day.

I hope this cavalcade of holidays and observances gives you something to celebrate this March. My apologies, but we can double down and make sure we celebrate the discovery of Uranus next year. Watch out.

Column 416, March 24, 2019

Presidential Lottery

In order to get out in front of the pack, I was going to announce my intention to run for president of the United States this week. At first, it seemed like an exciting idea, and in just forty-eight hours I have already raised $6 in pledges toward my candidacy during my preannouncement rallies.

However, after I found out that my brother-in-law is running, as is his sister and two of the neighborhood children, as well as one of their dogs, I somehow lost my enthusiasm for the position. This decline in enthusiasm is actually a good thing and ironically makes me even more qualified to be president, as I will explain.

For years, I have advocated that the only factor that should disqualify a person from running for president is the desire to actually be president. It can be argued that an appetite to be president is an indicator of questionable character or at least a craving for power that is immediately subject to the forces of corruption.

With this in mind, I have devised a new system for choosing a president that nobody will like. This is all predicated on my theory that if you can't please everyone with the outcome of an election, then the next best thing is to not please anyone.

In my system, every able-minded citizen would automatically be included every four years in the Presidential Selective Service Lottery, where we randomly select a good citizen to be president. The only people exempt from being chosen would have to fill out extensive paperwork and pay a hefty fee, which would publicly declare their exclusion from the presidential lottery. A randomly selected president wouldn't be beholden to anyone who helped them get the job.

The new president would be paid the minimum federal wage for their service, although we would not charge them rent for the White House. Of course, they would have an expense account (open to public scrutiny) and be offered all the protection and perquisites that comes with the job. They could pull in support and advice from any government or institute of higher education to help them make important decisions. At the end of their tenure, Congress could choose to give them a bonus package depending on how good a president they were.

There would have to be a robust system of impeachment, but it would kick in only after a year on the job. That should be enough time to determine if we randomly picked someone outside the bell curve who degrades the whole purpose of having a president.

It could be a viable system, as quite often I wonder who in their right mind would want to be president. Sure, you get to redecorate the White House and write executive orders, but there's the constant stress of being responsible for the well-being of 300 million people and, really, the world in general.

To make this work, all we would have to do is change our culture by educating everyone and instilling in our children that being chosen at random to be president is the ultimate call of duty where you must serve your country selflessly, and put all your attention into improving the well-being of the entire country ahead of all personal goals and aspirations. This terrifying sense of duty can always be tempered with the knowledge that it will last only four years, and then you can go back to being the self-centered whatever it is you were before duty called.

Imagine that the system is implemented and the first to be called to office is a middle-aged, female, Hispanic part-time history teacher from Detroit. What a wealth of normal, real-world experience and understanding of urban problems she would bring to the White House. She might also bring her twenty-eight-year-old unemployed son, who is living in her basement, and her daughter's baby, who she has to care for six days a week so her daughter can work two jobs to pay off her student debt. Who knows, maybe her disabled veteran husband will show up for his therapy sessions, which would be part of her benefits package as president. For her four years as president, she would be able to afford his medications. Do you think she might give politics as usual a different spin?

So as for my candidacy, let's just say that if chosen, I will serve, but for the public good, someone better get my head examined if I jump into this race voluntarily.

Column 417, March 31, 2019

Long Division

Before calculators, the threat of long division loomed large. It was an academic menace riddled with traps and pitfalls. It was the demon that could transform your report card from an asset into a liability, even though it might be decades before you learned these words exist.

Long division, for you youngsters, is a method of dividing long numbers on paper without any tools but a pencil! What's that? No, we will cover what a pencil is at some other time. Just imagine doing division problems *without a calculator.*

Our traditional method of long division was introduced around the year 1600 and was last used in 1992 by a hermit in Idaho who did it to thumb his nose at society. Do they even teach long division in schools anymore? If they don't teach penmanship and common courtesy, it's hard to imagine that long division could survive the curriculum axe.

In our youth, all of our teachers tried to convince us that the real problem was knowing *when* to multiply and *when* to divide, but for the elementary school proletariat, we knew that the true problem was the division itself.

Somehow, multiplication was more straightforward. If you followed the rules, kept the numbers in straight columns, memorized the multiplication tables, and effectively used your fingers as an abacus, you had half a fighting chance to manually solve multi-place multiplication problems.

But division was different because it involved guessing. They tried to call it "estimating," but I knew it was guessing and I was notoriously bad at arithmetic guesswork. Kids are naturally bad at guesswork. Ask them to guess how many eggs are in a dozen and they'll tell you anything from two to a dozillion. Teachers would ask, "About how many 9's are in 87?" Ha. Obviously 87 does not contain any 9's; there's just an 8 and a 7 there.

Early in life, I was mentally lethargic when it came to math. Problems were like chin-ups, and after just a few, I was down for the count, so to speak. As time went on, I fell on my head a lot and partially dislodged the blockage, allowing me to perform simple operations. Long division continued to be only slightly more preferable than a trip to the dentist.

It was just one of those tasks that you didn't want to do. It was a lot of work—not physical, but worse yet, mental work. How could that be so bad? You didn't work up a sweat or start breathing laboriously, yet dividing 123.456 by 39.298 was as painful as putting on a heavy pack and carrying it uphill over a rough trail, in the snow, barefoot.

The answer, by the way, is 3.141, courtesy of my pocket calculator. It was easier to find the calculator, replace the batteries, turn it on, and punch in the equation than it would have been to put pencil to paper and embark on the arduous and long, division journey.

No one even carries a calculator any longer, as they can be found on every desk and laptop. Smartphones, capable of running any number of calculator applications, will even take a math question by voice and respond with an answer as if it were not a bother. We are a society awash in calculators. Long division is dead.

At some point, however, long division will turn into an art form. You'll be able to sign up for classes called Meditation Through Long Division just like you can schedule a yoga session. Here you'll be given a paper tablet and two pencils with erasers. Beginners will have to master actually writing numbers *by hand*. At first, you will be able to work on a grid, but with practice, students will graduate to writing out number problems on blank paper. The best of these will be framed and displayed on the walls of the long-division meditation centers. Eventually, the movement will turn into a fad, with long-division establishments springing up in strip mall spaces.

Outrageous claims will inevitably surface proclaiming diseases can be cured and relationships saved through the practice of long division in the presence of incense, magnets, and crystals. Finally, the whole concept will come crashing down after enriching a few corrupt individuals who never cared about getting the right answer in the first place.

Oddly, now that I have mastered electronic calculators, the real problem seems to be knowing *when* to multiply and *when* to divide. Go figure.

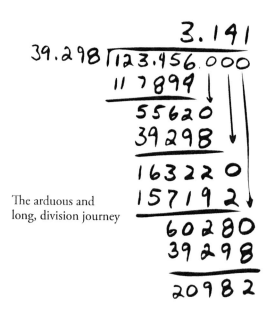

The arduous and long, division journey

Column 426, June 2, 2019

Doughnuts, Part 4

Everyone, please stay calm. People tend to forget it's coming, but hang on to your hats and loosen your belts because the first Friday of June is, at last, National Doughnut Day.

Besides apple pie and dieting, what could be more American than doughnuts? Now wait a minute, I can already hear the groans of people muttering, "Isn't November 5 National Doughnut Day?" Well, yes it is. You have to realize that this being America, we have two National Doughnut Days annually.

With a nation this big, it's really a wonder that the bureaucracy that deals with national days didn't inadvertently assign even *more* days to celebrate the doughnut. We're lucky that they have only one day slated for the Fourth of July, as they tend to keep better tabs on the more critical holidays when working people get the day off.

On the other hand, since doughnuts have been helping Americans get larger, their cultural importance has grown along with our waistlines to the point where maybe we need two National Doughnut Days. You would think one would be spelled National Donut Day but no, the spelling is the same for both days, unless it's not. We have a National Pie Day (January 23) and a National Pi Day (March 14), but that's something we should discuss on National Spelling Day (April 4). Soon I hope to discover we actually have a National "National Day" Day.

Anyway, aside from the fact that they are slowly killing us, what is there not to like about doughnuts? Everything about them is delicious: the texture and variety, the aroma of frying dough, the instant satisfaction and ease of eating the sugar-clad, fat-laden cake. Even the mathematical description of its shape is captivating. The idea that doughnuts could be killing us is a small price to pay in exchange for all of the pastry's glorious charms.

In truth, doughnuts aren't really killing everyone, they're just shortening the lives of some of us—those who shouldn't be eating sweets, fat, or processed carbohydrates. You know who you are. It is curious that our dietary restrictions just serve to heighten the anticipation of consuming the forbidden confection and elevate its perceived value.

But doughnuts aren't supposed to be nutritious. Their best use is as a rare treat or a quick source of energy for those engaged in something physically taxing, like overtime emergency work, or perhaps long-term endurance tasks like, I don't know, maybe driving across the country or commuting to work.

There apparently is little hope for making health-promoting doughnuts. A few years ago, in a desperate attempt to bring doughnuts into the realm of wholesome foods, my health-conscious daughter produced a batch of rye-flour donuts. During our serious tasting session, we carefully evaluated the future with an eye on what would happen if rye doughnuts were to take hold in our society.

When the rye doughnuts jumped off the plate and viciously attacked us, we quickly decided to incinerate the recipe and the leftover samples from this possibly illegal experiment and never speak of it again. The effort took all the magic out of doughnuts, brought down the lowermost level of culinary experience by an order of magnitude, and gave health foods a bad name—not to mention the bad taste in your mouth.

And yes, I know, a few years ago I did run a series of columns about doughnuts and even reminded everyone about National Doughnut Day—but that was when I thought we had only one. If you remember, I did confess that I own a doughnut machine in a mobile booth that is taken to various events, where we have produced up to fifteen thousand donuts in one weekend.

And no, I am not part of America's problem with fatty foods. I have a marginal, morally bankrupt rationalization for my defense: There are lots of people engaged in physically taxing overtime emergency work and long-term endurance tasks like driving across the country who need a good number of doughnuts. I figure fifteen thousand is a pretty good number.

And my contribution is but crumbs compared to the 10 billion doughnuts produced in the US every year. Do the math: that's 5 billion doughnuts for each National Doughnut Day. Divided by US population, that's only fifteen doughnuts per person per National Doughnut Day.

That's about right, if you're driving across country. Or commuting to work. Enjoy.

Column 435, August 4, 2019

Summer Job Tips, Part 1

Hey kids, it's late, but there's still time to snag a summer job for extra cash that, try as you might, you just can't wring out of your parents.

Working this summer will not only make you a few bucks, but it may even give you that rush of independence that comes with earning a living, the thrill of paying your own way, and a peek into the adult world of gainful employment. You may even experience an inexplicable incentive to jump out of bed in the morning to get to your job on time, but let's be real—probably not.

Let's get one thing straight—work is different from hanging out, goofing off, or going to school. Employers are not your parents, and they may expect you to act differently from how you've been acting up to this point in your life. This stems from the fact that they do not love you, but not to worry; outside of your family, hardly anybody loves you. It's normal.

You may find that you don't know the first thing about how to actually work or how to behave at a workplace. You will learn that you haven't memorized your social security number. Chances are good that you have no idea what you can do or how fast you can do it. This usually comes as a shock when you find out the landscaper who hired you expects as much effort from you as did your cross-country running coach.

Don't worry, people will roll their eyes or even laugh at you, but just ride it out. It's more fun than the backstabbing work environment you might encounter when you have additional experience.

Since you probably have no idea how to make your new employer glad that you showed up, I have compiled guidelines you might consider to take some of the edge off that first-job aura you will be projecting when you go to work.

Shoes. What kind of work will you be doing? If it's got anything to do with climbing ladders, lifting things, using tools, driving a vehicle, and the like, you're going to have to wear shoes. Yes, we all know it's unnatural, and I'm sorry, but when there is a chance you might have to use your feet, employers usually like to see some protection around them. They might not really care about your safety, but society demands that employers watch over you so that you don't do anything stupid like hurt yourself while helping them make money. By the way, flip-flops aren't shoes. They are merely portable foot pads.

Clothing. What you wear should reflect the job. Take note of what the other employees are wearing and how the boss is dressed. If everyone is wearing a clown outfit and the work site is not a carnival, reevaluate. Don't wear clothing that advertises, proselytizes, or insults, even if you know that it's really, really funny.

Phones. We all know your phone is your lifeline, but for the first day or week leave your phone in the car or in your backpack, turned off. You should look up the procedure for turning your phone off if you have never done it. You will still be able to talk and breathe, barely at first, but these skills will, in time, return.

Find out what the phone policy is and follow it. This is work time and not your time to be checking on any information your phone has to offer, no matter how valuable. If phone time pays more than working a regular job, reevaluate.

Next week, we will cover issues like when it is best to stand or sit, lunch, quitting time, and how to look interested in the work you are doing. But don't wait for more advice; get out now and start exploring the world of employment before you turn thirty and find that living in your parents' basement is not a charismatic lifestyle.

By the way, this is the time that *you* decide if work is a fulfilling, enjoyable adventure that prompts you to contribute your skills for the betterment of society or if work is endless drudgery that robs you of time and independence. Sure, it's unfair to ask a person your age to determine if your life will be upbeat and positive or dark and burdensome, but it's largely up to you to control your destiny, and this summer is as good a time as any to start making that choice. No pressure.

Column 436, August 11, 2019

Summer Job Tips, Part 2

Last week, I offered a primer with tips for the first-time worker with a part-time summer job. We covered what clothing to avoid, how to shut off your phone, and the fact that, against all logic, you will probably be expected to wear shoes.

Yes, it's been pointed out to me that the people who work for Google might not have to wear shoes, but a job at Google probably doesn't qualify as a first job and it's certainly not part-time summer work. For those new to the job market, you may battle two thousand applicants for a single job opening at Google later in life, and more power to you. Just be aware that you might lose your shoes in the fray.

This week, let's look at how to behave in a work environment.

Sitting and Standing. If you've scored a job at any active work environment outside an office, it's not usually appropriate to sit down. Go ahead, roll your eyes, but unless invited by your employer to have a seat, don't sit. If you haven't been directed to do anything for the moment, avoid flopping down on the closest place to sit; just stand around close to the work being done as if you are ready for the next task.

A boss who sees you standing may think, "Oh, great, I'm paying, and they're standing around; better get them something to do." But when the boss sees you sitting, they conclude, "I'm paying, and they're sitting around like my kids." You don't want the boss thinking this way.

For the sake of making a good visual impression, try not to stand around with your hands at your sides. Venture a pose like putting your hands on your hips or in your back pockets. Pay attention so that it doesn't look like you're daydreaming. This gives the impression that you're part of the project and not a bystander who is there for a look-see. It's body language that says you're alert and interested in the job.

Employers like to think you're interested or, hopefully, excited to be part of their team. It helps them validate their own questionable decisions to invest everything they have into a risky venture that they were warned would ruin them—often by their own parents. They don't need to look at the fifteen-year-old they just hired to be reminded that they are but one bad decision away from debtors' prison. On the other hand, if the business is going gangbusters, they don't need a teenage employee bringing down the level of energy in the workplace.

One last word on sitting down on the job: If, after standing around looking interested, you find you are being ignored, for heaven's sake, don't lie down, ever. I wouldn't bring it up, but the last guy I hired filled a lull in the workday by assuming the prone position, to my absolute astonishment.

Lunch and Quitting Time. Find out how long lunch break lasts. Get back on time. Don't invite friends over to the jobsite for lunch or a visit, and please don't come back from your lunch break and then eat lunch on the job between tasks (this also from a recent experience).

Avoid asking your boss or fellow employees for the time, and don't ask to get off sooner than quitting time. This is a job, not Saturday morning home chores.

General Considerations. Don't hurt yourself or anyone else, especially by doing something stupid. Stupid can be defined as an action that, once it's done and posted on YouTube, prompts everyone to comment, "Boy, that was stupid!" Refer to "fail" videos on YouTube if you need clarification.

Don't lie about your experience. If you don't know how to do something, ask for instructions. It's hard to be humble, but ultimately, it's better to be considered inexperienced than a lying blowhard.

Finally, if the work does not captivate your interest and the only positive aspect is getting paid, find another job. This is not the job you've been looking for. In the meantime, pretend you can do the work cheerfully without poisoning the work environment for the others. It's just the decent thing to do.

If you've never been employed, find a job that only lasts a day or two or one where you come in once a week. That way, you can recover from the shock of having to work and you'll have time to ponder how it is the world came to this point where most of us work for a living. Good luck.

Self-Checkout

Do you avoid the self-checkout "service" lanes in your large grocery, department, or home-supply stores? I know I do. It's not even a service as some stores make it out to be. As I see it, it's more of a lack of service or even a disservice on some occasions.

My snubbing the self-checkout lane is rooted in three very good reasons:

1. I'm an older guy who does not adapt well to new ways.

2.

3.

Okay, I'm working on 2 and 3 because I'm sure my age-related reluctance to try new things has very little to do with it.

Self-checkout is obviously another ploy by corporate retail giants to get the customer to do the work. You do the work; they get the money. You don't get a discount for the trouble (aka "convenience") of checking yourself out, so guess who really benefits from self-checkout?

It's like my car insurance company. They used to send me my proof-of-insurance cards nicely laminated and cut perfectly to fit into the don't-panic-if-you-are-stopped-by-the-cops paperwork packet that we keep in the car where the officer can see our hands. Then a few years ago, the company, which we will call "Stake Pharm" to conceal its identity, started sending me the cards on die-cut paper that you have to fold back and forth (and forth and back, I might add) to release the cards. The process takes a full minute, and it's just a way the insurance company has me doing their work.

If they issue a million cards that take a million minutes to release, that's like foisting off over sixteen thousand hours of work on the customers, and I guess it's because they feel we don't have anything better to do.

There are other examples: pumping your own gas, bagging your own groceries, and bussing your own table. It won't end there. I fully expect to be sweeping up after the movies and drawing my own blood for lab tests before the decade is out.

Then there is the suspicion component. When I get to the checkout with my cart, I wait in line for a genuine store employee to tally up everything I am purchasing. I back off just like I do when customs agents check my luggage at the border. I don't want any more trouble with the nightsticks and Tasers like the last time when I was just trying to be helpful.

Stepping up to use the self-checkout, I feel that the store automatically tags me as a potentially suspicious customer or as a suspicious potential customer in the case of more disenchanted retailers. I can just hear the security people watching on their video monitors: "No, he's avoiding our clerks…he's going to check out himself. Let's bring this suspect down. Set Tasers to 'maximum tingle.'"

Self-checkout feels like an honesty test. A lot of people can't pass an honesty test and have developed many self-scanning scams. The internet told me that self-scanning customers are five times more likely to try and cheat the system than those who are checked out by a clerk. Of course, the internet tells me a lot of things, but this statement at least seems plausible.

People try to scam the scanner by entering the code for bananas when weighing a steak, which, in case you are unsure or misinformed, is still wrong and contrary to our common sense of civilization and decency in spite of examples set by politicians.

Stores have been on alert for these scams. First, they installed weight scales that match the item you've scanned to its weight when you bag it. Now they are implementing visual surveillance systems that can tell the difference between a cantaloupe and a handbag or "see" if you have a case of red wine on the bottom of your cart that you "forgot" to scan. Next, they may be employing checkout clerks to tabulate all your purchases…hmm.

Eventually, we'll all be checking out when the grim reaper comes calling. He will likely be keeping a close eye on the self-checkout lane as we transition into the afterlife.

Since you can't take it with you, I'm sure you'll be able to get your supplies for the next world at the Hereafter Mart. There will be no sneaking merchandise past the scanner on that final day of reckoning. Good luck and Godspeed. I'll be over in the regular checkout line.

Column 445, October 13, 2019

Free Prize Inside Indeed

In my youth, I would get a box of Cracker Jack and tear it open looking for the free toy or prize that was included inside every box. What excitement! I seem to remember getting some pretty cool things like a spinning top, a magnifying lens, scuba equipment, and a .22-caliber rifle, although my memory may be a bit fuzzy because for a while there, I thought I got my first car inside that box of caramel-coated popcorn and peanuts. Later, I realized that it was not my first but my second car.

Hoping for a new laptop, one with a lightning-fast processor, too much memory, and massive solid-state hard drives, I recently acquired a new box of Cracker Jack. The experience was sweet on the tongue but underwhelming in the prize department.

I should have checked Wikipedia, which plainly explains that Frito-Lay, the company that has owned Cracker Jack since 1997, "announced in 2016 that the prizes would no longer be provided and had been replaced with a QR code which can be used to download a baseball-themed game."

On the front of the box, right at the top, it declares "PRIZE INSIDE!" I suppose there is no law that Cracker Jack has to use the word *prize* as defined by Merriam-Webster, which would be "something exceptionally desirable." They don't even have to use the word *inside* as conventionally defined. By those stuffy old definitions, there is no prize, and whatever there is, it's not inside the box.

Sometimes I tend to overanalyze things, but in this case, the entire product, from package to prize, deserves some up-close scrutiny.

Sailor Jack is featured near the top of the box with his dog Bingo. How is it that a sailor has a dog? I mean, if you have your own boat, of course you can have a dog. But Sailor Jack is dressed in a navy uniform, implying that he serves on a naval vessel, which would make having a dog problematic.

Furthermore, Sailor Jack looks to be about ten years old, twelve at best. Even in eighteenth-century England when boys were recruited to serve at sea (as boy seaman, 3rd class, or in other positions in the Royal Navy), they had to be at least thirteen years old, unless the boy was the captain's son, which would allow him to start his seamanship training at eleven. This may explain why Jack was able to keep Bingo, although the uniform with the neckerchief and white hat is clearly more reminiscent of modern times.

The only plausible explanation left is that this is the fantasy of a young boy who dreams about serving in the navy with his dog and happily eating caramel-coated popcorn and peanuts (because that is what they do in the navy) while enjoying a Major League Baseball game. The baseball game is suggested because the illustration on the box pictures Jack and Bingo half-emerging from a baseball like a stripper from a cake at a bachelor party. Well, not exactly like that, but who can resist the comparison?

So today, inside the box, we find not a laptop but a small sealed paper packet that states "Blipp a Surprise" and invites you to lift and peel back the corner. Inside are peculiar instructions about how to Blipp a Surprise, which clearly state:

1. Download the free Blippar app.
2. Aim and frame your prize inside.
3. Reveal a fun digital experience.

Right.

There was also a sticker that said "Surprise inside" and "Guess what's inside?" (I'm guessing a surprise), but there was nothing that looked like it could be a scanning code and nothing under the sticker. One thing for sure, I was in for a "fun digital experience" trying to figure out what to download, from where, and what to aim and frame.

Confusion ensued. I was directed to the wrong application and later got bogged down in the study of the massive Terms of Service and the Privacy Policy. There were too many probing questions and permissions. I never got to that electronic baseball game.

So, what have we learned? After a good deal of thought, we have to conclude that the Cracker Jack prize is really the gift of a valuable life lesson. Specifically: there is no free prize. And to help you get that bitter taste of a life lesson out of your mouth, there's always the caramel popcorn and peanuts. Not bad. Not a laptop, but not bad.

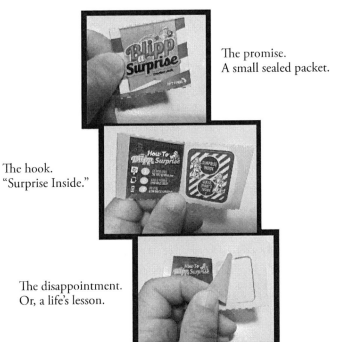

The promise.
A small sealed packet.

The hook.
"Surprise Inside."

The disappointment.
Or, a life's lesson.

Column 452, December 1, 2019

Lying

It seems like lying in public has become quite popular recently. Sure, lying has been around since cavemen learned to declare that the animal skins their partners wore did not make them look fat. But that was all private. Today, we have technology to disseminate lies far and wide, instantly making public liars out of the most remote members of the human race.

Lying seems to have become socially acceptable. You can buy time on social media to lie without fear, as no mass protests have materialized to shame public liars. Straight talkers, however, are finding it surprisingly difficult to get the hang of lying. You have to study politicians, dictators, and people in power to get the nuances and appreciate the hutzpah it takes to repeatedly tell bald-faced lies.

A "bald-faced lie" is a falsehood that after nearly everyone hearing it, knows it's a lie. This is different from "the big lie," which is a lie so ridiculously preposterous that people tend to believe it because they just can't imagine that anyone would have the audacity to tell such an untruth.

Lying, as it turns out, is really complicated. Just the word *lie* takes up pages in Wikipedia, where over thirty different types of lies are listed and interesting distinctions are made among half-truths, puffery, black lies, fraud, and bullshit. Many books have been written, movies produced, confessions offered, and still we lie. We even lie about lying. It's just one of our communication skills, although the spectrum of lies goes from harmless to criminal.

I for one, feel pressured because for years I have been telling lies in public, sometimes in the form of hyperbole, satire, or just your garden-variety bald-faced lies predominantly in this column. Now it appears other people have picked up on it. I can compete very well with your everyday amateur liar, but listening to the career liars, the public figures who are so practiced that they are no longer aware of their detachment from reality, has me put off. Constant lies from top officials desensitize the public and erode the value of my lying for amusement. Instead of public protest and indignation, people just stop believing anything they hear, even from legitimate sources, and we slowly descend into chaos.

You almost have to pity our poor politicians. They stretch the truth to the point where they have it inside out, and soon somebody calls them on it. Here they can backpedal and admit they were not truthful, which will dearly cost them the respect of all their lying colleagues. Or they can tell another lie to shore up what will eventually become their house of deceit.

A third alternative is that they bend logic so much that the lie becomes a truth by severely stretching the imagination. As a last resort, they can do what I used to do in fourth grade: claim they were joking. This pathetic option comes with a high built-in price—it defines you as a terrible comedian.

One other way to handle any accusations of lying is to call the accuser a liar. Since it's the job of the media to uncover who is telling the truth and whose pants are on fire, it follows that after so many political lies are reported, the politicians go after the media and accuse them of lying or producing false news. Here we find ourselves back on the elementary school playground. "You're a liar!" "I know you are, but what am I?" Oh, please.

On the one hand, our language is so nebulous that everything we say can be challenged. If you say the sky is blue, I can challenge you to define your terms and we can go on debating about what is obvious to both of us. On the other hand, we all have a gut feeling for what reality is, and often we can settle on an uneasy truce about the semantics.

Even though our terms are not perfectly defined and lies are repeated to the point of believability, we've got to trust ourselves to know that the sky is indeed blue and no matter how much a falsehood is spun and repeated, it is still a lie.

Okay. Forgive my little rant about lying. Next week, I hope to get back to the more amusing lies. I was just feeling threatened.

And no, that flag you've wrapped yourself in does not make you look fat.

Column 453, December 8, 2019

Christmas Carols Gone Awry

Again, it's that time of year when we are compelled to listen to Christmas-themed music we have known all our lives. With any other genre, these songs would be called oldies, sometimes prefaced with the words *golden* or *moldy,* but old Christmas songs do not suffer the same fate. These seasonal songs are now known as carols or hymns, but as much as we would like some of them to go away, they will never completely fade into history because they are all considered tradition. Since they are so ingrained in our society, it's curious we don't take more care in teaching the lyrics to our children.

We learn Christmas carols before we are old enough to even be familiar with all the words. As we turn these songs over in our heads, we seek out the meaning in the lyrics by twisting the song to fit what we know.

In the Christmas song "Jingle Bells," I thought the lyrics went: "Oh, what fun it is to ride in a one-fourth open sleigh." Hey, it makes perfect sense. You don't want to go riding in the snow completely unprotected, but then again, a sleigh ride in a tightly enclosed bubble insulates you too much from the experience. A one-fourth open sleigh would be open just enough, like a convertible where you can still have the windows up and the heat blasting. Oh, what fun.

In "Hark! The Herald Angels Sing," I was pretty sure I had the lyrics all figured out: "Glory to the newborn King, Peace on earth and earth be mild, God and sin, his second child." Yikes. Well, this deserves an explanation. (For those of you who think and hear like I do, and I can only pray that it's only a very few, the correct lyrics are "God and sinners reconciled.")

God, as I understood, had an "only begotten" son, whatever that means, and so as a kid I figured it wouldn't be much of an issue, God being all powerful, to have a second child. The church's reasoning had always seemed obscure, so this thinking fit in nicely. Going further, since God could have anything He wanted, choosing Sin as a second child couldn't possibly be a problem (outside of the certainty that Sin would indeed be a "problem child").

My other misheard Christmas song lyrics are rather mundane, but other people's mistaken words are quite amusing:

Frosty the Snowman is not only a jolly, happy soul, but he has a "corncob pipe and a butt and nose."

In "The First Noel," people have heard "No hell, no hell, no hell, no hell, Barney's the king of his Rhyl."

And, there are these classics:

Where the treetops glisten and children listen to hear *slave elves* in the snow...

Get dressed ye merry gentlemen, let nothing *through this May*...

Fall on you *niece* and hear the angel voices...

He's making a list *of chicken and rice*...

Oh, come *lettuce* adore Him...

In my youth, our very Polish family would get together on Christmas Eve and torture the children with the promise that gifts would be distributed only after a long, drawn-out, and formal dinner followed by the singing of carols around the

Christmas tree. First the Polish carols and then the English. How many carols? They would sing until no one could remember any more carols to sing. The wait for the presents was excruciating. One Christmas, if I remember correctly, the singing concluded around January 3. There was alcohol involved.

All this background is to explain that I not only misunderstood the lyrics of English carols but of the Polish ones as well. My Polish vocabulary was frightfully limited. There was one carol in particular about a speckled duck in which some of the words escaped me. I asked my younger sister what the duck was holding on her arm. My sister replied that she thought it was her breast. Fair enough, the duck was sitting on a stone with her breast on her arm and playing beautifully; never mind that ducks don't have breasts. Well, they do in the same way that chickens have breasts, but that's not how I was thinking.

Twenty, maybe thirty years passed and I got a correction from my sister. The word in the song she thought meant "breast" actually means "bagpipes."

Well, then…that makes a lot more sense.

Deck the halls with bras of holly!

Column 454, December 15, 2019

Consumable Gift-Giving

As I have said before, I come from a Polish peasant background where my people valued any material wealth they could accumulate. In the old country, if they found a piece of broken glass or a bent piece of rusty metal, they would squirrel it away because, as the old Polish idiom goes, "it will come in handy." Perhaps they could fashion some sort of shiv from the glass or sharpen the metal so that they could whittle a pistol out of wood they had stolen.

Peasant poverty was just like prison except there was no getting out early for good behavior. As a matter of fact, it was good behavior that kept them oppressed and poor. A lump of coal for Christmas was occasion for joy and gratitude. It would help them through the winter and maybe allow them to escape to the cities—or even to America.

Once in America, old habits were hard to break. The old folks still accumulated broken glass and rusty metal, warning the kids that they had better hold onto anything that comes their way because the feudal lords might come by at any time and take it for themselves—minus the 10 percent that, of course, had to go to the church.

And so we hoarded our Erector Sets, dollhouses, Chatty Cathy dolls, and Lincoln Logs. We would never let go of what pieces remained of Mr. Potato Head. The View-Master and Kodak Instamatic are still with us, as are all the snapshots that do not deserve to be called photographs which we made when film was king and the wallet-sized print was queen.

We are older now. We are Americans, and we don't really need anything. We may be broke, but we're material magnates. We are looking at concepts like paring down, downsizing, or simply simplifying, and now comes Christmas with its heavily entrenched and fortified tradition of gift-giving. There is no way to root it out and subdue it, but…come closer so that you can hear me: *there is a way around it.*

It's time to announce that we will no longer be humbuggers trying to restrict gift-givers. Bring on the gifts, as long as *all the gifts are consumables.* By consumables, I am not referring to consumer goods and durable items. No, we are talking about items that can be used up, spent, eaten, or evaporated. These are gifts that take up no space or disappear when used.

There is no shortage of consumables. Food and drink are always at the top of the list, and that can include things like dog food or a bottle of fine wine for the cat. Consider a grocery store as you would a gift shop that doesn't offer gift wrapping.

Entertainment bestowed will not end up in a storage box. Gifts of meals out, hotel rooms, travel, theatrical performances, concerts, and even fireworks qualify. Toiletries and personal-care products are something everyone can use and use up. Going a step further, you can gift people with personal services—hair, nails, massage, and those Botox treatments that no insurance policy will even think about covering.

Are your gift recipients remodeling? Then building supplies fall under the consumable category, but more stable people can always use fuel (wood, fuel oil, batteries) and new energy-efficient light bulbs. A payment on their utility accounts would be greatly appreciated, be it electric, internet, or dumpster.

There are many more creative ways to give gifts without the danger of people tripping over them later and sending them to the hospital or morgue. Charitable contributions in the name of your gift receiver are deeply rooted in the Christmas spirit. Memberships to organizations might be appropriate, and of course, education for fun can include gift certificates to cooking and gardening classes or, I don't know, shiv design and construction.

Some of your loved ones just don't want to accumulate any more stuff. If you gift them with consumables, they can be truly gracious, thankful, and appreciative. And after you leave, they can enjoy using up the stuff you gave them and—to put the icing on the cake—be rid of it.

Yes, bring us some figgy pudding and a cup of good cheer. Personally, I'll settle for a block of Tillamook cheese, a hunk of hard salami, and a bottle of Yukon Jack. That'll go a long way sharing with friends this holiday season and won't add anything to my substantial rusty metal pile.

Column 460, January 26, 2020

Musicians

Sometimes I think I should have buckled down in my youth and become a musician. I base this on the amazing thrill it was playing bass guitar in a teen band for a packed gymnasium where everyone was dancing. To see everyone in the room responding to the music I was creating was sublime. This was during the 1960s in the Detroit metropolitan area, where if you weren't playing sports, racing cars, or performing in a band, well, you weren't anywhere at all.

We called our band of five The Trespassers. It was a counterculture sort of thing. We wanted to be outside the law, but it turned out we weren't so radical that we wanted to be something like The Arsonists. No, we were more inclined toward misdemeanors than felonies.

We could have chosen to be called The Shoplifters or Disorderly Conduct, but The Trespassers implied a sense of adventure, which included travel to places off-limits. Shoplifting just gets you in jail. Anyway, we figured that every time people at church would say the Lord's Prayer, they would think of our band when they got to the "forgive us our trespasses" part.

If we had been more forward-thinking, we could have left our progressive rock behind and jumped on the discordant, aggressive, and destructive music genre of today. We would have needed a more sinister band name like The Kidnappers, The Enslavers, Forced Disappearance, or, wait for it…The Hit Men. (Oh, never mind, already taken; find the band's music on Bad Boy Records.) But it was a gentler time, we didn't want to hurt anybody, and we weren't even inclined to trespass much.

All we wanted to do was perform, but performing never paid well, if at all. Part of the problem was that performing induced such a rush, we would willingly do it for free. If you honestly account for the time it takes to get to the point where you can actually perform, any other job pays better. Most of the time, you actually pay to play.

For their dedication, career musicians are arguably the most underpaid people in modern society. Let's compare a piano player pulling in $16,000 a year to an engineer earning $72,000. They're the same age, but when they were eight, the musician was inside playing a torturous version of "Für Elise" on the keyboard while the engineer was figuring out how to get Mario and Luigi to flip over sewer monsters.

At age sixteen, we find the musician working up a sweat playing for his high-school prom while the engineer is chatting up the future homecoming queen.

It isn't until college when the engineer discovers that engineering is a real career. By this time, the musician has been involved in any number of ensembles, trying to balance different musical ideas while getting beat around by the business end of the music industry, all while dealing with the most difficult challenge: keeping the band together.

The musician emerges from college broke or broken, hardened to the business world, addicted to cigarettes and admiration while the engineer is fresh and ready to take on whatever corporate challenges are thrown at him as he stuffs away retirement money into his 401K. He takes on a job and learns as he goes. The musician keeps practicing and any work he gets in a club is often just above the pay scale of the dishwasher.

You've got to figure that there are nonmonetary rewards to being a musician that have to be worth something like $75 an hour or people wouldn't do it. But you can't pay your rent with the satisfaction of giving a good performance.

My buddy Kurt Reimann owns a recording studio. Over the decades, he's compiled a database of musician jokes that you can find by Googling "music jokes Surreal Studios." There are hundreds of jokes, and a great many are financially related, which tells a story in itself.

What's the difference between a musician and a US savings bond?

One of them eventually matures and earns money.

What's the most common thing a music college graduate says on his first job?

"You want fries with that?"

Okay, one more:

What's the difference between a dead trombone player lying in the road and a dead squirrel lying in the road?

The squirrel might have been on his way to a gig.

I guess as far as pay goes, I'm lucky that I'm not a musician... no, I'm a writer.

The Substance of Toilet Paper

In these times of uncertainty, everyone knows that toilet paper is one of the first items in high demand, but people can't quite grasp the logic or explain why. As soon as storms threaten or when other perils have us heading home to take shelter, people feel those pangs of panic and rush out to buy up all the toilet paper. As the demand gains momentum, even the concern over price is minimized and the expensive brands that we would never consider in stress-free times disappear from store shelves.

Except for rocks, leaves, and corncobs, we generally have no idea what there was before toilet paper. This leads us to one conclusion and explains the tendency to hoard these cleansing perforated rolls: Before there was toilet paper, *there was no civilization*. Whether it's on a conscious level or not, people hoard toilet paper in perilous times because they want to preserve civilization—if not for everyone, then just for themselves.

Civilization is important to us because it has brought us so many things we consider essential to the enjoyment of life. It's brought us washing machines and cell phones, *People* magazine and magazines for our assault rifles. It's brought us a respite from an early death, Fannie Mae home loans, escalators, and alcoholic beverages.

Actually, alcoholic beverages were a gift from times way before toilet paper, but with civilization, we got alcoholic beverages that would not poison us, at least not right away. Civilization gave us hip-hop, the Lindy Hop, the carhop, the lollipop, the IHOP, and Hopalong Cassidy. What's not to like about civilization?

Wherever there is civilization, there is toilet paper, and when there is no toilet paper, you are either exploring space, the final frontier, or you're in real trouble. But why toilet paper? It's really a process of elimination—if people are forced to choose, they would rather have toilet paper than running water, electricity, *Hollywood Squares,* or Facebook. When the trappings of civilization start to evaporate, people look for and hoard the most basic comforts, the common denominators we all need as humans to prove to ourselves that we are still civilized because we have the last vestige of culture at our disposal.

Sure, there are toilet-paper-free toilets. An automated wand cleanses your bottom side with a rinse of water that has a precise pressure and temperature. It may even have a blow-dry cycle, but I don't know because every time I come face to face with… no, wait, that's a terribly misleading expression. In this case, a better word would be *encounter.* Every time I encounter one of these most personal of personal-care robots, I decline to deploy their high-tech cleaning power for fear that something might go awry. I may even enjoy it.

The problem is that these personal depurating robots depend on electricity, hot and cold running water, and in-house sewerage. They may be the height of civilization, but toilet paper is the foundation. It's essential: it's closest to the bowels of civilization. And if you look around while you are seated and engaged with this dodgy future-of-personal-care device, you will notice that every advanced toilet has a roll of actual toilet paper within reach.

Picture this wilderness experience that I myself have witnessed more than once on remote treks: The boss signals the crew to stop and announces that this site is where they will set up camp. Everyone starts removing their packs. No one has been assigned yet to make a fire, set up a tent, or establish radio contact. The first order that goes out typically sounds like this: "Jackson, Schmitt; dig a latrine."

Even at the sketchiest and most hastily constructed pit latrines I have experienced, there is always a tree branch or a stick from a bush cut so that it will hold a roll of toilet paper nearby for the convenience of the user. It serves to remind us that in spite of the threatening circumstances, the difficulties we are now facing, and the odd sequence of events that brought us to squat on a log above a shallow, open cesspit, *there is hope*. There will always be civilization, as long as there is toilet paper.

———————————————————

Column 471, April 19, 2020

Life During Interesting Times

"May you live in interesting times" is a phrase of debatable origin, but it's generally viewed as a curse, like one you might hurl at your brother-in-law after he fleeced you in a friendly poker game. I've often wondered how fascinating the times have to be to qualify as interesting.

Well, I am finding out.

Here we are, four weeks into our pandemic lockdown. This sounds a lot like talk some of us have heard around the cellblock, except we're at home and the only warden keeping us penned up is this tiny virus made up of just twenty-nine proteins. This is all very interesting as I have never before been through a pandemic and by golly, my wife and I plan to make it through this one. We are being very careful to the point where we've decided not to invite the Latter-day Saints in, should they come by.

There is a bright side to where we are holed up. I mean, we could be in the penitentiary, a nursing home, a refugee camp, a homeless shelter, or a disaster area like the Pacific Island nation of Vanuatu, which recently was nearly wiped off the map by Cyclone Harold. We would have heard something about this tragedy if we hadn't been so deluged by coronavirus news.

We have it good. We live in Maine, in a house with a yard and trees. My wife and I get along partly because the house is big enough that we can work in different rooms and come together as often as we like. We have a computer, a TV, and liquor in the cabinet. And it's spring. We have it good. We can, and will, hold out.

The daffodils are starting to come up. And now, I see that it's starting to cloud up. Presently it's snowing—hard. The various forecasts predict an inch of slush overnight to more ominous predictions, but surely it won't get that bad this far into spring.

We go to bed, but I get up at first light to discover we were hit with eight inches of very heavy, wet, extra nasty snow. So here we are on pandemic lockdown with a punishing storm that left us what we call "plowable" amounts of snow. So far, so bad.

It's very quiet out. It should be. People are staying home, isolating because of the virus and now because of the storm. But it's very quiet; too quiet. That's because the power is out.

Okay. Situation summary: pandemic lockdown, a serious spring snowstorm, and now a power outage. No power means no heat, no lights, no internet, no cooking, and no water. No water means no handwashing, and even though we are stocked with toilet paper, no toilet flushing.

Trees are down in our yard. My snowplow is not hooked up to the truck. The driveway is full of branches. There is no hot coffee. The cellar is slowly filling up with water as there is no power to the sump pump. All the bars and taverns are closed.

Hey! Isn't this exactly the way airplanes go down? It's never just one thing. The captain thinks he hears a baby crying in the cockpit. He and the copilot look around but can't find a baby. The captain is called to the back to investigate a smoking coffeepot. In the captain's absence, the copilot turns off all alarms and annunciators so that he can listen for the crying baby. The captain returns just as a stowaway feral cat, which can sound like a baby, jumps onto the copilot's face, creating a scene reminiscent of the first *Alien* movie. The copilot falls on the controls, causing the plane to stall but no warnings are given. No alarms sound, so the plane goes down.

The smoking coffeepot or the feral cat weren't enough to bring the plane down. Each situation could have been easily handled. It's always a combination of small disasters and unusual events that bring the system down.

Or system failure could be foreshadowed by a large misfortune like a pandemic coupled with smaller crises like a tanking economy, a changing climate, a polarized society, mistrust in government, and unusual events like the public stocking up on toilet paper and weapons, the appearance of a pink moon, and the closure of all the bars and taverns.

Isn't that interesting? Do these qualify as interesting times? Did you just hear a baby crying?

Column 481, June 28, 2020

Fourth of July Musings

One of the overlooked beauties of fireworks is that you can shoot them at your neighbor's house and still maintain proper social distancing. It's a great way to let your neighbor know you are thinking about them while at the same time wishing them a lively and booming Fourth of July. Think of it as a way of illuminating your neighbor's almost certain dreary life without imposing your physical presence or violating any pandemic isolation protocol.

Fireworks stores are again open to the public. Growing up in a state that banned fireworks, I would have, at the very least, scheduled a negotiating session with the devil to have an opportunity to visit a store that sold explosives.

Now, perhaps with advancing years, I am not so keen on devoting my life to owning and operating pyrotechnics. In my last visit to a state-approved fireworks store, I examined all the merchandise, which included packaged mixtures of fireworks with names such as the "Stars and Stripes" collection for $39.88 all the way to the "Felonious Assault Assortment" for $222.88. I opted to buy only a length of fuse. This is what fuse-savvy people call visco fuse—the green, cord-like fuse that you see on quality fireworks. It burns with a spellbinding sparkle-flame you've seen in movies, even underwater. I don't remember the length, but fifty feet comes to mind.

No, I didn't tell my wife because (a) I am smarter than that, meaning she is not particularly interested in fuse as opposed to say, fabric, table linens or houseplants; (b) purchasing fuse is not the same as buying fireworks, which would require disclosure; (c) it falls under the "minor purchases" category that we do not have to clear with each other; and (d) she would immediately want to know why I bought the fuse and what I was planning to do with it—as if I ask her what she plans to do with the dish towels she buys.

It's extremely difficult to explain to people why you are buying fuse. If they understand, they would not ask, and if they ask, they will never understand. I have no immediate or even vague plans for the fuse. There is just this visceral need to have it in inventory. Now I know this part will sound ridiculous to the skeptics, but you have to have it, *in case the need arises.*

What's that? How many times has the need arisen?

Well, none so far, but I can conjure up some fantasy situation—I mean, some fantastic situation where I emerge the hero because only I can supply the fuse. There is no need to saddle you with the situational details, but in every case, you can hear dramatic movie music in the background and if you concentrate, you can pick out the theme from *Mission Impossible.* Oh sure, you might need some extra length to set off a backyard pyrotechnic display at your Fourth of July party, but when the real, serious need for fuse arises, it will be much more important.

One concern about having fuse in stock at the house is that when the search warrant finally gets approved and the FBI swarms the premises, they will probably locate the fuse, even though at this writing I can't put my hands on it hunting through the clutter which is my workshop.

We can be sure that people who execute search warrants are not likely to be those who understand why a regular guy might have a length of fuse about the house. The papers will come out and say "bomb-making materials" were found, even though no one with any technical sophistication has used traditional fuse to detonate anything substantial since the French Revolution.

In court, I will declare that the fuse was intended exclusively to celebrate our nation's freedom from the tyranny of the English king. The king forced American citizens to house British soldiers who would make sure that we were not in possession of fuse for some untold purpose.

Anyway, this wasn't supposed to be about fuse. We were wishing our neighbors a happy Fourth of July the good old American way: with fireworks. But before you go lock and load, it might be a good idea to evaluate how your neighbor will react.

Social distancing is one thing, but when it's called a restraining order, that's a different matter entirely.

Column 482, July 5, 2020

Pants

Apparently, this is a good time to bring up the subject of pants. A lot of people are now working from home and conducting meetings via the internet. My information, although anecdotal (meaning good enough for the White House), reveals that a lot of these work-from-home employees are not wearing pants. It's summer, they only have to look good from the waist up, and as far as we know, the dog doesn't really care. Going pants-free not only saves you time in the morning, it minimizes laundry and greatly extends the lifetime of the pants in your wardrobe.

Getting the most from your pants is important because I recently discovered a pair of men's denim jeans, Rag & Bone brand, for sale at $250 on Amazon. Could this be right? To be fair, there are free returns on some sizes and colors, and you can opt for $41.67 monthly payments for six months with zero percent interest. That has to be worth something.

These are brand-new jeans, although they look quite like the pants I am trying to replace—badly faded and about ready to blow out in all the normal wear spots. I thought they might have gold fibers incorporated within the fabric, but no, they are 98 percent cotton, 2 percent polyurethane, mid-weight, non-stretch denim. Have we lost our way?

There is one glimmer of hope for America in the listing as there are no questions posted and no one has yet offered a product rating or review. This may indicate that American men are not yet ready for $250 jeans. If the vendor will send me a pair for evaluation, I promise I will have something to say about them in short order.

Since getting out of diapers, I've always worn pants. I plan to continue until they put me back in diapers when things come full circle. Oh yes, I did try hospital gowns a couple times but found them breezy, although I did like the feeling of looking like Zippy the Pinhead. That might just have been the drugs talking. In a hospital setting, it's sometimes hard to tell.

As a result of careful observation, I have determined that pants and ego are closely related. This I learned in college but not as part of the curricula. Wandering into an off-campus store looking for jeans, I was confronted by a pair of red Levi's in my size. I said to myself, "Certainly, I can wear red pants," but it only took a day dressed in crimson to realize that it takes a special man to carry himself around in red britches. Likewise for plaid, checkered, and patterned pants, including those strange colored, pastel pants you only see on older gentlemen in Florida.

Have you noticed yet that we ignore many things in life until they start to affect us personally? Take for example, men's pant sizes. There has never been an infinite variety of sizes available. They just don't routinely make pants for a man who measures, say, sixty inches in girth with a twenty-inch inseam. It's just not a popular size. I don't know where Mr. Humpty-Dumpty would have bought his trousers, but it wouldn't have been off the shelf at Walmart if he wanted them to fit.

Warning to younger men: there will come a time when you will approach the limits of sizes available in your favorite brand. Oh no, you won't be wearing the same size in forty years, believe me. Steel yourself. Be prepared.

No discourse on pants would be complete without a tip of the hat to mathematicians who get intellectually ecstatic when confronted by shapes such as doughnuts, dodecahedrons, and circles. Math geeks are completely thunderstruck when delving into pants. Apparently, if you start out with a hollow sphere and cut three round openings in it and maybe shape the sphere a bit, you have what the math people call a "pair of pants": a surface that is homeomorphic to a three-holed sphere.

From this point, it's just pleasure-boating for the numbers people as they cruise around the topology of pants before slipping into something more comfortable like pants in hyperbolic geometry. You will have to pursue this aspect of pants on your own, but use discretion—it dips into Frobenius algebra, and it's probably not suitable for children.

Well, that's my rant about trousers. As Zippy the Pinhead said in regard to pants, "All of life is a blur of Republicans and meat." Loosen your belts and carry on.

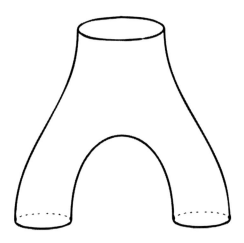

"A pair of pants represented in space." An image from Wikipedia. Wikipedia contributors. (2020, January 27). Pair of pants (mathematics). In Wikipedia, The Free Encyclopedia. Retrieved 04:52, June 28, 2020, from https://en.wikipedia.org/w/index.php?title=Pair_of_pants (mathematics)&oldid=937867823 By Jean Raimbault - Own work, CC BY-SA 4.0, https://commons.wikimedia.org/w/index.php?curid=50314235

Column 491, September 6, 2020

The New Photography, Part 2

I used to be a photographer. No, really. I had my own commercial studio and big corporate clients who would send over products to photograph and young models from modeling agencies to hold the products while the art director smiled and I snapped away. A photo agency handled my stock photos. I was put in helicopters and planes and flown about for different assignments, and I had to know what I was doing and so did my assistant. Yes, I had an assistant and lights and backgrounds and a darkroom. Yeah, that kind of photographer.

What's that? Yes, I had a darkroom. That was for when we used film and dismissed digital photography as a tool that would never approach the quality of film. The darkroom had enlargers, trays, and film washers. It smelled of fixer and acetic acid stop bath. I know darkrooms are old-school; yes, I realize I was part of the Dark Ages.

Starting in high school, I covered the classroom scene for the yearbook. If there had been a waterfront, I would have covered that, too. In college, I agreed to be the official photographer for the intramural sports department only because they offered me my own on-campus personal darkroom. Somewhere along my erratic career path, I was a stringer for a major Alaska newspaper, and I actually made a full-time living performing commercial photographic feats for a number of years. So you may think I know cameras.

Apparently, not anymore.

I needed a small shirt-pocket camera to replace my early digital model, so I opted for a fancy-schmancy type but without texting and voice mail. Even though smartphone cameras had become so easy to use and produced quality so stunning that it cancelled most people's desires to own a stand-alone camera, I had to have a separate camera. After all, I've never been without.

Whoa. The camera industry has been working very hard to keep ahead of the smartphone companies. Evidently, their strategy is to load the camera with features—or to be exact, to overload it with features. These higher-end pocket cameras are designed with the fringe techno-geek in mind. I may be a techno-geek, but I'm relatively mainstream.

The camera came with a four-page "getting started" guide: lite instructions to get you going in case you just want to *look* like a techno-geek to impress the girls—or more likely, other techno-geeks. If you want the 406-page manual, which is considerably larger than the camera, you have to download it from the internet.

I downloaded it. And to the worried amazement of my wife, I read it in bed like a romance novel. What is the point of having a sophisticated camera if you aren't familiar with all the features? But just like a 406-page romance novel, in the end all I retained were the really juicy parts.

The manual is divided into fifteen sections from "Before Use" to "Connecting with Other Devices." I seem to recall a section about how to send amorous signals via the camera to your mistress, but I can't be sure that wasn't from a romance novel. Besides being able to connect the camera via Wi-Fi to your smartphone and instantly send photos to social networks, the camera can walk your dog and represent you in front of the district attorney, I think.

Because I simply can't remember everything this camera has to offer, I had to save the manual onto my new smartphone so that I could have it handy in case I needed to adjust something or find out how to switch the pocket camera on. It's kind of absurd to be digging through the manual on my phone to look up something about the pocket camera when most of the time I can just take the image with the phone camera, which is first-rate. No need to focus, set f-stop and shutter speed. No calculating depth of field, factoring in film speed, or stabilizing the camera.

There is a point in getting older where you start to see that knowledge you have carefully cultured and accumulated over time is no longer relevant. Ouch. Newspapers don't have photographers anymore. Photographers don't use darkrooms. Soon, cameras will not need operators.

But it's all good. We are now free to concentrate on capturing the image. We are all better photographers.

I have to go. I think the camera signed me up for a Zumba class.

Column 495, October 4, 2020

Sourdough Mike, Opera, and The Bobs

Since the statute of limitations on socially improper behavior has expired, I suppose it is time to confess my heinous musical indiscretions.

I hereby publicly apologize to "Sourdough Mike" McDonald, who bestowed coveted opera tickets on my wife and me. We did not attend. I'm sorry. Worse than that…there is no way to put this delicately: we scalped the tickets to see another show. Shame on us.

My wife didn't really want to go, and truth be told, neither did I, but come opening night, I declared, "We shall put aside our prejudice, dress up, and attend the opera." Well, we dressed up and got ourselves to the performing arts center, and that's as close as we got.

I should, by all accounts, have more love and respect for the opera. My mother loved the opera and collected 78 rpm opera records in the 1940s. My grandfather loved the opera and even performed as a minor character in shows now long-forgotten. The family insists he had some social connection to the great Italian operatic tenor Enrico Caruso, but the details of the relationship have been lost. My family also insisted that in spite of our clear roots in abject Polish peasantry, we are descendants of royal blood. But as I got older, I found a lot of Polish village yokels make the royalty claim, probably along with the grand-father-Caruso connection.

I never succumbed to the allure of proper opera, although my sisters and I enjoyed my mother's record of Gilbert and Sullivan's *H.M.S. Pinafore* so much that we wore it out. Yes, I know the

Pinafore is opera's disparaged half brother, the operetta, and that it lives in the shadow of classical opera in the "musicals" neighborhood. But back to my confession.

The story takes place in Anchorage, Alaska, around 1987. Sourdough Mike was a drummer for The Fabulous Spamtones, the house band at the Fly by Night Club that was owned and operated by Alaska's impresario of sleaze and prime minister of the piano, Mr. Whitekeys. The club hosted a most irreverent show called "The Whale Fat Follies," and it often included a sketch where Mr. Whitekeys would verbally spar with Sourdough Mike in the ribald vernacular of the Alaska bush country. It ended with a challenge for the Sourdough to sing the state song of Alaska, "Alaska's Flag." At this point, the audience expected about anything to happen, but they didn't expect Sourdough Mike, looking like your quintessential gold-panner, to stand up and deliver a baritone rendition worthy of any opera house. For a minute before the crowd went wild, everyone sobered up and even stood as an emotional wave lifted the audience members from their seats. It was just like Victor Laszlo leading the crowd at Rick's Café to sing "La Marseillaise" in the movie *Casablanca*.

But that's another story. Actually, it's an entire collection of stories, more like a library that we'll have to save for another time.

It turns out Sourdough Mike had a serious sideline working with serious musicians producing serious opera. Who would have suspected? Since I was part of the production crew at the sleazy bar, he provided me with two tickets to the opera at no charge. Was it Puccini's *La bohème* or Verdi's *La Traviata*? I don't remember; it's opera.

Arriving at the Alaska Center for the Performing Arts, my wife and I spotted a sign pointing one way to the opera and pointing the opposite way to a concert on a smaller stage by The Bobs. We looked at each other, knowing we took pleasure in the music of The Bobs. We looked at our tickets. They were for the opera, and we were still young. We looked at the desperate people standing near the box office who were painfully sad, unable to buy tickets to the sold-out opera. A deal was quietly made where we were compensated for our tickets—enough for both of us to attend The Bobs concert, pay our transportation, and go out to dinner. And buy drinks afterward and go dancing. And maybe, you know, a little extra.

I'm not proud of what we did, but thanks to Sourdough Mike, I shall never forget that night; The Bobs put on an engaging performance.

Sourdough Mike passed away in 2002 and mercifully never learned of our indiscretion.

Older now, I wish there could be another opportunity to hear Sourdough Mike in the context of the opera. I would skip The Bobs and surely enjoy the experience of classical opera. Anyway, I've already been to a Bobs concert.

Column 301, January 8, 2017

Final Holiday Wrap-Up

Although it's very late, I would like to thank all of the friends, neighbors, complete strangers, and felons who attended our end-of-the-year gala for all the joy they brought to our household. Since the list of invitees was lost to the fire during that party night, I am writing this open letter to all who attended our holiday soirée with the hope of getting some things straightened out without the need for, you know, litigation.

Jack K. has sent me a note that someone left the party with his coat and left a jacket in its place. The jacket does not fit Jack very well in size or attitude, seeing that Jack is not a member of any kind of motorcycle club, angels notwithstanding. Please call us if you have Jack's coat.

Yes, the idea of putting all of the coats in one convenient spot is under review, and as soon as the police apprehend the individual who systematically went through the pockets and purses left in the pile, we should be able to let you know if any valuables were recovered.

I also have noticed that I am not wearing my own pants. If anyone went home with a pair of dress black slacks instead of what appears to be black pants with fresh yellow paint applied in stripes…oh, wait, I just noticed that these really are my pants; I just had them on backwards. That explains why I haven't been able to get them off.

One of the guests brought a nice hostess gift that we would like to thank her for very much. It was a beautiful box of small hand soaps scented like and appearing to be small chocolate bars. It would be fun to display the soaps in our bathroom. Unfortunately, someone put the box out on the dessert table, and we found it empty in the morning next to the chocolate brownie dish. Half-eaten bars were still on plates around the room, so please be aware that the soap is minimally toxic. The nausea, vomiting, and diarrhea should only be temporary.

If, however, you enjoyed more than one serving of the mushroom appetizer that some cad brought, it might be a good idea to seek professional advice if, say for example, you can't get your pants off or you feel that you have attended the party every night of the week. There was only one party.

Please don't worry, as we are not too upset about the furniture that was broken up and fed into the woodstove. It certainly seemed funny at the time, and God knows, Chippendale bookcases are just not in style like they were two hundred years ago.

In the future, we will require any fireworks brought by guests to be removed from the box and ignited individually. At the request of the town office and state troopers, we will require them to be pointed away from the house, the neighbors, and the guests at any future events. Also, we will not allow fireworks to be thrown into the woodstove, no matter how amusing.

I would especially like to apologize to the guests who could not find their cars. The valet parking was certainly a good idea, and many guests shared their enthusiasm for being able to pull up the icy driveway right to the front door. However, the decision to park the cars out on the lake may not have been the most auspicious, considering the last warm spell and how close the cars were parked to one another. It might be spring before an accurate determination can be made as to how many vehicles were involved.

The good news is that not all of the missing cars will have to wait until spring to be recovered. Some of the more expensive models were actually stolen. One has already been located at a chop shop that was raided last night in an adjacent state. That car will be returned to the owner as soon as the judicial authorities decide it can be released from their evidence lot. They also held out hope that they will recover the engine soon…and maybe the transmission.

I have to go. My pants are too tight, my head still hurts, and I feel like the party is starting yet again. If this is any indication what this new year is going to be like, we had all better buckle in and stock up on survival essentials. And, to whoever took the dog, we need to talk.

Alphabetical Index to Column Titles